MARXISM
AND
SOCIALIST THEORY

Michael Albert and Robin Hahnel

Vietnam

Neither high nor very far.
Neither emperor, nor king.
You are only a little milestone,
Which stands at the edge of the Highway.
To people passing by
You point the right direction,
And stop them from getting lost.

You tell them of the distance
For which they must still journey.

Your service is not a small one.
And People will always remember you.

Ho Chi Minh

To the Memory of Herbert Marcuse
and in the Spirit of his Life and Work

Acknowledgements

A number of people have read all or part of this volume in draft form and made various editorial and contextual suggestions. To enumerate their singular contributions would accomplish little and be quite impossible. For their advice has been instrumental in determining the ideas and the presentation of every chapter. Although it is also true that conversations with many people have greatly influenced this work, we would like to take this space to give special thanks to those who made direct contributions as a result of reading a part or all of the manuscript at some stage of its development: Robert Berko, Carl Boggs, Peter Bohmer, Sandy Carter, Ward Churchill, Herb Gintis, Jean Hahnel, Micaela di Leonardo, David Plotke, Lydia Sargent, John Schall, Steve Shalom, Sheila Walsh, and John Willoughby.

We would also like to thank Michael Prokosch for his design and preparation of the front cover.

Table of Contents

INTRODUCTION

The historical locus of the revolution is that stage of development where the satisfaction of basic needs creates needs which transcend the state capitalist and state socialist society.

Herbert Marcuse

In this first volume of the set entitled *Socialism in Theory and Practice*, we will deal with theory. An introductory chapter focuses on many of the philosophical problems associated with doing science in general and, in particular, social science and historical theory. It sets the stage for the work to follow. Next, the second chapter discusses the contributions of a number of contemporary Marxist theorists and presents the main contours of our own overall theoretical approach to understanding history and social change in a totalist manner. It provides the conceptual underpinning of the more critical and detailed discussions to follow.

There are then four chapters dealing in sequence with political, economic, kinship, and community theory. Each addresses *certain* of the predominant schools of thought, criticizes them, and elaborates our alternative perspective. These discussions are not meant to address *all* alternative left theories nor even to address any one in *complete* detail. Rather, by dealing with the main features of the most popular theories we hope to illuminate much of the texture and advantage of a totalist approach. Furthermore, we single out certain popular Marxist theories for more detailed treatment because their concepts—by and large—dominate the usual discourse about socialism and also serve to legitimate certain basic beliefs about socialism which we must overturn. These critical discussions are enjoined therefore, not solely in relation to the new theories put forth in this volume, but also as a basis for our criticisms of certain visions of socialism and our argument for a new socialist vision next volume.

1

Indeed, the *motivation* of this book, *Marxism and Socialist Theory*, is not at all theoretical. Rather, we are first concerned with *what is to be done* with the theory we are trying to elaborate. It is the second volume of the set, *Socialism Today and Tomorrow*, which provides our motivation for the effort undertaken here. In it we first present a very readable summary of the positive theoretical lessons of this volume and then proceed to three historical case studies: the revolutionary experiences of the Soviet Union, China, and Cuba. Each is treated in a major chapter and each is addressed in the framework of our overall theory including discussions of politics, economics, kinship, and community. Part One, including the theoretical presentation and three historical case studies, closes with a summary of the overall results and an argument motivating the immediate task at hand: elaborating a workable and desirable socialist vision for contemporary revolutionary movements. This vision is then presented in Part Two which deals sequentially with each of the four spheres of social life mentioned above. In these four chapters on socialist visions for economic, political, kinship, and community spheres of daily life we also address certain questions of socialist transition. Finally there is a discussion of the whole socialist transformation—how each sphere relates to the others in a whole—and then a concluding chapter titled "Neither Leninism nor Social Democracy" which draws certain strategic conclusions for the decade ahead.[1]

The Need For A New Vision

In our view, to constitute an effective movement for social change in the U.S. leftists must develop both a broad vision of what it is we desire to create and a comprehensive explanation of the inadequacies of "existing socialist" societies. First, people's motivations and their abilities to believe in their own ultimate potential depend upon reasoned belief in a goal, as does the task of elaborating a workable strategy. Second, the idea that "workers have nothing to lose but their chains" and that they will therefore be willing to struggle without a clear purpose is archaic. Instead, citizens of modern capitalist societies do have certain comforts and have generally come to believe that there is no possible way everyone could have substantially more or better. A reshuffling is considered possible, but not a change that makes almost everyone better off, much less one which is egalitarian, just, and liberating. So, given this view, why should one take serious political risks? Given, as many believe, the relatively little one can hope to gain, why work for social change at all; why risk losing what advantages one may already have?

This view, not unreasonable given the pervading atmosphere in our society, is a principal impediment to developing a serious movement for socialism. Until socialist relations are described in enough detail to demonstrate their feasibility and human content, few clear thinking people will commit themselves to activism. "Dissatisfaction is easy to have, widespread everywhere, and no doubt better than nothing... But what road leads from the initially psychological state of dissatisfaction to revolt?" Ernst Bloch answers his own question: "Dissatisfaction is not enough. One must know not only what one does not want, but also what one wants."[2] Without vision, activism requires a "leap of faith," which helps explain the almost clerical sectarianism of many Western leftists. Furthermore, without clarity about where we wish to go it is impossible to develop intelligent and coherent strategies for getting there. If our organizations of opposition, our consciousness and culture of resistance and our newly elaborated values are to move us toward socialism, then we must have a reasonable vision of the new society here and now, even as we begin to nurture socialism's roots in the present. And so we see the dual need for studies about socialism as it could be in the United States: for motivation and confidence, and to gain knowledge useful for the task of creating a new socialist strategy.

But why must we criticize existing models and established societies that call themselves "socialist"? For the most part they do not define where we wish to go, and with some important exceptions their history does not offer cause for hope and motivation. As a result these countries must be discovered as something other than socialist. Either that, or "socialism" will not be on the banners behind which a United States left marches. For insofar as the claim that these societies are "socialist" goes unchallenged, their authoritarianism raises a serious impediment to developing activist socialist movements in the capitalist world. And rightfully so, for there is no point in taking the risks of revolution in order to establish a new form of inequality. With regard to our spending substantial time criticizing other people's *ideas*, as Alvin Gouldner argues, "theory-work is not done 'just by adding another brick to the wall of science' but often involves throwing bricks as well; it not only involves paying one's intellectual debts but also (and rather differently) 'settling accounts.'"[3]

It is ironic that many Marxists hold that discussing future possibilities and aims is automatically utopian. They proclaim the need for sober scientific analysis yet preclude by fiat thought about future aims. They fail to see that a "vision" is prerequisite to effective criticism of the present. They fail to see that knowledge of where you wish to go is as critical as knowledge of where you start from, and that positive desires are as important to socialist motivation as hatred of current oppressions. Yet this denigration of discussion of future possibilities is slowly fading into eclipse. At a large 1977 conference organized by the Italian group *Il Manifesto*, leftists from both East and West Europe assembled to discuss "existing socialism" and possibilities for change in both the East and the West. Setting the tone in her opening address, Rossana Rossanda said:

> But I do want to say this: If the societies of Eastern Europe will not change without revolution in the West, there will be no revolution in the West without a thorough critical examination of the experience of the societies of the East. To ignore them, to draw back, not to get involved, would mean to refuse to understand what kind of society we want and will be able to construct here. It would even mean to renounce political theory itself. We must not forget that in the long and eventful evolution of the 'real socialist' countries—sixty years since October, more than thirty since the birth of the people's democracies, nearly thirty since the liberation of China, nearly twenty since Castro spoke of 'Socialist Cuba'—more than a mere hope has been shattered. The very idea of socialism, not as a generic aspiration, but as a *theory of society, a different* mode of organization of human existence, is fading from view. And here we come to the most difficult point of this discussion in the left: we must ask ourselves not whether these societies are unfree, but whether they are unfree *because* they are socialist or *because they are not socialist*. And if they are not socialist, what are they? There are those who deny that the question itself is legitimate.[4]

It is with Rossanda's spirit that we embark on the historical and theoretical tasks of these volumes. It is against those who deny the importance of such self-assessment by socialists that we make the claim that to ignore questions of what is and what isn't socialism is to ignore a chief problem of socialist revolution in the present.

Then what of the final question asked earlier: why haven't we focused solely on economics thereby attaining more detail while leaving other subjects for treatment elsewhere by people better equipped to the task?

A Totalist Approach

In our view the sharp division of analysis into myriad separate "disciplines" often seriously impedes clear understanding, not only of any "whole," but even of its component aspects. In our society social divisions occur along more than class lines, and these divisions affect all sides of life including the way people ask about and understand the world. Depending upon one's position in society, one develops a different view and has different experiences and needs. The understanding of a person who identifies first as a black, a woman, a worker, a Native American, a gay man, a professional, or a citizen each has a claim to legitimacy. Yet however relevant to a specific purpose, no such view is complete unto itself. From different life positions, different world views and theories emerge and they reflect different interests, sensitivities, values, and insights. Each reveals certain truths, but always less than the whole truth. On the left, some examples of such particularist theories are feminism, Marxism, nationalism, and anarchism.

A partitioning of perception and of contributions to our understanding due to different constituencies developing different theories exposes reality to diverse angles of investigation. Yet there must also be some means of social movements forming around a holistic understanding rather than only one or another partial understanding generated by a single constituency.

Coming toward society from a kinship, economic, community, *or* political perspective, an individual or group may develop a rich but partial understanding. To the extent these partial understandings can be encompassed in a larger whole, we believe this whole will be much more useful than the simple sum of its parts and that moreover the insight of each part will be enhanced as well. For example, socialist-feminism aims to be much more than a simple juxtaposition of socialism and feminism bringing new insights about both class and gender in our society. Class analysis, for example, is immeasurably enhanced by the new recognition that the economy cannot be understood purely from an economic perspective. Once insights from sexual, political, and cultural analyses are "infused" into the very roots of the economic view that view becomes more than it was before. And a similar process can also enhance feminism, nationalism, and anarchism even in their analyses of the family, the nation, and the state.

The different circumstances of social actors in our society thus yield a variety of left theories including orthodox Marxism, radical feminism, nationalism, and anarchism. How are we to approach this "menu"? One way is to assume a favorite view is basic and the others derivative and relatively less important. This yields either a strict monist orientation, where one factor causes all others or a more pluralist view where many factors are operative but one is "more equal" than the others. Another orientation is to juxtapose all the theories, arguing that they are separate pieces of a whole and must all be employed in turn depending on the problem to be addressed. Here the views are considered "complementary" and equal but the diversity is not a first step toward synthesis. Finally, one can agree that the views are often complementary but still feel that they must interpenetrate, and that there must be an encompassing orientation that embodies all four perspectives yet is nonetheless much more than their simple sum. This last view is ours and is elaborated in considerably more depth in the first chapter of this book.

Indeed, the first two chapters of this volume are quite abstract dealing with epistemology and general theory and the following four chapters are primarily theoretical as well. They assess different theoretical formulations and present a variety of new alternatives. But so far our argument in this introduction motivates a discussion of historical experiences and of social visions. It suggests need for a total approach. Why then focus on theory? Why can't we jump in to the practical analysis without a long abstract detour?

Theory can be pursued for pure reasons: its beauty, curiosity, or the pleasures of intellectual work. However, with regard to social and political theory our motivations are much more pragmatic. To assess a country's institutions or to say what kind of social setting we'd prefer to live in in our own future, we find theory an absolute prerequisite. It tells us society's most important attributes. It tells us how different attributes together form the whole and how different features of specific institutions influence the overall character of a society. Indeed, depending upon one's theory, one assesses history and thinks about human potentials in different ways. Therefore, though theory may be more difficult than description and less exciting, we mustn't leave it to others as if we have no interests in how it is developed. A detailed historical analysis is generally more readable than a discourse on concepts and their interrelations. Yet to do good analysis requires good theory and in turn the elaboration of good theory requires serious conceptual discussion, however difficult this might be.

Armed with the theories we critique in this volume, in our opinion even the most diligent analyst will elaborate less compelling analyses of the Soviet, Chinese, and Cuban revolutionary experiences than socialists need. Armed with these insufficient theories, this same analyst will also elaborate only a flawed vision for the future. It is a simple notion: if you use an inferior tool you will get inferior results. If you have an incorrect theory of how societies work and try to repair a society or to design a new one, you will fail. And a prerequisite to creating a new theory which can led to success will usually be a successful critique of inadequate prior theory.

As a result, in this volume, we are going to discuss theory. Our historical examples will only provide explanation and punctuation for theoretical arguments. As mentioned above, the first two chapters are the work's most difficult. In the first we focus on broad, abstract issues of methodology and philosophy and mastery of this chapter is not necessary for understanding the rest of the volume. Indeed, many readers will find that even given a cursury reading the first chapter will serve as a good introduction but that then it will flow much more easily and return more for the effort if read more carefully later as a conclusion to the whole volume. Further, readers who have little background in the physical sciences should not be deterred by the first chapter's arguments based on analogies with physics. For despite little familiarity with physics these can be easily understood so long as one doesn't get sidetracked from the structure of the overall argument to worrying over the full meaning of some of the allusions. For those who are familiar with the physics, however, hopefully there will be added enjoyment in the examples.

The difficulties of the second chapter, in contrast, stem from a different source. For in this chapter we try to argue for a totalist theory by describing its overall contours all in one place. This makes for some dense writing and also for a presentation which leaves many gaps which can only be filled in the succeeding four chapters. Another difficult part of the second chapter is the brief introductory account of the theoretical approaches of Raymond Williams, Jurgen Habermas, and Louis Althusser. This section is also "rough going" and while it situates our efforts and should be a useful introduction to these theorists for those interested in their work, it too is not a prerequisite to understanding the rest of the volume. Finally, the last unusually dense section runs for about twenty five pages at the outset of chapter four on economics. As the material appears elsewhere with more examples, however, hopefully no one will be too inconvenienced by the summary form of presentation here.

In sum, however, with these caveats about a few sections, we think the theoretical discussions in this book are accessible, important, and also suited to activists who want to develop socialist strategy and program. It seems to us that new visions and new strategies for reaching them depend on existence of new ways of understanding our societies and our roles within them. If this is so, and if our movements are to be participatory, it will not do to leave "the problem of theory" to treatment by select groups of academics. We will all have to deal with theory, not solely to ensure that there are no monopolies on a powerful and important component of socialist process, but also to ensure that socialist theory is invested with the lessons of real experiences beyond what academics have access to. Theory must be demystified at the same time that it is brought into contact with contemporary experiences of all kinds. Hopefully our efforts in this book will be a useful contribution to this process.

By making an analogy between a more complete totalist socialist theory and vision on the one hand, and a major architecturally innovative structure on the other, it is possible to delineate many of our feelings about *Socialism In Theory and Practice*. The need for the new building arises from the weaknesses of existing alternatives, yet these are not self-evident and for many reasons elude clear enunciation. The contours of the new building involve many innovations. Its construction requires quality work by people with very diverse skills and talents. As but two workers with considerable skill in some aspects of construction but much less in others, we are obviously incapable of erecting the entire edifice. What task should we embark upon?

If others are to exert the necessary energy and intelligence to create the new building as soon as possible they must feel, as we already do, that such a creation is both possible and desireable. The aim of our efforts must be to display enough of the foundation, enough of the main beams, and perhaps—in a few aspects of design and construction—enough of the detail to allow answers to two questions: First, with further work by capable architects and movement builders of diverse background, will the foundation and main structures be so improved to make the new building viable, strong, safe, and livable? And second, with the rest of the details elaborated, the contours filled out and the building completed including whatever alterations of the initial visions prove necessary, will the final creation be superior to existing alternatives and in tune with our most profound needs and desires?

At the same time as trying to provide enough argument to allow answers to these two questions, it is also necessary for us to avoid overextending. If we try to describe or construct too much of the foundation, too many of the main support beams, or too much of the detail, we will make so many errors as too necessarily distract attention from the worth of the initial conception.

This is the line we must uneasily straddle in these volumes. It means that there are parts where we felt greater confidence in our tools, training, and experience and thus went further toward detail. But there are also parts where we were hesitant even at many steps in the elaboration of rough contours. We can only hope that the partial structure we present will help inspire the collective and sustained effort necessary for elaborating a new socialist theory and vision for the eighties and beyond.

In Volume Two of this work our focus is primarily on four countries, the United States, the Soviet Union, China, and Cuba. We address the internal arrangements of the institutions of these societies and the different theories people bring to bear to understand these. And we make certain proposals concerning future possibilities as well. But we don't spend much time addressing the interrelations between the countries, nor their foreign policies and international affairs with other nations. As a result, imperialism is not centrally addressed. As imperialism is the context in which all political activism must occur and as it is the international phenomenon most responsible for pain and suffering on our planet, this is a serious omission. While we feel that it does not diminish the logic of our approach, we are concerned about the impact it may have on how our intentions are understood. For us, while the advance of the industrialized nations into a socialist future is a world historic aim, it is the elimination of imperialism as an international system which promises a still greater advance for a still greater number of people. The two struggles are obviously very intertwined. Here we would like to close this introduction with a substantial extract from a speech by Fidel Castro delivered before the United Nations in 1978. It evokes not only the horror of imperialism and the potential of humanity to overcome its ravages and move toward real civilization, but also the urgency of the project and the locus of responsibility for its success.

> Mr. President, distinguished representatives, human rights are very often spoken of, but we must also speak of humanity's rights. Why should some people go barefoot, so that others may travel in expensive cars?
> Why should some live only thirty five years, so that others may live seventy?
> Why should some be miserably poor, so that others be exaggeratedly rich?
> I speak on behalf of the children of the world who don't even have a piece of bread. (Applause) I speak on behalf of the sick who lack medicine. I speak on behalf of those who have been denied the right to life and human dignity.
> Some countries are on the sea, others are not. (Applause) Some have energy resources, others do not. Some possess abundant land on which to produce food, others do not. Some are so glutted with machinery and factories that even the air cannot be breathed because of the poisoned atmosphere. (Applause) And others have only their own emaciated arms with which to earn their daily bread.
> In short, some countries possess abundant resources, others have nothing. What is their fate? To starve? To be

eternally poor? Why then civilization? Why then the conscience of man? Why then the United Nations. (Applause) Why then the world?

You cannot speak of peace on behalf of tens of millions of human beings all over the world who are starving to death or dying of curable diseases. You cannot speak of peace on behalf of 900 million illiterates. The exploitation of the poor countries by the rich must cease.

I know that in many poor countries there are exploiters and those who are exploited.

I address myself to the rich nations, asking them to contribute. And I address myself to the poor nations asking them to distribute.

Enough of words! Now to deeds. (Applause)

Enough of abstractions. We now want concrete action! Enough of speaking about a speculative new international order, which nobody understands. (Laughter and Applause) We must now speak of a real objective order which everybody understands!

I have not come here as a prophet of the revolution. I have not come here to ask or to wish that the world be violently convulsed. I have come to speak of peace and cooperation among the people. And I have come to warn that if we do not peacefully and wisely solve and eliminate the present injustices and inequalities, the future will be apocalyptic. (Applause)

The noise of weapons, of threatening language, and of overbearing behavior on the international arena must cease. (Applause)

Enough of the illusion that the problems of the world can be solved by nuclear weapons. Bombs may kill the hungry, the sick, and the ignorant but bombs cannot kill hunger, disease, and ignorance, nor can bombs kill the righteous rebellion of the peoples. And in the holocaust, the rich, who are the ones who have the most to lose in this world, will also die. (Applause)

Let us say farewell to arms, and let us in a civilized manner dedicate ourselves to the most pressing problems of our

times. This is the responsibility, this is the most sacred
duty of the statesmen of the world. Moreover this is the
basic premise for human survival.

I thank you. (Ovation)

Though self-evident, it likely bears repetition that no matter
how democratic, powerful, and insightful, neither new theory, nor
new vision, nor even the two together guarantee any significant increase in socialist activism or success in the West or East. Necessary
though it is, theoretical innovation is not sufficient. Ideas and
dreams don't overthrow oppressive social relations nor create new institutional forms suited to human liberation. For that women and
men are necessary—to grasp theory, to embrace visions, and most
important, to forge bonds of solidarity and commitment sufficient
to sustain the war against "recalcitrant statesmen." Politics *is* personal. Strategies don't strike, workers do. Theories don't overcome
sexism, women do. Ideas don't make history, people do. And
however simple it may seem, the first wisdom of revolution is that
for people to make a new history, a human history, they have got to
trust one another, care for each other, want to win and all have faith
that they can win. To this end we certainly need ideas and
visions—yes, our minds must be awakened to revolution. But we
also need to awaken our emotions and revolutionize our personalities. Our society breeds competition, ego-centrism of the worst
kind, insecurity, aloofness, an incapacity to empathize, and a
generalized fear of freedom, but revolution requires the reverse:
sharing, solidarity, openness to criticism, humble confidence,
caring, and the courage to struggle and win. This turn around in
attitudes is primarily a matter of interpersonal practice, not intellect. Any movement which denies the need for theory and vision
would have us believe that a new world can be had without any work
of the mind. Absurd! But a movement which invests all its faith in
ideas would have us believe that a new world can be built without
any work of the soul, one might almost say, without any "labor of
love." Equally absurd! The fact that the volumes comprising
Socialism in Theory and Practice address primarily problems of the
mind should not be taken as a statement of their priority, merely of
their critical importance, and perhaps also of the imbalanced
development of our own areas of competance. In any case, what we
need is a movement with theory, vision, and interpersonal practice
sufficient to the monumental task at hand: socialist revolution.

ONE:

MARXISM, SCIENCE, AND SOCIALISM

> Concepts which have proved useful for ordering things easily assume so great an authority over us, that we forget their terrestrial origin and accept them as unalterable facts. They then become labelled as 'conceptual necessities,' 'apriori solutions,' etc. The road of scientific progress is frequently blocked for long periods by such errors. It is therefore not just an idle game to exercise our ability to analyze familiar concepts, and to demonstrate the conditions on which this justification and usefulness depend...
>
> Albert Einstein

In this chapter we argue that further progress in Marxism will depend in large part on how successfully a new generation of Marxists can break apart old Marxist categories and piece them back together in complementarity with new concepts derived from other till now disparate and irreconcilable schools of thought. The extent this occurs will depend, in turn, on the attitudes we have concerning what is a useful goal for Marxism, and how progress toward that goal can best be pursued. But we will argue that neither the implicit goals of most contemporary Marxists, nor their dominant views on how Marxism can progess are appropriate.

Since such methodological misconceptions about goals and progress as most Marxists hold are largely due to viewing Marxism as a "hard science" and to misunderstanding differences between analysis of the social and physical world, we will spend a considerable portion of this chapter exploring these issues.

We will point out that Marxists are right about certain similarities of the soft and hard, social and material sciences because of three themes that affect *all* theory: 1-the relationship between reality, theory, and the human mind; 2-the inevitable limitations of the perceptual and cognitive processes underlying all theorization; and 3-the similar contours of what constitutes progress in all scientific work. But at the same time we will also suggest that there are substantial differences between the social and material realms and also between social or soft sciences, and physical or hard

13

sciences: in short, the presence of consciousness in human relations makes social relationships far more complex than material ones. Relations in the sphere of social life and in history are far more interactive both over time and across space, than are physical relations. It is the social realm's greater connectivity due to the presence of people who think, remember, and plan, which 1-makes dialectical thinking more critical to social than to physical theory; 2-makes the aim of a "monist theory" less likely of accomplishment in social than physical sciences thus rendering the exclusively *economic emphasis* of most Marxism a dead-end orientation; and 3-renders what we will call a "totalist" theoretical approach based on the idea of "complementarity" the most useful way to address issues of history and social change and also the best basis for a further expansion of the relevance and power of Marxist theory.

Our aim is to address certain methodological problems plaguing most Marxists—how do our theories develop and how reliable are they, is Marxism a science, is dialectics a useful and sufficient methodology for analyzing history, is Marxism resting on a sound foundation or, is this foundation too narrow —and to show some implications of answers to these questions for current socialist purposes.

Perception and Conception

The world is an interconnected whole, but as finite beings at any given moment we can perceive and think about only small parts. To do this we necessarily draw borders, both perceptually and conceptually. We do not perceive the world-as-it-is, therefore, but only as we process it, and this processing occurs at a number of different levels.

In the first place, perception rests on a limited set of sensory organs which lie intermediately between the world and our awareness of it. These organs necessarily have tremendous impact upon the character of our knowledge. Consider the profound effect when one of our sensory organs is impaired. Or notice how different our world is than that of a bat guided by sonar, a mole guided by smell, or even than that of a scientist employing microscopes, and infra-red cameras. Our perceptual equipment is quite unique to our species, at least in its fine contours. Due to the impact of our sensory organs the map of our environment we form in our minds is not precisely the territory itself. Our view is not neutrally conveyed to our consciousness in a simple "transfer." Instead it is constructed there by our sensory organs including those within the brain itself.[1] It is a humanized recreated image that we finally settle on.

And this is not the only filtering that occurs before conceptual activity begins. We perceive very fine details with relatively coarse perceptual instruments. How does this occur? In fact, the instruments have "wired-in" search patterns. They are biologically attuned to construct some patterns rather than others. Given incomplete data, consistent with more than one interpretation, our sensory organs and mind will often fill in the gaps to yield a picture they were attuned to create in the first place. For example, when our eye perceives a wooden board, the mind does not receive millions of flashes but instead a construction indicating, among other attributes, the presence of a smooth edge where in fact, there is really only relative smoothness. In this perceiving there is a kind of biological inference between the world and our perception of it, an inference which occurs due to the very selectivity and processing character—both necessary and desirable—of our sensory system.[2] Thus, both perceptual and inferential biological biases affect our world view, even before we begin to process received data at a cognitive level.

Beyond automatic biological filtering, the first psychological manipulation of newly received data comes when we fit it to our already existing conceptual patterns. We look out a window. We do not perceive an undifferentiated whole—what is there—but instead "people," "trees," "clouds," "flowers," and "buildings," each separate from one another and each textured by our expectations. The mass of sensory data is "biologically processed" into smooth lines, and simultaneously into conceptual boxes corresponding to our most basic expectations and beliefs. In this "psychological processing" two biases are at work. First we automatically organize incoming data in categories governed by our prior beliefs. Second, we may bend the data to conform with expectations about how these more familiar categories should appear and interrelate. That these processes can involve a greater or lesser mutilation of "what is really there" should be clear. Not only does the map not precisely reflect the character of the real territory, but the name and thing named needn't perfectly correspond. In general, we perceive in terms of already adopted theoretical concepts. Furthermore, due to our particular experiences our attention is drawn more in some directions than others. Anticipating a certain event due to a deeply held belief, we may perceive just that event even when something different has transpired. Certainly this is common in interpersonal life, and also in political work where, for example, one often misjudges possibilities due to prior expectations and theoretical beliefs. Consider a Pentagon analyst seeing light at the end of pitch black tunnels, or a revolutionary seeing a politically aroused populace where there is largely apathy or a crumbling economy where there is only a mild disorder. Whole theories obviously embody this character as well. Neoclassical economics focuses myopically upon tendencies to stability and reproduction; Marxist economics looks first for contradictions and the possibility for revolutionary upheaval. Even in reading what is written clearly before us we often see other than what is really there because we process the words to fit prior expectations of what "must" or "should" be there. Marx himself is read anew with each set of differing priorities researching "scholars" bring to the effort. They rewrite his words on their mind's tablet to suit their own ends. What is truth? Whatever we can place in the tomes of God's revolutionary servant. At the extreme, Althusser the mystical worshipper even develops a theory to justify this twofold slip toward deism. For the sectarian scholar is really only "filling the lapses," "lunching on the lacunae," and "throwing light between the lines of the great teacher's efforts." How convenient that this requires no more than a pen and a lamp—no shovel—and can be tailored to any political expediency. But to return to the issues at hand, sometimes the ensuing errors are innocent and sometimes not, but in either circumstance perception is not only significantly altered as a result of our biological attributes, both sensory and inferential, and our limited conceptual dictionary, but finally it is also socially mediated by preconceptions of what is to be "seen," preconceptions derived from prior theoretical beliefs as well as subjective desires.[3] So, while we must accept that a division of reality into abstract parts is inevitable and necessary, we should also remember that the particular conceptualizations that occur are *not* preordained by what is "out there." Instead, they are a function of our capacities and of the world views and needs we take to our perceptions. This implies need for a very sober attitude toward our own most cherished perceptions—the facts we see—and toward the theories we base on them.

Debate Between World Views

Consider an individual with a complex world view. How does this view alter? If she perceives in terms of what she already has in mind, as we have just argued all people must, she will presumably never perceive anything out of synchrony with her current consciousness. The consciousness will be self-reinforcing. There will be no impetus to intellectual progress.

But what if another person comes along and argues that things are different from the way Ms. 'A' sees them. She is a feminist for example, and Mr. 'B' is an orthodox Marxist. Extrapolating from our discussion about the inevitable biological and psychological "massaging" new data receives, it would appear that he will see reality in tune with his theory, while she will see it in tune with hers. They will talk past one another. If either of the individuals could somehow imbibe the other's world view alongside his or her own, it would seem only a "taste-test" would allow a choice. For each view would be logically consistent, and empirical investigation wouldn't help because depending upon which view was held evidence for the other would tend to be perceptually and analytically ruled out.

As experience shows, the conundrum is false. It is not that un-communicative clashes of this type aren't common, they certainly are. But sometimes people with contradictory viewpoints do debate to a conclusion with one person's mind changed. Moreover, sometimes an individual's views change as a result of his or her *own* perceptions. The idea that world views are incommensurable except according to standards of how they "feel" is wrong, but it *is* held, for example, by many Althusserian Marxists. We will show why it is inaccurate before moving on to consider the broader questions at stake.[4]

In the first place, the fact that the world is perceived in terms of conceptualizations allowed by one's particular world view does not necessarily prevent one from perceiving things contradictory to that view. An example from physical science may help. A world view may contain as a thing-to-be-perceived droplet tracks in an instrument called a bubble chamber. Now even though the physical world view predicts that a certain experiment will yield tracks bending right, the experimenter could certainly perceive tracks bending left. There is no biological limitation to prevent this. Of course the experimental discord could be unnoticed, ignored, or consciously dismissed, and in certain circumstances conscious dismissal is even an intelligent practice.* But the point is, contradictions can be perceived and can compel an alteration in one's world view.

Consider a more political example. Orthodox Marxism predicts a falling rate of profit in capitalism, but includes recognition of offsetting factors. The profit rate is certainly a concept within the theory and therefore the theory does not preclude our perceiving it.

---

*C.F. Von Weizsacker (*The Unity of Nature,* Farrar Strous and Giroux, N.Y. 1979) relates a story about his teacher Werner Heisenberg which exemplifies this point nicely. A particular experimenter brings to Heisenberg's attention a series of experiments, very clever and apparently well designed, which demonstrate violations of the law of conservation of energy. Heisenberg replies, with no supporting argument whatever, that the experimenter is somehow in error, and proceeds to ignore the result. Later he is proved correct. (p. 85-86) Another story shows how taking results too seriously can likewise cause error. Newton, after calculating what should be the period of rotation of the moon based on the best available data about its distance form the earth, etc., and based on his newly developed theory of gravity, discovered a discrepancy between his result and the actual situation. He held his theory in abeyance for ten years on the weight of this discrepancy. Later it turned out that the data he was using in the calculation for the distance of the moon from the earth was in error, and it was this that produced the discrepancy between the calculated period of rotation and the actual period of rotation, not the new theory. Had Newton had Heisenberg's confidence in face of conflicting evidence we might have had the theory of gravitation ten years earlier. (p, 94-95) Imre Lakatos, in *The Methodology of Scientific Research Programmes* (Cambridge University Press, 1980) reports: "Scientists have thick skins. They do not abandon a theory merely because facts contradict it. They normally either invent some rescue hypothesis to explain what they then call a mere anomaly, or, if they cannot explain the anomaly, they ignore it, and direct their attention to other problems....Theories and paradigms or research programmes are not knocked out by recalcitrant facts alone, but only by recalcitrant facts *and* an alternative theory which explains them." (p. 4)

As this rate of profit fails to fall, a variety of possibilities exist. The analyst may refuse to notice or even claim to perceive a fall. This is mysticism, and while psychology may help us understand it, psychological pressures do not force its occurrence. The analyst may perceive the non-falling, but alibi it away. This may or may not be sensible depending upon "off-setting conditions." Or the analyst may become upset over the failure of his or her world view and modify it or even search for an altogether different approach. The point is that advance is possibile. It is not irredemiably precluded by biological or psychological factors though these may present temporary obstacles.[5]

But there are also more complex situations. There could be types of evidence of world view failure that *are* imperceptible from within the world view in question. To perceive such evidence could require an ordering of incoming data disallowed by the theory itself. Or correcting a world view might require asking questions which the theory fails to provide us a vocabulary to pursue. The orthodox Marxist, for example, is ill equipped to interrogate the capitalist factory to unearth kin-defined attributes or even to understand what these may be. His or her concepts focus on production activity and class relations and are sex-blind. As Paul Feyerabend argues, "The evidence that might refute a theory can often be unearthed only with the help of an incompatible alternative."[6] An important corrollary is that in testing a theory against experience "the appearance of success cannot in the least be regarded as a sign of truth and correspondence with nature."[7] Of course it can to some extent, but it doesn't constitute conclusive proof of full correspondence. The lesson is that even where subjective "need factors" don't operate strongly, it may be wise to occassionally "leap outside" our views and try what appear to be ridiculous contrary notions.*

For example, someone committed to the orthodox socialist vision and worried that his or her perception is too narrow to perceive inadequacies might sometimes think, "what if the socialist transition period is actually a relatively permanent resting ground,

---

*There is a more difficult version of this problem of choosing between alternative theories, but its relevance for us is marginal. For example, in modern physics the generally agreed view of spacetime is Einstein's, that is, spacetime is "curved," non-Euclidian and not like the geometries we learn about in our early days in school. However, it is also quite possible to

not a brief stage in an on-going process at all?'' Or an orthodox
Marxist might look at a factory and think about whether its work
roles resemble those of families or communities, and about whether
they might contain aspects explicable only in terms of kin or race
categories. Similarly, a radical feminist might wonder about non-
sexual determinations of male-female relations even within the
family itself. Such torture of one's habitual mindset can lead to
major revolutions in perception and understanding which would
otherwise remain quite unattainable. This is an important lesson for
anyone wishing to avoid stereotyped, sectarian thinking, yet it runs
against the grain of most Marxist attitudes. How many Marxists
would be eager, for example, to regularly juggle basic theoretical
concepts the way we have suggested? How many would be horrified
at such audacity, calling it frivolous, arrogant, or unscientific? Is the
root of the problem our emotional involvement in the import of our
theories? Does it have to do with the fact that for some thinkers
Marxist Science is a kind of "cultural capital" providing, status and
prestige on the left? Whatever the reason, the situation is ironic

construct a theory which says spacetime is flat, Euclidian and like that we
are accustomed to thinking about, and that it only appears curved in
experiments because there is a weak but universal and very peculiar force
which affects all measuring apparatuses. Or, in quantum theory there are
two formulations—one called after Heisenberg, the other after
Shroedinger—which again give *identical* predictions in *all* possible
circumstances. That is, the alternative geometric theories and the
alternative quantum theories are each indistinguishable one from the other
by *any* conceivable experiments. What is one to say? Are they the same
theory in different form? Are they different theories and if so, how do we
choose one as compared to the other? The philosophical problems that
arise from this conundrum are profound and unsolved, at least in our view.
However, for us the problems of choice are not often between theories that
are equal in all their predictions, and in any case, should they even exist,
different formulations that are theoretically equivalent could still be
distinguished for our purposes by their relative merits for *practical*
calculation in concrete circumstances. That is, while "ease of use" isn't a
reasonable criterion to allow choice between equivilent physical theories
however much it may predispose us toward one over another, it is a good
criterion for choosing between different social theories where our purpose
is not simply to understand the world, but to change it. For further
discussion of these issues interested readers might consult *Space, Time,
and Spacetime*, Lawrence Sklar, University of California Press, 1974.

indeed since theoretical physicists, for example, engage in this sort of creative juggling all the time.

In any case, though it was hypothetically suggested earlier, it is not true that only taste—how ideas feel, how I like them, how they make me feel—can affect a choice in a debate between alternative world views. Instead it is highly likely that given two views one can make us sensitive to evidence which can rule out its competitor. Indeed, this will fail only if both theories are equally successful in explaining all perceptible data, or if we subjectively distort our perception of information, alibi weaknesses, and remain intransigent in face of the possibility of improvement. In the unlikely case of equal explanatory and predictive power, or the more likely possibility that each theory has advantages and disadvantages compared to the other, both should obviously be retained for further scrutiny.*

But Where Do Correct Theories Come From?

Asserting that a clear thinking individual will find good reasons for switching from one world view to another whenever the latter is more correct—better able to explain events and predict future outcomes—is not the same as showing where such a better theory comes from in the first place. How are theories constructed?

In Albert Einstein's view and he is certainly an individual whose opinion should count for something in this matter, the question really has only the fuzziest of answers. In a letter to a friend explaining his thinking on this issue he drew the following little diagram:[8]

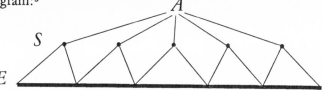

*Karl Popper has interesting comments on this subject in his essay "Normal Science and Its Dangers" in *Criticism and the Growth of Knowledge*, edited by Imre Lakatos and Alan Musgrave (Cambridge University Press, 1970): "I do admit that at any moment we are prisoners caught in the framework of our theories; our expectations; our past experiences; our language. But we are prisoners in a Pickwickian sense: if we try, we can break out of our framework at any time." p. 56.

The line 'E' represented experiences in the world. 'A' represented basic theoretical axioms. The 's' entries represented particular synthetic assertions deduced from the theoretical axioms. For Einstein the 's' are logically deduced from the axioms and are in turn testable by reference to the experiences 'E'. But the main problem was the transition from 'E' to 'A' in the first place. "Psychologically the 'A' rest upon the 'E'. There exists, however, no logical path from the 'E' to the 'A' but only an intuitive connection which is always subject to revocation."[9] The fact is that there are an infinity of possible experiences. To extract a subset and cull some relations from them, and then assert that these relations or some modified version of them represent a universal theoretical axiom is not logically supportable. For there is no reason to preclude the possibility that the experiences were special and that the "axiom" holds *only* for them if at all. In response to the notion that scientists work by strictly accountable deductive procedures, Einstein countered: "But a quick look at the actual development teaches us that great steps forward in scientific knowledge originated only to a small degree in this manner. For if the researcher went about his work without any preconceived opinion, how should he be able at all to select out those facts from the immense abundance of the most complex experience, and just those which are simple enough to permit lawful connections to become evident?"[10] And in particular, we might add, how does the theorist locate "connections" which indicate general rather than specific relations? What helps to guide this theoretical creativity of the scientist or of any theory-maker?

In part the issue is resolved by remembering that the theorist organizes data and reconstructs it in consciousness according to already held theories. But as a final explanation this involves an infinite regress and in any case it doesn't help when a real innovation is the issue. Another answer is to suggest that our minds are actually organized to more easily discern orderly patterns in some places than in others. In this view, our theories—or at least a subset of them—are in our heads before we begin. They are structured into the wiring of our brains, so to speak, ready to emerge when sensitized by data we are naturally predisposed to receive.[11] Still another explanation is to suggest that prior to our efforts to theorize, we have certain thematic dispositions which guide our activity.[12] Einstein, for example, often spoke about not only the relation between 's' and 'E' as evidence of the worth of a theory, but also 'A's "naturalness," "logical simplicity," or "aesthetic character."[13] The potential relation between this view and the prior "innatest" one should be relatively evident. For perhaps certain of these guiding themes—for example, what is "natural"—are a product of the fixed biology of our minds. In any case, in the hands of the philosopher of science Gerald Holton, these potential guiding themes become much more elaborate, encompassing such notions as synthesis, analysis, constancy, hierarchy, and holism. But for Einstein, after suggesting his criteria of "naturalness" or "logical simplicity" the issue really comes to a fuzzy close: "The meager precision of the assertions contained in the last two paragraphs I shall not attempt to excuse by lack of sufficient printing space at my disposal, but confess herewith that I am not, without more ado, and perhaps not at all, capable to replace these hints by more precise definition."[14]

But let us return to the social theorist trying to facilitate radical change in modern society. Confronted by a vast panorama of data, which subset should be "culled" from the rest to generate a new set of basic axioms? And more fundamentally, what factors *will* influence this choice as opposed to what factors *should* influence this choice? It seems wise to begin by admitting that a whole host of factors will influence the choice regardless of whether we would wish them to or not. Any theorist's personal disposition and experiences, as well as his or her previously held beliefs and theories will inevitably play a large role, though there may be nothing to recommend these over another theorist's particular personal influences. It is tempting to conclude that in light of this we should try to eliminate as many of these unplanned factors as possible and thereby base our choice of new axioms only on some set of historically warranted themes. But there is something unrealistic and "barren" about this formula.

It is unreal and unwise to think of ourselves as trying to transcend all influences we can not justify in the imperfect process of conceiving new theoretical alternatives. That process of human creativity is perhaps better left in its "imperfect state" without being subjected to a vigorous cross-examination, lest we leave it plucked clean of "unwanted influences" but also of likelihoods for success. Instead it is the products of fumbling creative efforts, the embryonic theories *after their creation* which we should subject to heated cross examination of how successfully the new 'A' generate 's' statements which can help us engender social change. Yet even this more realistic approach is incomplete. First, new theories must be given some time to mature before they are too mercilously tested against real world events. Second, there is the fuzzy matter of guiding themes raised by Einstein and elaborated by Holton. "Naturalness" or "logical simplicity" are more than an inevitable influence on theory creation but less than a conclusive criterion for theory selection. If it is not to be too facile, a self-conscious approach to the process of creating new theory must be flexible and yet cognizant of these gray areas of confusion.

Monism, Pluralism, Complementarity and Totalism

For theoretical investigation of all kinds, one guiding theme has often been the drive to synthesis culminating in what we might call "monism." Confronted by disparate data and realms of investigation that seem totally divorced, the analyst seeks ways of uniting the divorced realms under one set of explanatory axioms, or at least of situating them in a hierarchy where the rules of one level are more basic, the rules of each lower level more derivative. The idea is to deveop a minimum of theoretical axioms which subsume a maximum of types of data. The Newtonian synthesis brought the realms of celestial and terrestial interaction under the same theoretical rubric. Maxwell honed the phenomena of electricity, magnetism, optics, and radiant heat into one theory where before there had been many. Einstein broke the barriers between space and time, gravity, mass and energy. Nowadays many modern thinkers are struggling to join the disciplines of the hard sciences with those of biology, economics, and sociology through what is called sociobiology—a premature effort, to be sure. The idea of synthesis leads easily to the idea of monism. One searches for a single set of axioms that can generate 's'-entries sufficient to explain and predict all 'E'. In physics, the ongoing quest for a unified field theory is evidence of the power of this theme as a motivating and organizing guide of intellectual creativity.[15]

In the realm of revolutionary thought the ideas of synthesis and monism also have a powerful influence. Marxism has traditionally been understood and revered precisely for its economy of thought in developing a materialist analysis which can generate an understanding of countless realms of human activity—all from some basic axioms concerning economic relations and human behavior. Naturally not all Marxisms are monist, but the most prevalent orthodox version, a direct descendent of the Marxism of the Second International, certainly is. As Lucio Colletti has argued, for purveyors of a monist economistic approach, "production and social relations are...disposed of in chronological series, as *before* and *after*." There is a strict separation or exteriority and also a firm direction of causation. Colletti quotes Plekhanov regarding the critical factors in history and their "chronological sequence": "1. The state of productive forces; 2. the economic relations conditioned by these forces; 3. the socio-political regime established on a particular economic 'base'; 4. the mentality of men living in society...determined in part directly by the entire socio-political system that has arisen on that foundation; 5. the various ideologies reflecting the above mentality."[16] It is this type of analysis in *all* its various incarnations which is the primary object of our criticism in this chapter. And feminism and anarchism too, from different angles have similarly attempted to find *basic causes* and axioms at root of the most disparate relations.

At the opposite pole from synthesis we have analysis, and opposed to monism, we have pluralism. Analysis takes a complicated circumstance and seeks to break it down into component parts each of which may be understood on its own account. It is the analytic impulse which changes the synthetic field of study—humanities—into many, even dozens of disparate and inflexibly separate subject matters. Disaggregating, differentiating, and dichotomizing, are all methods of analysis.[17] Pluralism is an analytic perspective which is quite content with firm boundaries between disciplines. We have a taxonomy of fields to discern disparate intellectual realms from one another. Evolving many sets of disjoint axioms is fine. They need not be reduced and indeed they may not be reduced to one.

Actually, until fairly recently there were very few theoreticians who saw analysis as something other than a means to reach a synthesis. Pluralism was usually considered only a temporary expedient on the way to monism. One broke the whole into parts precisely to reconstruct it again with more knowledge in hand. However with the advent of the quantum theory this has changed. Where before there were diverse sets of axioms, diverse angles from which reality was to be viewed, diverse formalisms and sets of deductions, only as a means to a more unified end, now—according to some thinkers—this pluralism simply might be the best one can do.

The idea of "complementarity" arose in theoretical physics with the work of Niels Bohr. Confronted with a quantum theory which said that in looking at certain events—for example a collision of two atomic "particles"—only one part of the data one might want could be had at any given time, and this only exclusively of other data also needed for full knowledge, Bohr began to assert that perhaps the world could only be understood from different and complementary viewpoints. Perhaps no single viewpoint, no single interpretation, no single set of axioms could be sufficient to explain a reality which was more complex than we had previously imagined. Or, on the other hand, perhaps this requirement for more than one orientation was necessary for epistemological reasons alone—not because of the world's attributes but due to our relation to the world. Though the world might be knowable in theory, in practice, for real beings like ourselves, it might forever have aspects which are irreducible to one another and require diverse approaches for full understanding.[18]

Whether understood as an epistemological or an ontological necessity, many scientists have come to accept that complementary approaches will be essential to discern an all-sided picture of the world of atomic physics. And yet, for most, in a subtle way, this still hasn't meant an end to monism in favor of some sort of pluralist approach. This theory (which says that a particle is also a wave and that the features it has as a particle are complementary to or exclusive of those it had as a wave) is still encompassable within one framework, one totalist approach embodying within it a diversity of potential standpoints of analysis and organization of data.[19]*

---

*It is interesting and provocative to compare our social theory with current particle theory in physics a bit further. In our social theory, the components are people with innate and social needs and also institutions. In the physical theory, the components are particles and fields and the

So what is the analogy—for why else would we be travelling this difficult and arcane path—to the situation of revolutionary theory. It is far from a precise parallel, but in our view the lessons of recent decades have shown that the traditional monist approaches to social theory are bankrupt. Whether the reasons are epistemological only or also ontological is really of little consequence for the activist. It no longer suffices to take a subset of the whole experience, theorize it, and then seek to deduce all else from that. It no longer suffices to build a theory which embodies *only one angle* of perception and evaluation. Rather, it is essential that a new theory embody *complementary viewpoints*, those of all the most important oppressed sectors of society, while at the same time attaining a totalist orientation that can merge these into a single philosophy. There is no hope for a full social analysis, no hope for a movement which can attract disparate elements, and no hope for solidarity among these elements without this combination of autonomy and solidarity, complementarity and totality. In the United States there exist at least four approaches or "angles of focus" guiding the creation of largely disjoint social theories and movements— nationalism, feminism, anarchism, and orthodox Marxism. Each seeks its own particular "monist solution." Each is powerful but alone irretrievably narrow. While autonomy will be a frequent necessity, solidarity and the simultaneous encompassing of all these angles of focus within one broader rubric is a requirement as well,

"elements" here too have both intrinsic (innate) and environmental (social) attributes. In each case the two polar entities are both cause and product of the other and also both subject and object of change. In physics the dynamic relations are "forces," in social theory "interactions." Perhaps most interesting, in the physical theory the existence of *different* particles and fields is thought to be a product of the manifestation of a *single set* of defining relationships in diverse ways, and of course this holds true for the presence of differentiation in our totalist view of history as well. Actually, many more analogies can be drawn, though of course dissimilarities may be listed at length as well. The point of the analogy is to suggest that perhaps the employment of *like thematic norms* yields like theoretical structures no matter what diverse characters the addressed realities themselves may have in their deepest essence, a point that is consistent with certain of our earlier hypotheses about the origins of all theories.

not only for practical struggle, but to enrich analysis and vision. We have argued elsewhere why these four perspectives emerge as particularly important and how we think they may be interrelated and even made to subsume one another while each also retains its own integrity, and we will also address these issues in the rest of this volume. In this chapter, however, we will continue the discussion at a deeper and more philosophical level.

Events, Relations, Processes, and Dialectical Thinking

Most efforts to understand situations focus on "events": circumscribed sets of aspects that occur at a moment or at most over a span of some limited number of moments. For example, economic analysis often focuses on the event "production of a Chevrolet" or "consumption of a taco," or on a set of events like car production or dinner consumption. Events are localized in space and in time. There are a certain number of component elements and these are examined for their interrelations. Then, in due course, the theorist will also consider the event's relation to other similarly understood external events. The differentiation of the continuum of activity around us into disjoint events is a product of an analytic perspective. It is made workable by always proceeding to discuss interaction.

But this is not the only way to look at the world. It is not essential or inevitable that one examine reality only as a sequence of separate isolated events impinging upon one another from without. Instead, one can approach reality relationally. One can view each thing in context of its relations to other things, seeing that the very definition of any event, its character and meaning, depends on its interrelations with other events. In a sense the chosen event is seen as part of a spectrum of other events all interrelated and even co-defining.[20] Thinking relationally one seeks to understand each event in context of an ever-widening network of relations of which it is an inextricable part. Returning to the example above, the worker at General Motors who places rear-view mirrors on the chassis is "connected" in a network that includes not only the other workers on the line, the time-study men, the people who deliver the materials in the auto plant and their manufacturers, but also the consumers who buy Chevrolets, and the people who breathe the smog they create.

Similarly, rather than constricting an event to a moment or set of moments in time, one can perceive a trajectory. The event is only one part of a trajectory which traverses time. Its past and future are a part of its meaning in the present. We look at an act of production and perceive it in terms of a historical process, of which it is but a single part. With regard to Chevy production, we perceive the creation of the technology employed, the history of development of the labor force and of the consumer taste for cars, and the evolution of roads, car use in the future and so on. Where there is a continuum in space when one sees relationally, there is a continuum in time when one recognizes process. Again the event is expanded so we can discern elements in the past and future of its trajectory which are critical to its present meaning and potentials.[21]

Mechanical thinking, a powerful technique which reveals much about the world around us, consists of *analyzing* disparate things and events separately and then as they impose upon one another from without over time and through space. In our view, dialectical thinking consists of no more than developing a synthesizing understanding of things and events by expanding their scope via *relational and historical* thinking. That is, we seek to understand them as part of an out-reaching relational network and a time-spanning historical process. Mechanical thinking requires precise concepts whose meanings are fixed and whose boundaries are quite impermeable. Dialectical thinking requires flexible concepts whose meanings vary depending upon the nature of our concerns and whose boundaries are rather porous. *The two methods are likely complementary.* Their dual use is particularly beneficial if one wants to understand a complex subject matter, for example history and the dynamics of social change.

Employing both mechanical and dialectical approaches—viewing situations in terms of cause and effect and also relations and processes is another theme which should guide the development of Marxist theory in the future.

So What's a Science and Is Marxism a Science of History?*

Given what we have said to this point, what characterizes a science? Is it useful to describe Marxism as a "science of history"?

*Before reading this section it might be interesting to note a polemical jibe by Gustave Landuer written in 1911 and addressing the same issues: "For

Science is a process: the creation of theories sequentially better suited to understanding and affecting the world around us. But "a science" is something much more difficult to pin down. Jacob Bronowski says scientists "attempt to represent the known world as a closed system with a perfect formalism. Scientific progress is a constant maverick process of breaking out at the ends of the system and opening it up again and then hastily closing it after you have done your particular piece of work."[22] Following Bronowski's reasoning we could reasonably define a science to be any such formalism and also the whole body of deductions and data (and perhaps even guiding themes) giving weight to that formalism. There are linguistic symbols, semantic rules of interaction, and a kind of dictionary to translate deductions into statements about worldly phenomena. In a science some subset of the base symbols is held to be a foundation from which all the others and everything else as well, can be deduced. This basis corresponds to Einstein's 'A', the rest is 's', the dictionary takes 's' to 'E', and we might want to include some reference to the themes that guided the development of 'A' out of some subset of information from 'E'. The advance of such a science may be evolutionary or revolutionary. In the first case one methodically applies a particular theory to explain or predict a variety of worldly relations, perhaps maturing the theory through small refinements in the process. In the second case, one breaks the system to allow a leap from one systemization, from one 'A' and 's', to another, resolving old contradictions, explaining new data, or consolidating previously diverse understandings.

Since any axiomatic formalism is always incomplete it is reasonable to think that this process of opening up a science,

really, you are strange people, you Marxists, and it is surprising that you do not wonder about yourselves. Is it not an old and certain matter that even people of modest intelligence can learn the results of science once these results are there? What, then, is the point of all your quarreling, polemics and agitation, all your demands and negotiations, all your rhetoric and argumentation: if you have a science, cease these superfluous bickerings, take up the schoolmaster's cane and instruct us, teach us, let us learn and zealously practice the methods, operations, constructions, and as experienced, undeceived, and certain knowers, do what your Bebel tried as an honest amateur: tell us at last the exact data of future history!"
(*For Socialism*, Telos Press, St. Louis, 1978, pp. 52-53.)

revolutionizing it, and closing it, is never ending.[23] Perhaps the leap of insight becomes smaller with each new stage—there could be ultimate limitations on what the human mind can comprehend or limitations on the conformity between what our minds can process and real relations that exist in the world[24]—but even if the sequence of sciences should converge, there is no obvious reason to expect that we would ever reach the final end-point.*

We can also imagine various measures of worth of a science. How much data does it explain, how suitable is it to application and development, how simple and succinct is it, or how enriched is it in the sense of discerning "connectivity" in the world? But as socialists concerned with assessing the worth of a theory of socialism, of course our highest criterion has to be accuracy and use-value for intervening in social affairs.

Now is Marxism a science or not? Yes and no. It has often been a process of seeking to understand via the best known intellectual and practical methods, and this is "scientific." But it has not, *in general*, included an axiomatic codification purporting to completion within its realm of inquiry. Certain versions of orthodox Marxist thought—for example, historical materialism or the labor theory of value—are perhaps of this sort, and we may choose to call them specific sciences. But Marxism as a whole, as we mean it, has been open, encompassed contradictory viewpoints, and has not been at all a science in this systematic sense, nor has it meant to be. Perhaps at its best it could be better labelled an intent, a heritage, a framework and a haven for the intellectual creation, improvement

---

*The notion that an area of scientific investigation might actually come to an end has come and gone but was recently most compelling when many thought that physics had come to an end with the solidification of Newtonian mechanics. The idea wasn't that there could be no further analysis in physics; Newtonian theory could be used to explain new phenomena ad infinitum. But instead, what people felt was that the theory itself was final, that there was no need for further theoretical work because the laws of mechanics were known and that was that. Of late, certain physicists have begun thinking that we may be on the verge of closing out the entire discipline of the study of basic physical laws of nature in an analogous way, though this time with more complex theories, to be sure. What the physicists don't generally suggest (or admit?) is that the reason we are reaching what seems to be the end of the line in physics might not be

and recreation of new sciences. As E. P. Thompson argues, "Marxism has been one possible development, although one with only an attenuated relationship to Marx. But the open, exploratory, self-critical Marxist tradition has been another development altogether. Its presence can be found in every discipline, in many political practices, and in every part of the world." And about Marxism taken as a science of history, Thompson says, "Marxism has for decades been suffering from a wasting disease of vulgar economism. Its motions have been enfeebled, its memory failing, its vision obscured. Now it has swiftly passed in a last delirium of [Althussarian] idealism, and the illness must prove terminal. Theoretical practice is, already, the *rigor mortis* of Marxism setting in. Marxism no longer has anything to tell us of the world, nor any way of finding out."[25] And in agreement with Thompson, part of our work here will be to show that this scientific Marxism is outmoded and to give insight into means of its eventual replacement within the broader Socialist heritage.

Scientific Progress and Stagnation

Science was born in its modern format with the advent of astronomy and in due course Newtonian mechanics. This genesis was likely no accident, for the stars provided a set of "events" which were regular, recurred over and over, and which revealed their orderliness after a relatively brief analysis, at least as compared to most other systems.[26] But once scientific analysis and synthesis were well established, once many theories existed and the elaboration of new theories and of innovations in old theories became a common practice, why then did advance occur along certain axes faster than along others?

because we have "perfect theories" that represent the "whole truth," but instead because we have simply exhausted our capacities of theoretical innovation or comprehension in this discipline. Which of these explanations will prove more compelling should physics actually end as a theoretically innovative discipline—still only a possibility, to be sure—only time will tell. In one view we will know the laws of nature. In the other, we will know only the most encompassing laws that we are humanly able to know, and cunundrums and confusions will persist.

Why is there generally more theoretical progress in "hard sciences" than in "soft" ones. One answer, borrowing from Noam Chomsky, is that the human intellect may simply be better adapted to certain kinds of investigation and theorizing than to others.[27] Contrary to popular belief, physics may simply be easier for people than anthropology, psychology, or economics. It may well be the relative difficulty of the latter studies which ironically keeps the level of their discourse so shallow that they have the appearance of being actually simpler than physics. But even if this is so there is another way of asking the question about differential development that is perhaps more important for our immediate purposes.

Why does quantum theory replace classical mechanics as more correct, the latter being retained only as a useful approximation of limited (if immensely important) applicability, while in political theory, economic theory, and anthropology for example, old world-views seem to never pass on? New ones arrive, to be sure, but the old ones hang on too, and not simply as previous "champions" or "useful approximations" but as "legitimate current contenders." You'd think if there were objective ways to choose, people would simply get on about the task of doing it. Why do we read classics almost solely for historical interest in the hard sciences, while in the soft sciences we read classics as the frontier of knowledge and, at least among many Marxists, to quote them as scripture?

The irony is that the soft theories are actually *much less* complete than their hard counterparts. Indeed, those that aren't easily refuted leave so much underdetermined that it is always possible to assess failures in prediction to factors which haven't been analyzed. In these instances taste appears to become a much more important factor in choosing between theories.

But it isn't so much taste as it is use-value. What does the theory help me to do? Although a social theory can help one understand and change the world, it can do this in a variety of ways and toward a variety of ends. Incomplete social theories can frequently be quite useful for particularist ends. A sex-blind theory can serve male ends in a patriarchal society despite or even because of objective inadequacies. A particularist theory may leave out or distort embarrassing information one wishes to obscure. Or, alternatively, whether flawed or not, a theory may bring prestige (knowing a theory others deem important whether it is or not), power (in an organization which holds to the theory), tenure (in a university where knowledge of the theory is requisite irrespective of one's belief in its actual merits), or self-esteem and identity (if others don't know the theory). In such cases the theory may of course be held in a sectarian manner. The aim of perception becomes to bend reality to confirm the theory and thereby preserve its legitimacy *and* the personal privileges it bestows. It is the theory's maintenance and often monopolization, not understanding nor intellectual advance that becomes paramount. The individual engaged in this behavior is not usually aware of it, but such people, and they are not a mere few, "quite naturally confuse knowledge with mental rigor mortis."[28]

In the hard sciences, where there is recourse to controlled and repeatable experimentation, it is far more difficult for individuals motivated by these subjective factors to defend incorrect theses, though it does occur sometimes even by manipulation of data. However it is not at all unusual in the hard sciences to see the direction of investigation adversely affected by subjective interests. One can only wonder, for example, about the focus of cancer researchers, the emphasis on military technology, and other similar distortions of intellectual creativity. But in the human and social sciences, where controlled experiments are limited, vested interests and psychological pressures of all sorts can affect not only the direction of inquiry, but also the conclusions and even what is labelled viable or unviable theory.

Why do many rush to call themselves a Marxist, Leninist, Maoist, or Trotskyist? Would one call oneself a Gallilean, Einsteinian, or Heisenbergian in physics? Perhaps philosophically to refer to certain underlying themes, but not to identify one's scientific (axiomatic) allegiances. The use of such labels in political theory may be a clue that what is going on is often more doctrinaire than scientific. Too often advocates of one or another revolutionary analysis are principally concerned with preserving a body of thought by seeing reality in ways which conform to this thought, rather than with understanding reality and continually bending their thought to conform with it. Major clashes over strategic and theoretical problems—the role of the state, the structure of the party, class analysis, and the implications of establishing a dictatorship of the proletariat—are invariably studded with classical quotations rather than reference to worldly events and relations. The intellectual test of new formulations in this orthodox world—and it is a world which includes more of us than is comfortable to admit—is a matter of the exegetical fit of these formulations with theories laid down long ago.

There is one last point we would like to make in this section about theories and our relations to them, a point relevant to the issue of the development of a science and to criticisms of science. There is considerable difference between a well-established world view and one in its earliest stages of development. Adherents of the former should be exceptionally sensitive to evidence of its failure. In this case intellectual progress depends upon people's willingness to make alterations and consider major change—however perceptually, psychologically or even materially wrenching such change may be. With a well-developed theory, to go back to Bronowski's formulation, we must be sensitive to the possibilities of breaking it open at the ends. Constantly rushing to affix new wrinkles or epicycles everywhere discord appears is not the path to progress. Rather, one should consider revamping basic assumptions or developing a new theory. Critics, in this case, have a right and responsibility to be merciless. If orthodox Marxism seems to ignore many sides of life critical to the development of social movements in the West, if it makes many predictions that aren't borne out, if it seems to narrow one's vision in ways that are politically counterproductive, then instead of making alibis at every turn, it makes more sense to search for *basic* weaknesses causing these problems, whose correction may pave the way for a new theory that brings new insights and practical advances.

But on the other hand, a new world view can't possibly be adequate to all evidence. Here it is first necessary to develop and close the theory so it may then be compared to predecessors on a "fair" basis. What is in order is for the adherents to plod along as effectively as possible, at least for a time even against evidence, for further thought may surely account for temporarily conflicting evidence one way or another.* This has often been the practice in the "hard sciences," and is part of the reason why young physical

*"One must treat budding programmes leniently: programmes may take decades before they get off the ground and become empirically progressive." (Lakatos, op. cit. p. 6) "Given a new theory, we must not at once use the customary standards for deciding about its survival. Neither

theories have been able to attain sufficient stature to "unseat" their predecessors. The quick dismissal of counter-evidence to an established world view, and the quick dismissal of a new world view because of insufficiences in some areas are both "sectarian" acts conducive to a diminution in intellectual and practical advance. Remarkably—and this is a function not of necessary biological or psychological forces but of social interests, habits, and pressures—the reverse conservative priorities are usually dominant in the social sciences and most ironically even in the world of revolutionary thought.

For example, one need only consider the extent to which new social theories are greeted with supportive energy aimed at improving them, or with hostility aimed at subverting them as quickly as possible. Or, contemplate the lengths to which adherents of established theories go to defend themselves, even ignoring the most reasoned criticism, discounting it, or claiming it doesn't apply or matter, but never taking it seriously. The response of orthodox Marxists to feminists, or of adherents of the labor theory of value to neo-Ricardians or of either of these schools to "social relations" theorists are cases in point, as is the manner in which bourgeois theorists of all kinds cavalierly dismiss Marxists and other radical critics. In each case the issue is not the ultimate worth of new ideas—some will be valuable and some useless—but the reactions people have to their presentation and the implications of this for the advance of social theory. An excellent recent example on the left is provided by the furor that greeted the attempt by Barbara and John Ehrenreich to amend our understanding of class and class struggle in the U.S.* Their essay on professionals and managers as a "new class" couldn't be ignored into oblivion, so it had to be buried in vituperation. Wouldn't it have been better if everyone had begun with a mindset to explore the merits of the Ehrenreich thesis, and

blatent internal inconsistencies, nor obvious lack of empirical content, nor massive conflict with experimental results should prevent us from retaining and elaborating a point of view that pleases us for some reason of other." (Paul Feyerabend, *Against Method*, New Left Books, London, p. 183).

*The Ehrenreich's article and a set of responses make up the volume *Between Labor and Capital*, (South End Press, 1980), and other responses to their essay may be found in issues of *Socialist Review* and *Radical America* among other journals.

even to expand and elaborate it rather than quickly chucking the whole innovative endeavor? There is a related and even more cynical phenomenon all too common to Marxist theoretical work. A new insight described by an activist in relatively informal terms is ridiculed for its uninformed naivete, only to reappear later, dressed up in suitable scholarly rhetoric but stripped of its most important political content, as the contribution of one or another "scholar." Torn from the context of their birth, and made nearly incomprehensible to the activist community, the ideas now serve more as cultural capital for the scholar than as theoretical weaponry for the movement.

Alvin Gouldner discusses many of these issues in a way nicely illuminated by his concept, "cultural capital," however much we may disagree with some implications of the usage. For example, he argues, "A view of theory as cultural property not only helps explain what happens to anomalies once discovered, but how and why they are generated, who is more likely to do the kind of work that yields anomalies, and who is more open to them once they are produced...The younger generation's milestones are the older's tombstones. Intellectual life, in our time, is a contest for the protection or reallocation of cultural and intellectual property between competing generations...The older generation seeks to muffle and defuse this contest by controlling the education and careers of the younger, by advancing only those whose work promises to support the property and career interests of the older generation, winnowing out doubting Thomases who resist the old paradigm."[29]

The body of Marxist theory is obviously ill, "in crisis" as the phrase goes, and the unwillingness of the majority of Marxists to look with favor and support upon ministrations and efforts at alteration are akin to a sick individual brushing aside potentially useful medicine. No matter the pressures to preserve cultural capital, we must bring to health a powerful theory of society, however revamped, not an unchanging and time-bound geriatric doctrine, however jaded and inapplicable.

A Further Analogy Between the Hard and Soft Sciences?

Granting our inability to clarify precisely how one moves from experiences to new axioms and a whole new theoretical system, is there anything more one can say about the sequence of such openings and closings as we go from a theory to its "child," to its "grandchild," and so on?

In the hard sciences there certainly is more to be said. According to Werner Heisenberg, for example, in a formulation similar to Bronowski's, a theory develops until it reaches a "closed" condition.[30] This state is characterized by the theory's inability to be further improved without making it a new theory. The structure is mature. One form this takes is for the theory to be axiomatized (remember Einstein's 'A'). Then change means change of an axiom not simply the use of the axioms to deduce another 's' to explain additional events. Such an alteration will reverberate through the entire theoretical structure, yielding a new theory.[31] Kuhn's "natural science" is, in this view, simply the process of the last stages of closing a new theory or of employing the newly closed theory to explain ever greater reaches of experience. His "revolutionary science" on the other hand, is the process of opening theory via an overthrow of one or more axioms, leading in turn to a new structure superior to its predecessor.[32] For Heisenberg, the form of this "superiority" is clear—at least in physics. In his view each new theory incorporates the one that went before as a specific case. The new theory synthesizes at a higher level than the old, and also contains the old as a subcase applicable under particular restrictive conditions.

According to Heisenberg, when we employ a theory "normally," eventually we encounter data which cannot be incorporated under the umbrella of the original theory. Analysis with the theory leads to evidence of its own limits. A new synthesis, incorporating the new data under the umbrella of a new set of axioms is called for. According to Frederick von Weizacker:

> ...physics develops from unity via plurality toward unity. The term 'unity' is used in two senses here: at the beginning, we have the unity of the basic scheme. It is followed by the plurality of experiences that can be understood in terms of the basic conception, indeed whose systematic experimental proliferation is made possible by the basic scheme in the first place. The insights gained in these experiences in turn modify the basic conception, and a crisis ensues. In this phase, the unity conception

constitutes itself, which now encompasses in detail the plurality of the newly gained experiences. That is what physicists call a true 'theory'. Heisenberg coined the expression 'closed theory'. A theory is not the unity of the scheme prior to the plurality, but the unity of the verified conception in the plurality.[33]

This procession is a logical one which holds quite closely in the physical sciences.[34] According to von Weizacker another characteristic of this progression is that in each succeeding theory the axioms are more inclusive and more generalized. The synthesis, analysis, synthesis sequence leads, in the terms of an earlier section, toward "monism," first within a particular discipline and then presumably for the totality of all knowledge and experience.[35]

In this book we will attempt to move the locus of Marxism from a focus on economic activity to activity in general. We will elaborate what might be called the "initial conditions" of historical theory by positing a more complex human agent endowed with sociality, consciousness, self-consciousness, and the peculiar practical attribute we label "praxis." Hopefully this will help lead to a solution of what has been called "the crisis of Marxism."

For the crisis, in our view, has been precisely that orthodox Marxism—understood as the historical materialist theory of history and the labor theory of value—has run up against the limits of its applicability. This has taken a host of forms. Analysis of value leads to use-value and exchange-value which slowly escape the perimeter of the labor theory's reach. Analysis of history runs up against patriarchy and racism whose importance cannot be denied but which are beyond the scope of historical materialism. And finally, "existing socialism" belies the predictions of orthodox Marxism—the working class is not in control and the state is not withering away.

The new synthesis must be more than diverse theories jammed into one small container under a new name. We do not need eclecticism, though in a crisis period eclecticism is more likely to yield insight than an outdated monism. Hyphenated orientations are a good start but a new theory will have to be a *synthesis* of *complementary orientations* based on a fuller theory of human nature. Out of this will emerge, we believe, a broad conceptualization of human practice and history. People engage in social praxis to meet needs. This involves the elaboration of social relationships in at least four spheres corresponding to different innate human needs and potentials. The ensuing economic, kinship, community, and political relations will have to either accommodate to or co-reproduce each other. Humans, social relations, and institutions, will all be both subject and object of history. Each will mold the development of the others, though only the people have consciousness. Furthermore, these social relations will cause distinctions between people who share similar enough circumstances to have like needs, consciousness, and behavior patterns along class, gender, race, and party lines. These groups will be collective agents of history.

What will be different from the old historical materialist view is the primary focus upon a single sphere and a single kind of human praxis. The old theory, as expected, appears as a special case of the new.[36] Whether the new theory should be called Marxism at all is no more than a semantic problem. Among people calling themselves Marxists, those who approve the direction of development will say yes; the rest will say no. Whether the new insights into economic, kinship, community, and political relations that emerge will be sufficient to warrant strenthening and ''closing'' the kind of new theory we are talking about remains to be seen. That we should hope so, since some such ''revolution within the revolution'' is a prerequisite to practical advance, seems obvious.

A Fundamental Difference Between the Hard and Soft Sciences: Theoretical Scope, The Usefulness of Mechanical Versus Dialectical Thinking, and the Importance of ''Connectivity''

A fundamental theory of physics would apply to all elements, explain all physical occurrences, at all times under all circumstances and in all places. Less comprehensively, one could imagine a theory which would apply to the whole but only under restrictive conditions. There could also be theories of a sub-realm of the whole which might apply generally or only under restrictive conditions.

Examples of a generally applicable but restricted theory include non-relativistic quantum mechanics and special relativity. Examples of restricted theories with a circumscribed realm of applicability include the theory of heat and temperature and Maxwell's theory of electromagnetic radiation. Einstein's theory of general relativity *may be* an unrestricted theory with a circumscribed explanatory realm. The comprehensive fundamental theory that would unite all "sub-theories" is still only a hope of practicing theorists.

What allows a theory to usefully explain a subrealm of the whole physical world? Since the whole is entwined, when we extract a subrealm its analysis can only prove useful if the connectivity between the subrealm and the "rest" is relatively weak. It must be possible for example, to think usefully about electromagnetic radiation while paying no attention to gravity. Gravity's ultimate presence must not so bias the definition of electromagnetic concepts nor so affect the operation of electromagnetic dynamics that the sub-realm theory is inadequate, even though of course it will have some effect. In the social sciences, sub-theories could be focused on economies, kinship systems, legal systems, cultures, or of course any of countless other subrealms as well. For such sub-theories to have merit either they must be fundamental themselves—all other realms are built up of the dynamics of the chosen one—or, not being fundamental, they must be relatively free from influence by the rest. Their concepts must be applicable without redefinition because of the presence of other realms, and their laws of interaction operative even in context of the interactions of other realms. This is not to say that interactions between realms would be absent, but that they would be additive in a simple manner like the addition of gravity to an electromagnetic explanation.

Another analogy between social theory and physics may help to explain the various ideas being broached in this section. Physicists employ the concept "atom" (in the classical sense of an object occupying a small volume) as a useful theoretical tool for explaining many real world phenomena. Yet it is not a perfect tool for any context, and in some types of analysis its meaning must be enriched or the concept even replaced by others that are superior. For example, quantum theory tells us that the simplest meaning of "atom" is imprecise and therefore always only approximate, and that the error will become significant whenever we are talking about situations that defy analysis by classical mechanics. This correction is of a general kind in the sense that the concept in question is always inaccurate when understood in its classical sense, but nonetheless often adequate to the degree of accuracy the analyst requires. Another alteration comes when we consider possible changes in the environment of an analysis. For example, in the presence of very strong electromagnetic fields we must recognize a fine structure within the atom rather than simply treating it as a uniform entity, and then in a context where the temperature goes high enough the concept "atom" becomes inapplicable in any version because the thing it means to designate simply ceases to exist as a possible physical entity. This kind of correction has to do with the increasing importance of factors that could be rightfully abstracted when they were of minimal impact, but which then interfere as they grow more important such that not only are calculations involving familiar concepts affected, but literally what kinds of concepts or what revised meaning of a particular concept is sensible for understanding the setting in question is affected.

Moving to the realm of social theory we can find similar situations of many kinds but it will be most useful to consider an example that bears upon our discussion of Marxism. An orthodox Marxist economist defines the concepts "use value" and "exchange value," for example, with a certain abstract context in mind. Within that context the concepts seem powerfully suited to analysis and even prediction. This is like the physicist using a classical concept of "atom" in a context where it seems fully applicable. Now along comes a theoretical advance which demonstrates that this orthodox usage of these economic concepts is only approximately accurate even in the context for which they were designed. For example, the classical definition of "use value" may be shown to be insufficiently sensitive to the social relations that affect taste, and the classical definition of "exchange value" may be shown to overemphasize one social relation while neglecting the importance of certain others. This would be like the quantum theory advance in physics in the sense that it would be a general innovation demonstrating that the original conceptualization was intrinsically flawed and therefore always at least somewhat inaccurate. Alternatively, another analyst comes along and says, with regard to a setting in which there are men and women, and members of different cultural communities, the impact upon economic relations not only influences how we must calculate how "use value" and "exchange value" interact and affect phenomena, but also how they themselves must be understood and perhaps redefined. This is like the change in temperature affecting the definition and then even the applicability of the concept "atom." In the less abstract setting the orthodox concepts become misleading or even inappropriate. The crucial point of this example, however, is the difference rather than the similarity between the physical and the social cases. For in the physical case, the abstract setting in which the classical concept "atom" is useful, is a setting that actually corresponds very closely with conditions that appear very often in reality. In the social case, on the contrary, the abstract context in which the orthodox concepts are applicable, is purely fictitious. It does not correspond to conditions that regularly appear in reality. Rather, only more complex conditions exist in which must more complicated interactive concepts are required. And this is a function not only of the error in the orthodox designation of the concepts, but more important for our discussion here, due to the complexity of interaction between different aspects and levels of the social world as compared to the physical one, such that abstract concepts are often exceptionally useful in physical studies, but often quite misleading in social analyses.

Orthodox Marxists assert that the realm they theorize is fundamental.* This is an exaggerated claim. As a result they fail to see that many of their concepts must be redefined in context of a whole social formation, and that many of the "laws of motion" they proclaim are false due to the entwined relation of different social realms. Sex blind economic concepts and laws, for example, are not analogous to "gravity blind" electromagnetic field concepts and laws. Where the latter can generally explain their focused realm

---

*A stark and succinct expression of this monism comes from Plekhanov, *The Fundamental Problems of Marxism*, (London, 1969, p. 52): "The characteristics of geographical environment determine the development of productive forces, which, in turn, determines the development of the economic forces and therefore of all other social relations."—But such formulations are not confined to theorists of the Second International, even if modern variants do often enlarge the causal cornerstone to include "class struggle" along with more "objective" material relations. For this sort of advance, see, for example, Samir Amin's *The Law of Value and Historical Materialism*, Monthly Review, 1978. Longer but less insightful works that take a "monist" approach and are contemporary, if backward looking, include Melvin Rader's *Marx's Interpretation of History* and Cohen's much heralded *Karl Marx's Theory of History*.

because gravity has only additive impact upon electromagnetic interactions, by ignoring sex the orthodox Marxist economic concepts leave out too much to sufficiently analyse even the capitalist workplace. For they obscure the powerful defining impact of patriarchy (and other relations) on economic institutions.

This is not to say there are no economic relationships that can be usefully theorized in the abstract, just that there are fewer than usually thought, and that they are of less significance to the overall motion of the whole social formation than previously realized. The same problem plagues certain *exaggerated* claims of many social theorists, for example, feminists, psychologists, nationalists, sociologists, and so on.

The issue here is what we might call connectivity. The entwinement of social realms is seemingly greater than that of physical realms. Therefore, the error introduced by abstraction in studying history is much greater than that introduced by abstraction in studying particles. This is what makes it relatively more difficult to piece together a theory of history by analysis and then synthesis. For the analysis always leads to too few useful results because viewed in isolation the abstracted subrealms are always underdetermined.

And why this extra connectivity in the social and historical world? We think the explanation lies in the presence of consciousness in the social world but not in the physical one. Consciousness spans time and space in ways that physical forms of interaction do not. It enhances the connectivity of social events far beyond that of inorganic and even organic but unconscious events.

This means that the effort of social theorists to learn from the experiences of natural scientists has often been misplaced. There are lessons but analogies must be drawn more carefully than one might first imagine. Not only should it *not* be presumed that mechanical thinking alone will suffice equally well in the social and natural sciences. Not only is it far less likely that a monist general theory can be achieved in the social than in the physical sciences. But the path toward scientific progress inherited from the natural sciences—synthesis, analysis, synthesis—will be inadequate for the social sciences to the extent that even the most useful and basic concepts within any realm are influenced by the most appropriate set of concepts from other connected realms. Moreover, a pluralism of fields will be much less fruitful in the social than the physical sciences since the dynamics of each will be less capable of simple additive combination and instead, more interactive. In light of these differences between hard and soft sciences we draw the lesson that progress depends on a different kind of breaking apart and piecing back together in the soft than hard sciences. We need something along the lines of what we have been calling complementary conceptual development. We also draw the lesson that neither monist nor pluralist visions are suitable for social scientists and for Marxists in particular, the former being unrealistic and the latter inadequate. Instead something more along the lines of what we will call a totalist orientation is required. The conclusion, therefore, is a strong impression that Marxists must dispense entirely with economism. To overestimate the monist importance of the economy as a sole determining sphere of activity alone or to fail to perceive that the economy itself is fundamentally affected by other spheres is debilitating. Instead we must begin anew, reassessing existing concepts and incorporating new ones from complementary studies of politics, kinship, and community. We must aim not for monism but for totalism, not for synthesis but for complementarity, and not for dominance of one perspective but for autonomy within solidarity.

In this context, we hope that the lessons of this chapter concerning human perception and conceptualization, the origin and development of theories, analysis and synthesis, the importance of "themes," complementarity and totalism, open and closed theories, and connectivity can serve us well as underlying themes for a new study of social formations and possibilities.

A Concluding Comparison of the Physical, Human, and Social Sciences

Physics: Within the study of particle physics the "data-base" is a vast mountain of information regarding the behavior of tracks in bubble chambers and other similarly arcane second order representations of the activity of truly minute entities called elementary particles. The study of this data has led some exceptionally creative thinkers to hypothesize very elaborate theoretical structures which presumably explain or model the most basic forces and interrelations of nature. At present there is a catalog of literally scores of particles, a few of which are deemed in some sense more basic, and of four elementary forces: the electromagnetic, strong, weak, and gravitational. The particles are arrayed by physicists into what we might call "phyla," much like the phyla naturalists use to clasify living things. There are those who take a monist view seeking to show that one or another force, and one or another particle, is most basic and that all else is derivative.[37] There are others who are more pluralist, feeling that each force must be understood separately and that no most basic single force or single type of particle will be found.[38] Finally, it is also possible to take what we would call a totalist approach, arguing that though the particles are separate and different, and though the forces are also separate and different, they all exist so interactively and interdependently that a totalist view is required—not a view which relegates most attributes to a position of secondary importance to some main cause, but a view which sees the whole diverse collectivity as simultaneously a single elaborate entity and also a collection of many complementary parts.[39] In any case, the absense of consciousness *and the relatively lower connectivity between physical subrealms has always enhanced the ease of discovering useful natural laws.*

Moreover, debates among physicists have always been subject to a kind of collective public evaluation. Theory was testable against experimental data. Certainly, subjective inclinations pressured some theorists to move one way or another, caused some to be lax about noticing evidence contrary to their pet theories and others to be overeager in perceiving evidence contrary to competitor's theories. But possibility of repeatable experiments under strict controls meant that given time, energy and sufficient financial resources theories could be shown true or false fairly readily. Moreover, the influence of popular, government and corporate pressure hardly ever goes so deep as to significantly influence experimental outcomes or interpretations. Rather, it often influences what questions are asked and what kind of equipment is made available for experimentation, but with very rare exceptions, political pressure doesn't really care much one way or the other what deep physical theory holds sway.[40] The lunacy of a Hitler attempting to outlaw general relativity bcause it was the product of a Jew, or of Stalin finding the same theory idealist and threatening to his ideology are the exceptions that tend to prove the general rule.

Biology and Psychology: The human sciences, biological and psychological, are obviously far less developed than physics. Here the data base is simply we humans, our ailments, behaviors, dispositions, reports concerning ourselves, x-ray scans, organs before and after detachment, autopsies, and so on. It will be useful to pick out for discussion a single aspect of the whole of the human sciences, the study of a particular organ and its associated functions and activities—the brain.

The subject is the material brain and its acts—the formation and use of language, the process of perceiving visually, aurally, etc., the formation of concepts and then of elaborate theories such as general relativity, and so on. In the long run it would be most desirable to have not only a behavioral theory of perception, language, communication, and intelligence, but also a biological theory of the underlying operative physical aspects of the brain itself.[41] But the approaches scientists are taking to such an ultimate quest are quite diverse. Some believe, monistically, that various human faculties—for example the ability to deal with numbers, to form symbolic concepts, to make analogies, to create language, to learn it, to remember—will *all* prove reducible to one general learning capacity, all therefore proving subject to the underlying influence of but one set of physical attributes of the brain itself.[42] Other analysts feel that it is more likely that capacities for visual perception, language use, and mathematical manipulation, for example, will prove no more similar to one another or reducible to a single underlying common characteristic than do capacities for walking, sexually procreating, and breathing. These analysts expect to find relatively autonomous organs responsible for each faculty, expect only minimal similarties of operation and form, and don't see any reason to attempt to reduce or otherwise confuse one process with another.[43] And finally it is also possible to view the whole matter somewhat differently, in a manner of speaking hedging a kind of fence. Yes the capacities are different or expected to be so, and yes the organs are expected also to be different, but no they are not simply autonomous. Rather they operate in such an entwined manner—memory and conceptualization playing a role in language use and vice versa—and have so structured the development of one another that while they may be usefully addressed and studied separately, they can only be *fully* understood by a totalist approach which sees each element as but a complementary part of a complex single whole. In our view the debate here is over the applicability of the concepts "connectivity" and "complementarity."

Interestingly, whatever theoretical viewpoint proves most effective, in the biological and psychological sciences, the extent of public resolution of theoretical debates is diminished by the difficulty of doing controlled and repeatable experiments—and, at the same time, the influence of political wills and programs becomes more pressing and operative not only in determining the direction of inquiry, but even in determining which answers will be accorded prestige and which relegated scorn. For while theories of minute particles only rarely carry philosophical or ideological overtones of political import, theories of how people think or conceptualize often do.[44]

Historically, for example, the impact of racial agendas on genetic theory has been overwhelming. To address a long and sordid story summarily, in the early part of this century it was believed that if one species was the superior descendent of another then the individual member of the superior species would have traits as a child that the member of the inferior species only showed as an adult. If the theory was to serve racial ends in the U.S., it would naturally be necessary to show that white children had characteristics similar to Black adults. So the scientists set out on their search and amassed a huge list of characteristics that filled the bill and in their eyes proved beyond a doubt that white children "recapitulated" the features of Black adults—anatomical, behavioral, psychological—and then, of course, matured to their own superior adult levels. But then a theoretical revolution occurred. Recapitulation is incorrect. In fact, remarkably, the reverse is true. A superior descendent species effectively stays young; the adult individuals of the superior species show common traits to the children of the inferior species.

For the racists it must now be shown that white adults manifest the characteristics of Black children. The fact that the precise reverse had already been shown to everyone's satisfaction, thus (by the new theory) proving Black superiority to white, was simply ignored. The same naturalists, after throwing their old lists away, developed new ones suited to the task at hand. What a remarkable commentary on the ethics of "scientific investigation."[45]

But there is no absence of present day examples. Behaviorism is now heralded because it provides the perfect rationale for the behavior of a military and government gone wild—we are merely reinforcing desired behavior among the peasants when we bomb their communities and farmland back to the stone age and face barbed wire inwards to prevent escape from the centers they are forced to run toward to escape this rain of explosive terror.[46] Similarly, sociobioloby is heralded as the ideal new theory of social life. Everything that is, in the sociobiological viewpoint, from the prevalence of rape and other violence against women and the sexual division of labor, to hierarchies in politics and the current density of crime, and even to levels of mental instability and alienation, is ultimately a product of our genetic make-up. Social responsibility and reform, much less revolution, are unnecessary and likely to do more harm than good. Sociobiology is a useful analysis for those benefitting from the status-quo and one which therefore in turn benefits from their sanction, however flawed its premises may be.[47]

Predictably, the hypothesis that is most anathema to authoritarian political powers of all sorts is the one which says that people are neither "blank slates" nor "greedy malevolent egotists" —the former person requiring leadership and outside domination to attain anything, the latter needing restraints lest he/she destroy civilization—but instead creative social beings with diverse, desirable innate characteristics. This, of course, is our premise, here and in other work. A study which shows the extent of the dogmatism which enters into this debate, and which at the same time argues a position akin to our own, is Noam Chomsky's recent *Rules and Representations*.[48]

History: Regarding the study of history, we needn't review the diverse theoretical approaches, nor the monist, pluralist, and totalist alternatives people use to understand how different spheres of life activity intersect to compose human experience. We have already argued that the presence of consciousness and great connectivity in the social sciences makes the totalist alternative most compelling.

But it is worth mentioning that experiments are even less possible in the social than biological and psychological sciences because of the numbers of variables involved and for ethical reasons as well. (The exception is perhaps a maniac like Milton Freedman collaborating with the junta of fascists in Chile to make that country's entire population a captive subject of a more or less controlled application of his economic policies to see what their effects might be;[49] or the U.S. high command deciding to bomb Hiroshima to see the effects of an atomic blast.[50]) Likewise in the social realm theoretical results are even more important to powerful political elements.

Since this becomes all the more true as social relationships that serve such powerful elements show themselves to be failing, the decade ahead is likely to be a time of extreme struggle for any diversity of opinion to prevail in the area of the social sciences. Where the church used to be threatened by physical science which dethroned the earth in the universe, capital, patriarchy, racism, and authoritarianism are threatened by social sciences which demonstrate the potentials of humans for a better social arrangement promising greater human dignity, creativity, and equity. Though the particle accelerators are not likely to soon be threatened, and though the sociobiologists and behaviorists will be handsomely rewarded, the human scientists with integrity and especially the social scientists with critical and innovative insight are soon to be subject to scrutiny, ostracism, and repression throughout the West. It will be a horrible calamity if we are unable to coalesce in face of this threat. We must move from academia to activism not solely in self-defense but to help create a new world.

TWO:
SOCIETY AND HISTORY

It is our understanding that revolutionary thought must take a new course; it is our understanding that we must leave behind old vices, sectarian pursuits of all kinds and the positions of those who believe they have a monopoly on the revolution or on revolutionary theory. And poor theory, how it has had to suffer in these processes, poor theory, how it has been abused, and how it is still being abused. And all these years have taught us to meditate more, analyze better. We no longer accept any 'self-evident' truths.... A whole series of old cliches should be abolished. Marxist literature itself...should be renewed, because by repeating cliches, phraseology, and verbiage that have been repeated for thirty five years you don't win over anyone; you don't win over anyone.

Fidel Castro

Numerous social theorists have been enthralled by a conundrum: If individual people each possess a will of their own, independent from that of any other individual, how could such a vast network as a society evolve and persist? How could such a multitude of independent actors become an integrated whole unless each was subject to forces beyond themselves? Even the individual molecules of air within a balloon form the structured sphere only because of the pressure of the confining walls, an outside force. How much more true must this be for millions of people with consciousness and wills capable of generating independent programs of action? Yet if social order is the result of forces beyond each individual, what becomes of the role of human will? If we exist in a social network not by the creativity of our separate wills but instead due to large scale pressures within which our wills are constrained only to function in particular ways, then doesn't the character of history transcend the personalities of its starring players? Do we create freely, the subjects of history, or is our creativity but a facade, its product foreordained, ourselves but the object of history?[1]

Our answers to these questions will emerge in this chapter as we address issues of human nature, society, and history. In short, we will argue that each individual does create his or her environment and even, to an extent, him or herself, and that the fact that this creativity is accomplished by people with a shared human nature acting in a setting which is also largely shared, leads to common projects: the construction of diverse networks of social relations which in turn themselves then act as both beachheads and also limitations for further human creativity. To introduce our general theory and motivate it as well, we would first like to make a brief survey of some other efforts to move beyond the limitations of orthodox Marxism.*

The Problem of Totality
In Four Modern Marxist Approaches

In the orthodox view "base" refers to the mode of production and encompasses both the forces and social relations of production. "Superstructure" refers to political, familial, cultural, legal, and other institutional and ideological relations which are deemed to be both derivative and reflective of the society's base. The mode of production determines class relations and the contours of class struggle—society's laws of motion derive from the interaction of class struggle and the imperatives of the mode of production itself. The superstructure must accord with the requirements of the economic base.[2] Many new readings of Marx, however, including those we will address here, have in common a rejection of the "base/superstructure" conceptualization which they find too mechanical and too insensitive to issues of culture, consciousness, and the importance of the state. The aim in these new theorizations is to retain a powerful understanding of economic relationships while further developing an analysis of other aspects of social life.[3]

*We have chosen these four perspectives not because we think them necessarily superior to all others but because in sequence their examination provides a useful introduction to some of the theoretical problems our own approach seeks to overcome.

One line of thought, followed for example by Raymond Williams, is to broaden the conceptualization of production to include cultural phenomena. Williams effectively eliminates the conceptual differentiation of base and superstructure by assimilating the latter into the former.[4] A different strategy is to make the boundary between these spheres even less penetrable than it is in the orthodox view. The economy is set off distinctly from all other realms which may then be investigated not as derivative but in their own right. On the one hand, this investigation can be unitary (ala Habermas) and on the other variegate (ala Althusser).[5] For Habermas, there is simply the economy on the one hand, and the non-economic, more subjective sphere of society on the other. For Althusser, there may be diverse autonomous spheres of social life each requiring attention, for example, not only the economy, but also a polity, culture, and so on. Finally, the practice of the new left also addressed the same underlying issues as these three theoreticians.[6] For the new left, the relevant boundaries between social spheres were seen as porous and firm simultaneously. For some purposes, an approach blind to the demarcations of separate spheres was useful, but at other times clear recognition of differences was essential. In any case, here we would like to briefly address these four orientations in turn, in order to situate our approach within modern Marxist theory as well as clear up possible confusions over what we mean—as opposed to what others mean—by certain concepts.

Raymond Williams: The Theory of Production and Holism

One problem many critics of the orthodoxy focus on is its relative insensitivity to the importance of culture. Marcuse, for example, says that in the orthodox framework "a devaluation of the entire realm of subjectivity takes place," and that "it is all too easy to relegate love and hate, joy and sorrow, hope and despair to the domain of psychology, thereby removing them from the concerns of radical praxis." And he goes on to point out that while, "indeed, in terms of political economy they [the emotional states] may not be 'forces of production,' for every human being they are decisive, they constitute reality."[7]

Raymond Williams has elaborated a reading of Marxist theory aimed at overcoming this deficiency. He argues first that the notion that culture and ideas are but a "reflection" of material relations arises from a misreading of Marx's original formulations. This misreading "is not materialist enough."[8] By adopting the metaphor of reflection by a mirror, a passive process, the orthodox view "succeeds in suppressing the actual work on material which is evident in cultural creation. By projecting and alienating this material process to 'reflection,' the social and material character of artistic activity—of that art work which is at once 'material' and 'imaginative'—was supressed."[9] Williams' point is straightforward: The reflection theory relegates cultural production to a passive role when actually it is an active process itself. Like any other activity, cultural production is material and significant in its impact, both due to its product, and more important, due to its effects on the people involved in the activity, the "workers." For example, the creation of the painting *Guernica*, the novel *Catch 22,* or the movie *Apocalypse Now,* all affect the diverse participants in creation (production) and appreciation (consumption). Surely Beethoven's *Ninth Symphony* and Dylan's *Highway 61 Revisited* are both art, but also parts of economic processes. The social relations of aesthetic production and consumption are a priori no less important than those of the factory or market.[10]

Williams' reinterpretation of Marxist theory is centered on a redefinition of what we mean by "production." Where most orthodox Marxists use the term to refer to industrial labor, or at best to wage labor, Williams means all activity related to the "production and reproduction of real life."[11] Production of "social cooperation" is production. The parent, preacher, and politician all work. Production of social knowledge is production. The author, artist, and philosopher are all workers. In each case, we not only satisfy needs but also produce "new needs and new definitions of needs." We produce "ourselves and our societies" via many forms of activity and, in Williams' view, each of these activities is a kind of "material production."[12]

This certainly constitutes a severe break with the orthodoxy. The lens Williams uses to scour society for important relationships is different. Now, for example, "establishing a political order"[13] is a kind of production, and therefore part of what should be the primary focus for Marxist analysis. It is "beside the point" and misleading to isolate the creation of material commodities in industry from the creation of "law and order," "welfare," "entertainment," and the arts in general. They are all acts of human production and all must be centrally addressed. In this view "the concept of the 'superstructure' was then not a reduction but an evasion."[14] For what had been relegated to the superstructure was for Williams as much a critical part of society's foundation as industrial production. It is all of one piece. Certainly, it must be agreed, with this view one is no longer as likely to fall into the trap of downgrading the importance of "subjectivity," "joy and sorrow, hope and despair." Williams has developed a relational approach which extends previously stagnant, narrow concepts to new reaches and power. Society is a whole. The base/superstructure metaphor may be useful for particular analytic purposes but to reify our overall perceptions of reality according to this demarcation is misleading. We must examine all sorts of production as critical, not simply that which takes place in industrial factories. We must approach the interrelations between different productions with a more open mind rather than simply assuming a priori that they are hierarchically arranged in an order whose "top" and "bottom" we know *in advance* of examination. A more totalist approach is urged: "Determination of this whole kind—a complex and interrelated process of limits and pressures—is in the whole process itself and nowhere else: not in an abstracted 'mode of production' nor in an abstracted 'psychology'."[15]

This theory of production embodies improvements whose virtues we should retain in any further efforts. It is important to realize that temporary conceptual differentiations (base/superstructure) shouldn't be fetishized. The lines dividing such concepts are drawn for specific purposes and may be misleading for others. It is also important to realize that the concept "production" can be extended to encompass all forms of social activity. Indeed, a brilliant analyst might develop a compelling theory of society as a whole and of its various "parts" as well by following just such a course. But alas, it is not likely. For the approach gives no more guidance to such an analyst than would an excellent motion picture. Like the picture, it is too undifferentiated *and* too comprehensive.[16] With no boundaries and nothing "left out" there are no guides and ultimately little explanation. It is useful to learn from Williams the art of successively extending the domain of a particular concept toward the outer limits of the whole.[17] But to do this with only the concept "production" and claim this as a theory of all society is insufficient. The approach fails to recognize that if we want to understand society to change it, some types of activity and some institutions *are* more important, more causal, and deserve more focused attention than others. Williams can write without allusion to specific qualities of the "production and reproduction" of differences between men and women, adults and children, people of different races, and people of different religions. Thus all the concrete work remains to be done with this approach. An error is overcome, but by using a new insight to move back toward the starting gate and not forward down the track. A full theory of society must certainly address economic, cultural, and political activity (and other forms as well) alternating between a treatment of each activity in-and-of-itself and in relation to one another—becoming steadily richer with each successive round. But if we wish to intervene and transform society, it won't do to act as if all kinds of activities and social divisions arising from them are one—that all activity is productive activity and all social divisions class divisions.[18] For not all divisions feel the same, have the same roots, generate the same social dynamics, or yield the same sorts of organizing possibilities. We say all this while also recognizing that as we make differentiations we should also remember the point Williams is impressing upon us and remain sensitive to "entwinement."

Let us not belabor. The relational approach Williams uses can help us overcome the mechanicalness of orthodox Marxism and push us past old conceptualizations.[19] His efforts to extend the concept "production" should suggest the possibility of other "starting places" for a non-myopic approach to society. For "production" is not the only concept which can be made comprehensive. We could, for example, begin an analysis from the concept "cultural creation" or "socialization" or "politics" and elaborate their pervasiveness by demonstrating the possibility of encompassing the bulk of social relations within *their* domains. Indeed, perhaps it would be useful to develop a conceptual dictionary that would allow us to come at any society from a number of directions. In each case, we would work toward an understanding of the whole somewhat differently, along different paths, though in ways that overlap and augment one another's insight. For beyond production, we will find other types of activity from which to usefully interpret any social formation. And so this is another insight which emerges from a critical evaluation of Williams' extension of the theory of production, though the extension itself is insufficient.

Jurgen Habermas: The Divorce of Culture and Economy

This is not the place nor are we especially equipped to attempt a full summary of the theoretical views of Jurgen Habermas and the school of critical theory.[20] Despite having considerable difficulty with his style, we have learned much from his work and that of the whole Frankfurt School. But here we need to address only one aspect of his approach.

As we understand him, social activity has two forms for Habermas: "subject/object" and "subject/subject." In the first, the main relation is one of appropriation. A thing, the object, is appropriated—made, altered, used—by a person, the subject. In the second form of interaction, it is two actors who encounter each other. The relation between them could be one of understanding and equality or of domination.[21]

The first type of social activity constitutes the main locus of orthodox Marxism, at least in Habermas' view.[22] The orthodox theory addresses the interaction between people and nature, people and economic inputs and outputs, people and wealth, people and economic institutions, and so on. The theory is well conceived, the analysis, by and large, is powerful and important.

But the subject/subject realm has got to be addressed as well. The reproduction of the species, the socialization of children, the creation of culture and its dissemination will otherwise be accorded too little importance. Instead of "base/superstructure" it is desirable to see that there are two realms of social activity—and more than likely different sites where one or the other type is more preponderant. But according to Habermas, neither of these two types of social activity should be viewed as more important, or prior, to the other.

Thus the result of the orthodoxy that most irks many modern Marxist commentators—that it asserts the dominance of economics over other aspects of life and the reducibility of these other aspects to economic causes—is overcome by Habermas too, though by a route opposite to that travelled by Williams. For Habermas, that is, the material realm has one kind of fundamental interaction, subject/object, while the cultural and socialization realm has another, subject/subject. Obviously the latter is *not* reducible to the former. Finally, we are forced to understand the latter in its own right.

This advance should not be minimized. The orthodox framework tended to lead analysts to ignore all that was most human about societies. The orthodox analysis of change could hinge only on largely technical contradictions within institutional forms leaving little place for human desire, need, and will. With Habermas's innovation these aspects rightly reenter the analysis. Contradictions may now arise from the complex relations between people and from the production and reproduction of consciousness, behavior patterns, and even myth and ideology.[23] It becomes necessary to ask questions about what distinguishes people from "objects," and why people are subjects even when they are "done-to," more than "doing."

But there are still grave problems. Is the economic realm to be relegated to essentially the same mechanical treatment as it received at the hands of orthodox Marxists? Are there no significant subject/subject relations established in the economic realm? Are people only actors, and market institutions only acted upon? And in socialization, for example, aren't there subject/object relations as well as subject/subject relations that should at times be kept in focus? Are we to relegate socialist economic activity to subject/object analysis—perhaps calling it the time of necessity—and only worry about revolutionizing subject/subject relations outside the economy, in the realm of possibility? For Habermas, in fact, this is the right course to follow. For him the main step to establishing socialist relations has to do with ensuring that subject/subject relations—communication—are free, equal, and honest. Change of the economy is secondary and not likely to significantly overcome workplace alienation in any case. For this is intrinsic to subject/object interaction, to be ameliorated only by shortening the workday. But there is something very misleading about a sharp division of society into realms divorced from one another.* There is

---

*There is another, more subtle dimension of inadequacy in Habermas's approach, pointed out to us by Ward Churchill after he read an early version of this work. The subject/object, subject/subject pantheon of

too much commonality among all forms of human activity to be adequately reflected in a conceptual framework of disjoint sets. What is wrong with the orthodox approach isn't merely that it misunderstands culture *outside* the economy, but that it ignores the existence of cultural aspects *within* the economy and therefore the need for economic relations themselves to be free. Habermas' subject/subject formulation can propel us to reinsert what is most critical about human characteristics into our understanding of social activity. But it is wrong to suggest a *permanent divorce* of social life into two realms, even with the proviso that neither is subordinate or reducible to the other. It fails to recognize that all types of human activity are more complex than simple materialist analysis lets on. It fails to discern that in all interaction each agency is always *both* subject and object. And it fails to assist us, again, in discerning just which types of interaction are most important to look at. From the point of view of the activist who wants to change the world, Habermas' concepts are just too far from the issues that must be addressed daily. The dynamics of race, sex, class, and authority divisions do not fit easily in a world of subject/objects and subject/subjects.* As with Williams, the concepts are too far from the ground on which our practical political decisions must be made.

Louis Althusser: The Theory of Levels and the Last Instance

Althusser charts another solution to the problem of discerning alternative types of social relationships. In all societies he sees a political, economic, and cultural level corresponding to the existence of separate and distinct political, economic, and ideological

relations relegates the person/nature interface to the same instrumental realm it occupies in Marxism (and virtually all other "Western" thought). The conscious people appropriate unconscious separate nature to their own ends. But what of a subject-object/subject-object understanding—people and nature as parts of the same undifferentiated whole—that could allow an ecological perspective? What is perhaps paramount in Native American and many Eastern and African cultures is here ruled out a priori in the guiding conceptual structure.

*At the risk of this note being torn from context to demonstrate that we are mindless empiricists, readers of Habermas' published volumes in English will certainly have to admit that very few pages are given over to discussions of racism and sexism and that few of the discussions of class or political relations adequately treat the concrete conditions of organizational work.

practices. Here, labor as understood by more traditional Marxists provides a kind of metaphor for the development of a broader—and to Althusser, non-economistic—theory.[24] For as work involves the transformation of raw materials into products by a "determinate human labor, using determinate means of production," so we can see political and ideological activity in similar terms.[25] As there is a mode of economic production encompassing the social relations of economic transformation so there is a mode of political and a mode of ideological production. Science too is merely the product of a "theoretical mode of production," or mode of production of knowledge.[26]

So for Althusser there is an economic, an ideological, and a political practice, and associated with each a set of "raw materials," a set of forms of activity and technique, and a set of institutional relations—the whole of which constitute three distinct structures, the society then being a "structure of [these three] structures."[27]

Of course there follows the issue of the interrelation of these structures. Each contributes to the determination of the social whole, and that whole in turn contours the characteristic features of each of its component parts. Moreover, as each structure has a certain autonomy due to its practices being separate and distinct, so all social outcomes are affected by three factors and thus "overdetermined."[28] But Althusser doesn't stop with this seeming pluralism which is already economistically infected since the concepts for understanding each practice are constructed not with specific regard to the different spheres but simply by transposing economic categories.[29] Althusser goes on to reassert that the economic level is determinant "in the last instance." That is, while each level has a certain autonomy, one will be dominant in any particular social formation. And for Althusser, in any society it is always the economic level that determines which of the three will be dominant. So in feudalism the economy makes the political realm primary, while in capitalism the economy makes itself primary.[30]

The economy remains "determinant in the last instance" for Althusser, but in his theory some other spheres have histories of their own as well. It is only the relative importance of these other structures that is finally determined by the economy, though of course all of the structures are permitted to influence one another. So Althusserians *might argue*, for example, that as politics is relatively autonomous from economics, in the Soviet Union the economy may still be socialist even in face of the obvious existence of a totalitarian polity.

Althusser doesn't make the "holist" mistake of reducing all activity to one. He recognizes this is just too high a level of abstraction for useful social theory. But, like Habermas, he draws dividing lines that are too impermeable. Specific practices and their structures are bound so tightly together that the interpenetration by each structure of other practices is ignored. There is no understanding that activity in the economy, for example, entails cultural or political practice as well. For Althusser the structures push and pull one another only from without. The relations are exterior. The practice of each structure is confined to that structure alone. But this is too rigid. The economy does not just produce goods, but also produces people. The political sphere includes economic as well as political practice. There is cultural practice within both economic and political institutions. Of course, particular practices may be predominant in one institution in a society—for instance, kinship activity in the family, or production activity in the workplace—but in general, any practice can appear in any institution and for many purposes this is a critical insight. In other words, there is an interpenetration of practices into diverse spheres and even further, each practice embodies elements of the others.

Althusser is attempting to overcome economism, but he has failed miserably. Tempering the economistic notion that production directly governs history by his "in the last instance" interpretation of historical materialism *is* a step forward in that it begins to discern the need to recognize other spheres of social life which are also causal. But it is an unfinished attempt. The main stumbling block seems to be that Althusser has been able to reach into new sides of human interaction only via extensions of economic concepts—everything is compared metaphorically to production. There is intrinsic to this an inability to discover the *new features* which characterize the social relations surrounding socialization and culture. Indeed, these spheres are understood only in their economic—perhaps better "economistic"—dimension.*

---

*Beneath the above perspective lies Althusser's particular epistemology and structuralism. His epistemology allows him to be one of the most

This could be a simple theoretical error, or perhaps an error of habit. But there is also a possibility that political/material interests might be acting as a propellant for such "inaccuracy."

For by confining practices to separate spheres and making the relations between them exterior, Althusser preserves the orthodox analysis of the economy largely in tact. His economic structure is to be understood economistically permitting no new insights from feminists, nationalists, or anti-authoritarians to intrude. With the orthodox theory of the economy thus preserved, Althusserians can be quite liberal in their tolerance of feminist, nationalist, and libertarian analyses of the family, community, and state since Althusser has already concluded that the economic structure is determinant in the last instance and also always dominant in capitalism. When push comes to shove, therefore, those who theorize the economy and "lead the working class" will attain dominance.[31]

So while Althusser leads us in the direction of treating non-economic activities seriously, he ignores Williams' relational insight entirely. But how can we utilize both lessons? How can we focus on autonomy and yet on interpenetration at the same time?

New Left Intuitions

One can certainly become sensitized to diverse types of social activity, institutions, and social divisions, through theoretical discourse—but this is an inevitably abstract and tortured route. It is simpler to look out the study's window. Better yet, one can go through the door and participate in change itself.

One strain of development in the U.S. new left which was particularly strong in our own training ground of Boston, was a

extreme idealists on the scene even while laying claim to the mantle of "materialist science." His brand of structuralism leads him to explicitly write people out of history—an advance in honesty over the orthodoxy which kept this mass purge a secret. Althusser sees history as subjectless save insofar as we might want to attach the term "subject" to social relations. There is no human agent in any case. But the ignorance and harmfulness of Althusser's idealism and anti-humanism have been dealt with elsewhere and, since neither of these trends represent the slightest advance over even the most mechanical orthodoxy, we needn't add our own critique of these weaknesses here.

simultaneous sensitivity to what was called "totality" and "autonomy."[32] There was class struggle, sexual struggle, struggle over race, and struggle over political power. There were movements and organizations centered around each of these foci. While debates over priorities never ceased, it was agreed in general that each focus was critical, each was to be respected, and none were subordinate. Yet there was a continual emphasis on "finding the connections," "drawing the links," and "understanding the whole." For example, the sexual struggle was not relegated to the family, but expanded to encompass all of society. Somehow, everything was implicated in everything else. Yet, at the same time, it was essential to guarantee those people most involved with a few key areas an autonomy in elaborating the struggle in their own areas.

It would be wrong to say the new left produced a theory consistent with its practice. In a sense we were all much too busy. The theories we used were all less advanced than the practice we haltingly elaborated. Orthodox Marxism was predominant in intellectual discussions, even if it seldom determined the actual programs and actions people took. Even so, the theoretical contributions of the new left were profound.

Foremost, the daily confrontations of the sixties showed perceptive theorists that whatever their other innovations, they had better address class, race, sex, and authority relations centrally. Otherwise, they would be talking a language unsuited to the tasks of the day. "The personal is political" shed light on the interpenetration of kinship and cultural aspects into all spheres. The women's movement questioned both political and economic forms, seeing patriarchy in the different options they offered both men and women. To continue with this enumeration would be to present this book in an alternative form. For our theory is only an attempt to make more formal the ideas common to the new left and created in its collective experiences.[33]

But why seek to formalize these ideas at all? First, it is necessary so that they may be used by ever wider circles of people. Second, it is necessary so that they may be systematically strengthened. And third, it is necessary so they can compete. For among the many reasons for the decline of the new left was the lack of a common language and framework that would allow clear analysis, a comparison of thought, and a ready approach to facilitate solving problems rapidly. With their orthodox Marxism, Leninist sects could always generate "answers" more quickly, reach agreements and communicate more swiftly, and argue more "logically." In contrast, new leftists had only good intuitions, and this was not enough. In the "next round" we must confront the status-quo and the orthodoxy not only with energy and intuition, but with a new theory as well. Finally, it is also true that clear expression of a political approach is necessary if the approach is to be democratic. To be democratic, that is, new concepts and ways of thinking have to become the property of all members of the movement and this cannot happen if they are always clouded in mystery, or presented only in the most obscure language.

For Marxists throughout history, attention to the woman, national, and democratic questions is evidence of a practical awareness of the importance of spheres beyond the economy. But insofar as these issues have been addressed as "problems" to be analyzed with a powerful theory that is already developed, success has been impossible. To address the question of socialism—what is the character of the societies which deem themselves socialist and what might socialism be like in the United States in the future—we need an approach that extends beyond economic determinism, simplistic holism, and all particularisms of the past.

The early development of Marxism eventually led to the solidification of historical materialism and the labor theory of value as whole, "closed" theories. They were elaborated as far as they might be. Minor alteration or slight redefinition would no longer lead to improvements. At this point the task was to apply these theories to ever widening concrete problems and to the development of sub-theories of ever more diverse realms of social life. At first this was rather successful. Such areas of investigation as anthropology, aesthetics, law, politics and the problems of the state, the relations between men and women and the dynamics of nationalism were all powerfully elucidated by the new theory. But in time the study of these diverse realms got out of control. The new insights unearthed in this investigation began to escape from under the umbrella of the sponsoring theory. New realms seemed to be beyond the reach of historical materialism and the labor theory of value. After a time, therefore, analysis destroyed the prior synthesis. The monist, materialist theory could no longer encompass the insights to which its applications had given birth. The ensuing crisis has led to such attempts at reconstruction as we have discussed in the prior sections and many others as well. Althusser gives autonomy to diverse structures but saves economics as main focus by suggesting that it has a determining position. Williams attempts to redefine the classical concepts so the words and formalism may be retained—with only the meaning changed. Habermas seems to give up the original plan entirely. By positing two separate realms he forgoes the prior materialist priorities. The new left looked to retain plurality in context of some sort of new and enlarged unity.

We will follow the last course as well. Rather than looking for a new synthesis which replaces economics by a new "master science," we seek a synthesis *without* the old kind of pinnacle. Our aim is to simultaneously combine analysis and synthesis to create complementarity within totality. We orient ourselves rather differently than is common for most socialist approaches and as a result innovations in focus and conceptualization will be necessary right from the outset. Thus, to develop even suggestions of a new orientation, we must start at a new beginning, at the root, with a new understanding of human nature, people, and what we mean by history itself.

The Importance of Human Nature

Humans have biological, genetic characteristics whose impact extends beyond determination of physical appearance to psychological and cognitive attributes. Recently many Marxists are seeing the obvious reality of "human nature" and likewise "rereading Marx" to uncover his use of the concept as well. Melvin Rader's discussion is representative, as is his view of the late Marx that "he by no means abandoned the view that there is a relatively constant human nature that is fettered by the inhuman condition of existence. He still thought of man as alienated in capitalist society, and he still used the terms 'human nature' and 'species being'."[34] Of course, contrary views on Marx's own opinion and supporting textual evidence for them can also be found. Of more importance than the argument over what Marx truly believed, however, is the relative merit of the opposed conceptualizations themselves.

Within biological science the idea of innate genetic characteristics affecting not only such physical attributes as our having arms and not wings, or of our developing mature reproductive organs only at a certain stage of bodily development—and also perceptual, conceptual, linguistic, and even emotional attributes, is not uncommon. Note, however, we do not mean the kind of biological determinist arguments of Edward O. Wilson and other sociobiologists.[35] Rather biological studies assert that *our genetic endowment provides a rich and also restrictive foundation* upon which our personality, skills, knowledge, etc. develop socially. For example, Noam Chomsky quotes two neurophysiologists in a way supporting our general (and his linguistic) conception:

> By this we mean to emphasize that the developing nervous system is not a tabula rasa, free to reflect whatever individual experiences dictate. Rather, the development of the nervous system is a process sharply constrained by a genetic program. At certain points, the genetic program permits a range of possible realizations, and individual experience acts only to specify the outcome within this range.[36]

The use of the word "only" is relevant for the neurophysiologist's point, of course, yet it is precisely the choosing from a range of possible outcomes that leads to all human diversity. In our idea of human nature there is therefore both constraint and potential—the two in fact being intimately related and basic to human progress. Humans are able to elaborate intricate shared conceptual schemes and behavior patterns because their genetic endowment disposes them toward these accomplishments as some among the "many potential outcomes within the range" their natures allow. At the same time, outcomes outside this range are simply unreachable. Chomsky's view is one from which we have learned a great deal:

> Consider again the question whether cognitive functions are both diverse and determined in considerable detail by a rich innate endowment. If the answer is positive, for some organism, that organism is fortunate indeed. It can then live in a rich and complex world of understanding shared with others similarly endowed, extending far

beyond limited and varying experience. Were it not for this endowment, individuals would grow into mental amoeboids, unlike one another, each merely reflecting the limited and impoverished environment in which he or she develops, lacking entirely the finely articulated, diverse and refined cognitive organs that make possible the rich and creative mental life that is characteristic of all individuals not seriously impaired by individual or social pathology—though once again we must bear in mind that the very same intrinsic factors that permit these achievements also impose severe limits on the states that can be attained; to put it differently, that there is an inseparable connection between the scope and limits of human knowledge.[37]

In our view, beyond simple features like the need for sustenance and the power and proclivity to reproduce, people also innately have more distinctly human characteristics: a highly developed sociality, a capacity for empathy, a need for freedom, love and community—and unique capacities for conceptualization and communication which allow us literally to change ourselves while also changing our environment. This last attribute, it should be added, distinguishes us not only as acutely social beings, but also as beings of ''praxis.'' The fact that the particular biological basis of these traits has yet to be understood makes us cautious, but it in no way precludes our developing a general theory built around the ''human nature hypothesis'' yet not completely dependent upon it. From here on we will be assertive about only a few traits taken to be a part of human nature, though a compelling case could be made for using a still longer list.

We are *social* in that to meet our needs we require social interaction and to employ our capacities we require collective involvement. Even more important, previous accomplishments always form the basis for each new human advance. Thus, unlike other organic creatures, far from continually starting from scratch, humans are historical. We build upon our understanding and experience of past human achievements in a way that makes us the social subjects, as well as the social objects of history.

On the other hand, we are also beings of *praxis* in that we consciously act to change our historically bequeathed environments and in doing so change ourselves as well. That is, even though our genetic make-up has changed little in historical times, our human personality, skill, and consciousness can change over periods as short as a day. These attributes are a cumulative flexible imprint of our life histories and also largely determine our future options. A product of past praxis and foundation for future praxis, our activity always affects our beings. Therefore, though personality and consciousness are often persistent, they are never totally fixed. In short, as beings of praxis, changes in our activities engender changes in the historical fingerprints that compose our social natures, and this constitutes one basis for human progress both for individuals and for the species as a whole.*

Human Development

It seems to us quite reasonable to hypothesize that people have an intense "built-in-need for positive self-image and for social recognition."[38] The creation of an identity, of purposefulness, and of a path of action is dependent upon this. We act. To be satisfied with ourselves we have to be able to see our actions as intelligent and good ones—the more so as they become more controversial and involve more of our time, energy, and identity. For this reason, behavior can affect personality and consciousness as much as the reverse. That is, we often mold our consciousness to rationalize prior behavior. As but one example, to retain a place in our circle of

---

*The contrast between our own view and that of various orthodox schools—for example, the Althusserians or revivers of Second International theories—should be clear. For us the individual is a subject who acts on him or herself and on society and social relations simultaneously. Moreover, the individual has a species and even a personal biological nature meshed inextricably with a historical being that is a product of social interaction and in turn acts—within certain given conditions—as a cause of further interactions and changes. For the orthodox schools, however, individuals are only ciphers for external causes—we imagine ourselves to be cause but that is an illusion. Furthermore, our beings are entirely—at least for all historically relevent discussion—a function of imposition from without. Colletti says of Plekhanov's view (one which is always refreshingly clear, if often also wrong): "The argument could not

friends, we might act as they do in response to the detention of U.S. citizens by Iranian students. This could be relatively thoughtless, just an action designed to retain access to friendship and community. Yet shortly later, to preserve our dignity we may have to justify our act on its own terms. Our consciousness may take a reactive racist turn.

It is critical to see how in this way traits may develop not only through individual error or coercive imposition, but by intelligent accommodation to the limits of our social environment. In certain settings, to obtain essential food, shelter, and clothing we may have to act in ways detrimental to meeting other equally human (though immediately less pressing) needs. This can engender personality traits and consciousness unsuited to ever fulfilling the latter needs. Moreover, these alienated characteristics, "self-developed" in restrictive settings, may survive long after those settings disappear. The street urchin, ex-convict, or child from an upper class home may make necessary adaptations to their immediate environments which will nonetheless restrict their fullest development in a more general setting.

In acting upon the world, therefore, we also develop our consciousness and personalities. Initially, changes are rooted in particular human purposes, of course, but in time they can come to have "roots" of their own. We become what we once were not, and it is not necessarily to our advantage. Still more serious, in an alienated environment there is no escape from the conditions generating detrimental consciousness and personality. In context of particular combinations of ongoing institutional relations it may be that individuals can achieve fulfillment of one type *only* by accepting or even self-inducing oppression of another kind. For example, to gain wealth we must often sacrifice integrity. To have

be clearer: man who in his own *consciousness* imagines himself to be the cause, is *in reality* the effect and nothing but the effect....Freedom for Plekhanov, repeating Engels and through Engels, Hegel, is the 'recognition of necessity.' Freedom, in other words, is the consciousness of being determined." (Lucio Colletti, *From Rousseau to Lenin*, Monthly Review, 1974, pp. 68-69). Whatever one may think of Colletti's inclusion of Engels in the indictment, his critical assessment of a prevalent view of human non-agency is a useful counterpoint to our own formulation.

children, we may have to sacrifice our own careers and identity. To maintain friendships and social recognition, we may have to conform to views we know are false. And so on.*

Four Moments In All Human Practice

Any human activity can be seen, in relation to the whole society, in a number of ways. To describe the different realities revealed by different angles of view, so to speak, we use the term "moment." A ball thrown fifty feet across a field by a person five-and-a-half feet tall travels in a single line—a curve. But it's affected by different physical forces—the earth's gravity pulling it down, friction with the air slowing it, and the muscles which sent it across the field in the first place. In physics sometimes these are loosely described as different moments of force which together create the ball's trajectory. We think human activity must be viewed in terms of at least four *social moments*:

> 1-To one extent or another all human activity necessarily involves creation and use of material objects and this production and consumption defines the *economic moment* of human activity.
>
> 2-As humans produce other humans, human activity also embodies what we (following many feminists) call a *kin-*

---

*The difference between our view—changes of personality and derived needs on top of an essentially fixed biological human nature—and that of orthodox Marxists—there is an infinitely malleable human nature; nothing is fixed even over human lifetimes—must not be minimized. Its essence might best be understood by meditating upon the following brief formula quoted from G.A. Cohen's very much heralded defense of the orthodox historical materialist orientation, *Karl Marx's Theory of History: A Defense*, Princeton University Press, 1978, p. 103: "Society continually alters human nature, and it may become part of a man's nature to want a deodorant." For this is only an exaggerated and depressing variant on the many kinds of dehumanizing notions that emerge once one adopts a logic denying the existence of any essentially fixed biological human nature. It is remarkable and worth contemplating that on this point—the denial of human nature—orthodox Marxists and the worst of Skinnerian behaviorists share the same fallacious reasoning despite the complete absence of scientific evidence to support their claims.

ship moment principally involved with the reproduction and socialization of people themselves.

3-As social beings our activity is meaningful only in inter-action with others (or with an environment in which the history of others is embedded) leading people to elaborate a collective social and historical identity. This aspect of activity encompasses what we might call the *community moment* of human behavior.

4-It is also the case that human activity must be organized with reference to extension over time. We are influenced and act in terms of both our past and our projected future and our activity has a related *political moment*—the regulation of what is socially acceptable (or outlawed) and thus to be encouraged (or punished)—aimed at regu-larizing outcomes to obtain social stability.

So in general, though particular human activities are often more consciously oriented toward one of the "spheres" of social life than others, every activity can nonetheless be viewed from each of four angles to reveal in turn its economic, kinship, community and political attributes. In the factory, for example, activity is usually thought of in terms of its economic features, yet workers' personali-ties are altered, cultural norms are affected on the line, and rules are continually elaborated, obeyed, or broken. In the family, by the same token, activity is usually conceptualized in terms of kinship relations yet goods are consumed and dinners produced, cultural and religious norms obeyed or altered, and political attitudes incul-cated. Similar examples of multiple effects could be pointed out within community and political activity, but the essential point is clear: the price of abstracting from the "secondary" moments of activities that are classified to be of "one particular sphere" is too high to endure in all but the most peripheral instances. Each type activity incorporates all the others—none is isolatable.

So while we often usefully label factory production "economic activity," and electoral involvement "political activity," it is important to remember that each process actually displays all four moments. We can certainly find a principal purpose or defining feature for any activity and then classify the activity accordingly into one particular sphere for particular analytic purposes. But in the end we must always retrace our steps and interpret all activity as fourfold if we are not to fall into a one-sided, narrow, and innacurate understanding of the full dynamics of social life.*

Four Basic Spheres of Social Involvement

People have material needs and productive capacities. In all societies they will always and inevitably engage these and this requires entry into economic relationships. This much we know even before investigation. To know, however, the form these relationships will take—for example whether they will be feudal, capitalist or socialist—requires specific examination. People must also reproduce the species, procreating, nurturing, and socializing. With diverse sexual needs and capacities, people must enter social relationships to fulfill these ends—kinship relationships—but

---

*Although the approach we are formulating is quite different from the hallmark of most orthodox Marxism with its priority for a class and mode of production focus, it is interestingly in tune with the logic of a particular criticism Marx applied to Proudhon in the *Poverty of Philosophy*, in the *Collected Works*, Vol. 6, International Publishers, pp. 166-7:

> "M. Proudhon considers economic relations as so many social phases, engendering one another, resulting one from another like the antithesis from the thesis, and realizing in their logical sequence the impersonal reason of humanity. The only drawback to this method is that when he comes to examine a single one of these phases, M. Proudhon cannot explain it without having recourse to all the other relations of society; which relations, however, he has not yet contrived to engender by means of his dialectical movement. When, after that, M. Proudhon, by means of pure reason, proceeds to give birth to these other phases, he treats them as if they were new born babes. He forgets that they are the same age as the first. . . . The different limbs of society are converted into so many separate societies, following one upon the other. How, indeed, could the single logical formula of movement, of sequence, of time, explain the structure of society, in which all relations co-exist simultaneously and support one another?"

For this is the critique we have made of economism and other reductionist approaches and which we have attempted to transcend by an approach we call "totalist."

whether these will be matriarchal or patriarchal, nuclear or communal, is again a matter for concrete investigation. As social beings who can and will empathize, who require self-respect and a social identity, people necessarily enter into communities with shared customs, languages, and cultural solutions to problems of situating themselves in history. Whether the lines of demarcation between communities will be ethnic or racial, religious or national, and what the character of the communication across these lines will be is again a matter for investigation in each society and each epoch. Finally, all societies have some form of political decision-making institutions necessitated by the conscious and social nature of human beings. But again, the exact form these will take—dictatorial, democratic, bureaucratic, or participatory—must be discovered through direct investigation.

Every society has economic, kinship, political, and community spheres of social involvement. But why do we divide human activity and society along these particular lines? The critical thing about economic, kinship, political, and community activity is that *each* calls forth complex forms of involvement leading in turn to the development of elaborate institutional networks having profound implications for how we think, what we feel, and what we are capable of doing in any given society. Moreover these particular spheres of social life have generated time and time again important "we/they" distinctions between people (class, sex/age, race/national/ethnic/religious, and authority divisions) which are in turn very critical to social reproduction and social change. Thus, the argument for focusing on the above four spheres is that these foci will be most useful in helping us understand how and why people act as they do in particular societies, and how and why there might be qualitative changes.

To avoid mechanical pitfalls, it is critical to realize that each of the four institutional networks is, when fully extended, made up of the same pieces. As in the example of family and factory above, *all* of society's institutions ultimately appear in each network. Yet each network also has its own central and defining "key" institution(s), the production/consumption, kinship, state, and community units—each of which is in turn more or less replicated in the more peripheral institutions throughout its sphere. Thus, viewed as a part of the economic network, in its economic functions the family in part replicates the factory, viewed as a community institution the state replicates many cultural norms and interfaces, viewed as a kinship institution the factory embodies familial characteristics, and so on. In essence, as we look at society from the perspective of a particular moment of activity, we can see all its institutions as a network. Depending on our perspective, each time they are clustered around a different key institution. From the feminist's viewpoint all society's institutions cluster around the family and are extensions of kinship requirements. From the orthodox Marxist orientation the factory and class relation are the hub. For the anarchist the state is featured, and for the nationalist, the community. But in fact since major institutional networks are coextensive these separate analytic approaches can yield important but *only* incomplete truths about society. They will fail to discern, among other things, important limits upon what kinds of social relations are historically possible, an idea we must now investigate.

Society's Center and Boundary

At the risk of overwhelming the reader with spatial metaphors, we will also make use of the terms "center" and "boundary" to describe and understand social relationships. By the human center we mean the people who live within the society including their needs, powers, personalities, skills and consciousness. By the institutional boundary we mean a society's framework of interconnected social roles serving to organize social activity and also the natural and human-made material objects which exist within the society.

The line we draw between these two aspects is imposed by our act of conceptualization and not intrinsically present in reality. Nonetheless, the demarcation can prove useful in analyzing key aspects of social life. It is important to note, however, that given our definition, a society's human center depends on *both* innate human characteristics—our species nature—and also on the historical processes of social development of people's personalities, consciousness, skills and derived needs. The center in the United States for example, consists of our innate attributes but also of social products—individualism, sexism, etc.—we embody in our personalities and needs. Similarly, the institutional boundary depends upon the natural laws of interaction of material entities as well as on the social laws deriving from the historical formation of these social institutions. The economic system in the United States is partially dependent on technical material relationships affecting production possibilities, etc., and also on social outcomes and relations governing the development and operation of specific institutions like our market system. Furthermore, the market boundary and worker/consumer center both define and affect each other. In general then, we expect both center and boundary to play a subject (active/initiating) and also an object (passive/affected) role in historical development.

Institutions are defined by conglomerations of social roles which delimit the available options for behavior if one is to benefit from social intercourse. For example, to benefit from the existence of a market one must fill the legitimate social role of a "buyer" or a "seller." It should be clear from what we have said about the relation between activity and human development that the particular role offerings in a given society—first by defining available activity options, and then second, by thus defining consciousness and personality possibilities—largely determine how people can live their lives, what they can achieve, and what limits they must endure, at least for as long as the role structures remain in force. Examination of such role offerings via examination of boundary relations in economic, kinship, community, and political institutions is therefore a straightforward route to an understanding of the human implications of any particular social formation.

Societal Stability

What defines a social formation is its continuity or the "enduringness" of its main features. When such continuity exists it is a product of a complex mesh between boundary institutional offerings and center human expectations and also between the respective institutional/consciousness "pairs" arising in different spheres, for example those arising in the economic, kinship, community and political activities of daily life.

For a society to be stable people must generally expect and accept (not necessarily happily) what they get and have to do. On balance, we must choose activities that are compatible with society's role offerings: there must be a "fit" between the human center and the institutional boundary. Imagine the contrary: society's roles require advanced formal knowledge but its citizens are all illiterate; social roles presume equality among all citizens but the citizens themselves believe some sectors of the population superior and others inferior; production requires obedience without question yet people's personalities are highly rebellious. It is easy to see how any of these situations would be unstable. A change would necessarily occur either in people's characters or in the characteristics of their environment.

But why would people choose behavior that generates alienated personality traits and detrimental consciousnesses? Even if this is required for the human center to "mesh" with an inherited oppressive institutional boundary, we certainly can't be suggesting that people intentionally "sacrifice themselves" in the interests of social stability.

No, instead there are incentives. Some are blatantly coercive, as is the case with many laws, but the most important are intrinsic to the very high cost of refusing to participate in society's institutions. The idea is simple. Refusal to behave in accord with society's accepted roles excludes the individual miscreant from social interaction and from whatever benefits it may afford. Born into an institutional setting inherited from our predecessors, if we are to enjoy the fruits of society (however objectively meager they may be) we must fulfill society's role expectations. But by behaving in this way we produce character structures that yield a human center that conforms to society's boundary, even should those institutions be oppressive. Families, schools, places of work, markets, churches and social clubs all involve roles we must step into if we are to belong, and in adopting these we create ourselves as "conformists." This is the fundamental dynamic that "reproduces" societal stability as a historical outcome.

Core Characteristics

To further investigate this dynamic and the issue of the interrelations between the four institutional networks we mentioned earlier, it is useful to employ still another analytic concept, "core characteristic." A core characteristic is a societal attribute, set of attributes, relation, or set of relations which has a defining impact upon the lives large numbers of people are able to lead. It is a feature or set of features which *is basic* to the determination of people's interpersonal relations, life options, and their demarcation into social groups. For example, in a particular society if certain social features were intrinsic to all relations between men and women and determined a basic inequality between them then these would likely define a core characteristic. They would determine much of what people are and can be, what needs they perceive and can fulfill, what limits are placed on their development by social relations and by their own consciousness. Core features of this sort would come to penetrate both a society's center and its boundary.

Determining the core characteristics of a society is an empirical process. They cannot be known a priori. However, we do know in advance that there will be core characteristics and that they will be present in both center and boundary.* And we can further deduce that to maintain a condition of relative stability, any two core characteristics in a given society must be at least mutually compatible. For example, suppose women were subordinate to men in the family relations of a particular society but the hierarchy in economic units placed women above men in income and power. Obviously the society would be simultaneously pushing people in opposite directions. Moreover, having both a kinship and an economic moment, every institution would be a seat of this contradiction. The limits and possibilities imposed by one core characteristic would be contrary to those of the other. There would be instability and a change such that some kind of conformity would finally result. Obviously roles and people's expectations and also institutions of different kinds in a given society may be frequently out of synchronization with one another. The dynamic we describe is more powerful as the disjuncture is greater in magnitude.

---

*This theoretical insight, like the one that there is a center and boundary in any society, is not really a priori in the Kantian sense; it is simply pre-investigative of any *particular* society. The results derive instead from our knowledge of the human condition and the general requisites of social life and social interaction. Here we shall occasionally use the word ''a priori'' in just this way, meaning, in essence, known prior to any concrete investigation of the society in question. We do this not to confuse the issue, but because this distinction between what is socially known ''a priori'' and what instead requires specific inquiry is often confused.

Accommodation and Co-Reproduction

Now we can usefully address the question of the relations between the institutions and consciousness associated with the four spheres of life activity. In most historical settings economic relations beget class divisions, kinship relations beget gender divisions, and community relations beget race, ethnic, national and religious divisions. There is no intention to suggest that class is acultural, community devoid of sexual content, etc. We are talking at an abstract level about the primary seats of certain demarcations, not about their complete genesis or determination. In any case, when people are divided along these lines, diverse historical forms of classism, racism, sexism, and authoritarianism generally become core characteristics of the society, and the involved groups become potential collective agents of historical change.

In a stable social formation, economic requirements can't severely contradict those deriving from political, community, or kinship forms, and similarly for all other permutations. "Can't contradict" is of course too strong to be precise. Rather, minor contradictions continually resolvable by an on-going flux of the social relations are always present, but stability should be understood flexibly to include this low-level of continual evolutionary alteration. More important, there can also be significant objective contradictions between or within spheres which don't immediately impact on people's lives and consciousness in ways prompting resolutions. When they do, however, the dynamic factors described in these paragraphs come into play, and this rather powerful result applies to the institutional arrangements in each sphere and also to the consciousness people develop from acting within the roles dictated by those institutions. You can't have one world view resulting from your economic activity, and another generated by your kinship activity, where the two pull in seriously conflicting directions. Rather, there must at least be minimal accommodation. Without such accommodation the institutions and consciousness—of one sphere or the other—or both—must change. But there is no apriori reason to argue that the accommodation in such changes will always proceed in one direction. For example, there is no reason to assume that the economic sphere is the fundamental "driving force" such that everything accommodates to the economic moment which therefore can be presumed to dominate in all conflicts.

But it is quite possible that the different moments are more interactive than simple accommodation. We have already seen that each of the four moments is a potential aspect of all activity. In this general case each type of institutional network is involved in accomplishing functions central to the other networks in addition to its own. So the factory also socializes when its technology and role definitions deskill workers and compel competitive and instrumental relations among them and the state also produces when it creates highways, missiles, schools, etc. Another way of viewing society that sensitizes us to situations where features of the four networks are co-defining and co-reproductive is to see one single institutional network with four different moments and, in a sense, four different foci. Depending on the situation we will feel free to employ either the one network with four moments conceptualization or the four networks each with a principal moment as well as three secondary moments conceptualization. This complementarity of approach is designed to insure the most complete and all-sided analysis as well as tools suited to different needs.*

But what is the difference between "simple accommodation" and "co-reproduction?" With accommodation, as we have discussed, it is "merely" necessary that the social hierarchies which evolve in community activity, for instance, are not contradicted by economic relations, and vice versa. If community life places whites above blacks institutionally and in consciousness, then economic relations must honor this asymmetry. But it is possible that beyond "honoring" this hierarchy, economic relations help reproduce or aggravate the asymmetry. In this case, the very definition of

---

*Couching a theory in more than one formalism has a variety of uses. One formulation may spur innovation more effectively, or have more useful psychological or philosophical content than another, even as the two are logically indistinguishable in their predictive and explanatory content. It may be easier to find error criticizing one formulation than another—the error may be isolated as one "axiom" in one formalism, and embedded in many in another; or, on the contrary, one may be easier to use and therefore reveal new capacities of the theory. This multi-expressability of theory actually pervades our analysis and is quite common to many other disciplines as well.

economic roles and the content of their requisites would be a function of the racial core characteristic as well as the class core characteristic. And in this situation we speak of co-reproduction and co-definition. Or imagine a society where economic roles embody kinship divisions—workers fulfil roles mediated not only by class criteria, but also by family ones—for example, in the hospital where women "pick up" and "support" as well as type and clean up. Here it is not simply kin-blind class requisites that are defining the division of labor but also patriarchal ones.[39]

Such a tight fit among the different hierarchies is not inevitable in all societies but is a real possibility and is one reason we should be very careful about neatly classifying institutions into four spheres. For this demarcation can blind us to the more complex determination wherein a set of core characteristics merge to a single social totality, this totality then being at the root of the definition of all institutional and consciousness relations, rather than only the various parts of this totality being at root in the different institutions in turn. Thus, as a hedge against this oversight, we should try as much as possible to employ the twofold approach to looking at society outlined above.

One of the implications of our understanding emerges in the following logical sequence, which in turn provides the context in which the coming theoretical analyses should be interpreted. 1) The nuclear family, bourgeois state, private firm, and nation are each key institutions in the social network as we view it in turn in terms of the social relations of kinship, politics, economics, and community. 2) In any actual society, as these institutions and their associated activities interpenetrate, they must also at least accommodate and may even co-define and co-reproduce. So 3) none of the four can be *fully* understood in isolation from the rest, or in abstraction from a particular social formation with its own history. Thus, 4) there can be no *comprehensive* general theory of abstracted economic, kinship, political, or community relations, nor even of the central institutions of these types of social involvement. So 5) it follows, at least in our view, that at most what we can abstractly develop are theoretical insights generally relevant to an activity or institution in the abstract, and also a set of conceptual tools to help in more specific analyses aimed to generate theory of actual historical social relationships. This will therefore be one of our main aims as we proceed in later chapters.

We understand that, in trying to develop terms that allow us to describe a reality that is more complex than most orthodox analysts admit, we have come up with concepts and metaphors that are certainly unfamiliar and probably unwieldy. These metaphors do have a certain internal logic though, and by way of summary it is useful to describe how they fit together.

Imagine four spheres—four transparent globes if you will—representing a society's arrangements for dealing with the economic, political, kinship, and cultural moments of activity. The surface of each globe is a map of all the institutions the society has evolved. On each of these globes one institution becomes the focus from which others are seen to eminate as one might see the ocean dominating a globe of the earth. The surface maps, however, are not the whole story of the spheres—merely the boundaries. Inside each globe are complex webs connecting the surface institutional arrangements to the center, which in our scheme represent the human beings. These webs hold the sphere together; without them, each must alter or explode; without a proper fit between human center and institutional boundary a society must change.

But no one of these globes defines the society; actually all four are necessary, and the points on one map are located—with different names and arrangements—on each of the others. They must be combined, superimposed in an entwining fashion, to give a true picture of the whole society. And here again if the society is stable, there will be a fit; in a sense, the oceans on the kinship map will overlap in size and shape the oceans on the political map though water temperatures will be different and mix. What historical process created this relative conformity, only further study of the spheres will reveal.

Finally, we must have features to use in summarizing the nature of the spheres, and in comparing them to see whether they fit together both at the boundary and at the human center. These are the core characteristics, analogous in a way to core samples of the earth's crust, only drilled in our globes not a few miles "down," but all the way through.

Social History: Evolution and Revolution

Human activity is free—it is an outgrowth of the conscious application of human power to meet human needs. And it is also not free—it is constrained by the historically bequeathed institutional boundary and human center we cannot individually will away. Hence human beings are both the subject and object of historical processes. We apply our powers and mold ourselves and our environments as subjects, and are in turn molded by them as objects. When this ongoing process is sufficiently constrained by the contours of the status-quo to reproduce the defining features of those contours over and over, we have evolution. Details of life alter while core characteristics are reproduced essentially unchanged. But when the interplay between people and their social environments yields a change in at least one core characteristic, we call this social revolution. The society is no longer essentially the same. A new social formation exists, and life's options are different. Thus, the Russian revolution, Chinese revolution, American revolution and Cuban revolution were all revolutions in these terms too. But so were the industrial revolution, the American Civil War, and the transition from Victorian to post-Victorian (patriarchal) kinship relations.

Societal reproduction rests on the tendency for people to behave in accord with the roles defined by society's institutions to receive the benefits of social interaction and from the rationalizing forces of human consciousness formation. Against this background there are also, of course, conscious and sometimes coercive efforts by groups of people who are the relative beneficiaries of existing social structures to preserve those existing relationships. Revolutionary social change rests on the fact that humans are not infinitely "malleable" and that the conformity between center and boundary in all societies to date has been to some degree oppressive. All previous societies have rested on the denial of some subset of human needs and capabilities while partially fulfilling others. The "mesh" between center and boundary has never been without friction: society has always placed a round peg in a square hole, so to speak, but the peg never entirely loses its resiliency. There is always at least unconscious individual rebellion, even among those who accept their place. And against this background there can also develop conscious efforts by groups of people who are most aware of their deprivation by existing institutions to transform them in revolutionary ways. In sum there are both relatively automatic unconscious forces and also conscious human efforts at play in pursuit of both social stability and social change.

To translate these general tendencies into concrete analyses of actual historical experiences is an empirical task. But there are some further things we can conclude about revolution that are applicable to most social formations. A revolution occurs 1) when there is a contradiction which either cannot be or appears unable to be overcome without alteration of at least one of society's core characteristics, and 2) when this contradiction is overcome by human agents who succeed in effecting just such a transformation. In other words, there are two issues: there must be a deep contradiction and it must be translated into effective human activity. The type of contradiction which can generate such an outcome is not completely specifiable in advance, but we know it must involve society's core characteristics as well as social groups capable of being historical agents.

There is no particular need to discuss here the different kinds of contradictions as well as the different forms they might take in different societies since we will continually address the issue in later chapters. But who can we expect to be the agents of social revolution who will transform social institutions and norms? Since core characteristics determine life possibilities, and since contradictions focused around core characteristics are central to social change, we expect precisely those groups defined by core characteristics to be critical actors in social change. Thus a crucial task is to identify people according to the different places they occupy with respect to society's core characteristics. Contradictions which cause arousal of needs society can't meet, awakening expectations inconsistent with role offerings, delegitimation of institutional structures, or other similar disjunctures can cause these social groups to undertake rebellious activity which can in turn fuel the awakening historical process.   Thus, for example, with respect to the economy the definition of classes should be undertaken in light of this kind of process and of the need to delimit the actors who could become crucial to it—and similarly for locating critical groups defined by political, kinship, and community activity. The purpose in mind, that is, when we develop concepts which demarcate certain groups within society, is that of locating and understanding potential agents of historical struggle and change.

The main distinction between our approach and that of more orthodox Marxists about revolutionary agents should be fairly clear.

In the orthodoxy, economic relations are most basic, economic contradictions most critical to social struggle and change, and therefore economic classes are the most important collective agents of revolution. In our view, beyond economics, kinship, community, and politics are also central to social change. So not only class but also kin, race, national, religious, ethnic, and political divisions can yield groups with critical revolutionary roles. For example, the division of people into party and non-party members, men and women, or blacks and whites could all become critical just as the division of economic actors into capitalists and workers can.

However, beyond broadening the focus with respect to identifying important collective actors, we also differ from the orthodoxy in our understanding of class relations themselves. And though this will be elaborated in much greater detail later, an introductory discussion must appear here as a basis for certain assertions to be made in chapter three.

Where orthodox Marxists focus their attention on ownership in determining class relations, we address all differences in economic situations sufficient to generate differences in world views, values, motivations, and skills as well as incomes which pit groups against one another in ways relevant to potentials for social change and possible economic transformation. This leads us to address differences in the quality and type of work, as well as in the character and quantity of remuneration. In particular we identify a "new class" of "coordinators": individuals who have considerable control over their work and often the work of others, who have substantially greater incomes than workers and also substantially more status due to greater specialized and general social knowledge, and whose work is largely conceptual rather than executionary. Members of this new coordinator class include managers, engineers, and social planners, philosophers, ministers, and "intellectuals" of diverse types. Under capitalism this class is between and in certain ways opposed to both capital and labor and, as we shall see, in societies which call themselves socialist, this class often attains a dominant economic position.

The Problem of Social Transformation

For one reason or another a society that was previously stable enters a period of instability and revolutionary upheaval. Before there was a social formation with considerable conformity between boundary and the center, and between the relationships in different primary spheres of social activity. During the period of transformation this meshing of society's core aspects unravels and contradictions become paramount. Struggle between diverse agents ensues—some groups seek to reenact the stability that had previously reigned, others seek to overturn prior norms and establish new core characteristics in context of new social relationships in one or more major institutional networks. But what if there is more than one new direction to travel? What if the period of flux can have more than one outcome, can lead to changes ushering in more than one new organization for society? Then, the period of struggle can become quite complex. Rather than a simple dichotomy between forces of reaction and forces of change, there can be forces seeking *different types* of change. In this case, confusion may arise. People desiring one type of alteration may act in ways conducive to another. In our second volume we will investigate socialist possibilities for advanced capitalist societies. But we will also address the heritage of social transformations in some countries which underwent anti-capitalist revolutions while having relatively underdeveloped, non-industrialized economies: the Soviet Union, China, and Cuba. In each of these countries the initial conditions were different. And for all of them there were considerable differences from the kinds of conditions we may anticipate in a country like the United States when we embark upon the construction of a new social formation. In the "first world" as compared to the "third world" there are very different levels of industrialization, different political heritages and political institutions, and different kinship and community forms. It is quite possible that while certain options are foreclosed by under-industrialization or a generalized lack of literacy and technical skills among the populace of one society, they are present for another, different one, *and vice versa.* * In these volumes we will try to develop an understanding of the processes in the three countries mentioned above, of the movements' successes and

---

*In particular, it is interesting to notice one possible advantage that may hold for the non-industrialized countries as compared to, for example, the United States, should each "decide" to embark on a path toward a true socialism. For if such a society will be characterized by self-management, social solidarity, and diversity of cultural and social forms—and therefore,

failures, of the forces favoring socialist outcomes and of those favoring something else entirely and of their respective accomplishments. But while we will specifically address the situations of these three countries in their own right, we will also seek lessons that bear upon the likely future situation of industrialized societies to help develop a reasonable model of socialism as it may be enacted in our own future.

A Totalist Approach to Social Theory

In the totalist perspective there are four principle spheres of human activity and institutional relations—the political, economic, community, and kinship spheres. In a given society these all exist together in a single social formation and are therefore intricately interrelated. Furthermore, the four spheres have the same elementary components and roots: individual people with their particular diverse needs and potentials and also institutions and their social role structures. This sharing of elements and the same social space and time means that the characteristic features of each sphere must minimally accommodate to one another's dictates and may reproduce one another's basic features. They are actually manifestations of the same totality of entwined phenomena.

This fourfold character of social divisions may be understood as a product of the fourfold character of human needs we all share due to our species nature. We have economic needs related to the provision of sustenance and means of survival, kin needs associated with reproduction and sexual/emotional requirements; community needs arising from desires to understand our situations and evolve social identities; and political needs deriving from our social and

by an architecture, technology, and distribution of resources suited to equity, human scale, dispersal of control, etc.—it is possible that the transformation from agricultural "underdevelopment" to this new organization will not only prove relatively simpler than industrialization on a Western or Soviet model, it may even, as Mao Tsetung was perhaps intimating, prove simpler than would the transformation from industrialized/massified forms to a real socialist alternative. The Marxist catch-22 however, may be that the creation and production of the new socialist technologies will require the industrial know-how and capacities of the industrial infrastructures even if this creation may be their last act.

praxis natures and their implications for establishing regularity and clarity of norms of activity. But, in fact, as the expression of any one of these needs is always entwined with the presence and expression of the others, so too the four different types of activity are also always carried out in context of one another.

But doesn't the fact that each type of activity is entwined with, co-defining of, and sharing aspects of all other types mean that we could analyze society from the angle of any one type and yet arrive at an understanding of all four? Imagine someone beginning with the community orientation. Society is seen as a compendium of communities each defined by the interrelations of its own group with various other groups, and by the role structures of the community institutions it has evolved. The definition of community would be enlarged to include the collective elaboration of solutions to *all* kinds of interpersonal and collective social problems so divisions between men and women, minorities, classes, and political elements could all be discerned as different manifestations of community relations. But would the analyst recognize *all sides* of the less cultural and more economic, sexual, or political moments of society's different activities? Likewise, the anarchist using only power divisions, or the orthodox Marxist focusing on only class divisions, or the feminist emphasizing only kinship divisions must answer the same question.

It is possible that there is a *timeless* ontological reason why a fourfold approach to understanding society cannot be dispensed with even by someone who is especially adept at a rich single sphere approach. Whether this is true or not, however, we believe there are definitely strong ontological and epistemological reasons to prevent any singlefold approach from being penetrating enough to perceive all sides of all social relations. Basically, the fact that we all grow up and learn to think in societies that are multiply fragmented in ways affecting not only our material, social, and psychological interests, but also our very ways of looking at, understanding, and framing theoretical questions and concepts means that we each embody diverse biases in our thinking, and these biases will only be aggravated should we employ a theory which runs the risk of being similarly myopic. This is one critical reason why we have argued the need to elaborate a theory with a fourfold orientation. There is also an intimate relation between the structure of our concepts and the ultimate intellectual framework they compose on the one hand, and our activities, movement structures, and dispositions toward one another on the other. Single focus theories employed by citizens of societies that have fourfold frameworks of core characteristics won't yield solidarity nor preserve mutual autonomy for diverse groups. Yet these complementary aims must be accomplished within the same revolutionary process if we are to attain socialism. The kind of totalist theory we have argued for is, however, consistent with this sort of strategic project.

Ecology and Method: A Case Study

To see some of the benefits of the approach we are proposing consider different possibilities for developing an ecological analysis and program relevant to modern society. Among leftists, the orthodox Marxist will approach the problem from the orientation of class division and capitalist motivation. The culprit is twofold—on the one hand the capitalist's drive to employ all means possible for enlarging profit and on the other the capitalist's relative obtuseness to all but the most crass economic calculations. For the former compulsion pressures the capitalist to consider strip mining, dumping wastes, and risky and polluting ventures, and the latter ensures that no inhibitions about human well-being will stem the tide of such destructive profit-seekng. What will be absent from the analysis, however, is attention to issues of the qualitative side of ecological balance and, as a result, upon attaining power the orthodox Marxist is likely to pursue "expansion of the forces of production" in equally ecologically devestating ways. A feminist approaching matters of ecology will likely develop an analysis stressing the "male mentality" which sees nature as something to be "mastered" with no attention to the consequences. Similarly, community analyses might focus attention on the way nature is treated as only a "thing," thereby alienating it of its importance in the biological and cultural scheme of life. Finally, an anarchist is likely to stress the authoritarian moment of ecological destruction and its relation to hierarchical forms and mindsets.

Each approach has insights and power lacking in that of the others. But due to narrowness, each approach alone is susceptable not only to errors of ommission but even to the commission of faults on a par with those being challenged—witness the results of orthodox Marxist hegemony in the Eastern countries. Perhaps most important, in seeking to develop strategies for ecological movements, each orientation alone will prove insufficient. The problem is that programs worked out with a particular viewpoint will be insensitive to other non-focused roots of ecological crimes and also to the multiplicity of factors essential to keeping a powerful movement effective in a fourfold core characterized society. The alternative we suggest is the totalist approach which would ask how do class, political, kinship, and community relationships help to determine ecological contours and how must movements for ecological change encompass the lessons of analysis from all four angles simultaneously? Obviously this is not the place to do such an analysis. But it should be evident to people who have been active in ecological struggles that failures to adequately understand simultaneously class, political, sexual, and community factors relating to ecological destruction and to the formation of social movements have frequently been even more of an impediment to success than the admittedly substantial defensive efforts of major polluters and the state.

What are the implications of this totalist approach for further theoretical work and for major questions facing socialists? Without previewing the lessons of each chapter to come, perhaps a few points should be made here concerning overall implications that will emerge rully only in context of the whole study we are undertaking. First, the idea of categorizing societies economically (or along any other single axis) will be seriously undermined. It will become clear that one cannot say a society has this or that kind of economic network and claim to thereby have understood and classified it. Instead, we will see that every society has four intertwined networks of institutions and spheres of social life which must each be described. Likewise, though these spheres will affect one another's historical alterations, they need not always change simultaneously. While basic alterations of any given sphere will usually lead to basic change in other spheres or be reversed by the lack of alteration of other spheres, in other instances major alterations in one set of dynamics may cause only minor changes elsewhere. In either case, a simple stage theory of history is rendered obsolete. More important, the idea of laws of motion of a particular sphere, while certainly valid and important, cannot be mistaken for the idea of laws of motion for a whole society. In addition, due to social connectivity, laws of motion for an abstracted sphere, for example, capitalist economic relations, will have to be given less weight. Logical analyses of economic tendencies abstracting from politics, community, or kinship can yield important insights, to be sure. But they will also yield results which may need to be reevaluated when other relations are taken into account and likewise fail to reveal relations that are important only due to the interface of economics with these other social spheres.

Program of Analysis and Evaluation

The main aim of *Marxism and Socialist Theory* is to elaborate a theory suitable for analyzing the societies that call themselves socialist but are not, and for formulating a desirable socialist vision for implementation in the United States. In this chapter we have presented the main outlines of such a theory.

With regard to analysis this theory presents a clear injunction. In any society we should begin by investigating the features of center and boundary in each of the four primary spheres of life activity: economics, politics, kinship, and community. We should try to understand the nature of the four interrelated institutional networks, their role offerings, and the associated personalities, consciousness, skills, and perceived needs people have. We should identify the core characteristics and determine their effects upon quality of life. We should determine the kind of connections between the four spheres: simple accomodation, co-reproduction, or some variant of these possibilities. Last, we should address the society's historical characteristics. What has been its evolution? What are the stabilizing forces, what are the contradictions, what are the social groups that are potential agents of change or reaction? What is the balance between unconscious and conscious forces in stabilizing and destabilizing the society, and what is the overall balance of strength between reproductive and revolutionary tendencies?

But while we have given some arguments for this program, we have said relatively little to motivate its choice in place of more familiar approaches. Furthermore, we have only elaborated the most general contours of the theory. What does this abstract framework tell us about specific economic institutions or about real families?

Before we can usefully employ it to understand the historical experience of anti-capitalist revolutions or to guide us in elaborating a vision of how a socialist United States might be structured, it will have to be substantially filled out.

In the following four chapters by contrasting our framework with that of other leftists we simultaneously make a case that our approach can yield original insights the other theories obscure, and also fill out the totalist approach so that a more exacting analytic process can begin. But when we finally address the Soviet, Chinese, and Cuban experiences in Volume Two, and elaborate our own models of socialist institutions and relations, analysis alone will not be sufficient. We will need to be evaluative as well.

What do we feel about "existing socialism" and alternative models? The problem of evaluation must be taken up first from the perspective of human fulfillment. Most simply, a society is more desirable the more it promotes fulfillment of human needs and enrichment of human capabilities. However, many needs and capabilities are social products. We must therefore look not only at whether a society allows people to meet expressed needs, but at the conditions which govern what needs will "speak out." We need to assess not only whether people's aroused potentials are elaborated into positive social outcomes, but also whether the best potentials are being expressed. In short, a good society must not only allow and help its citizens meet their aroused needs, it must also allow the continual development of needs and of human capacities that are most beneficial to its citizenry. But it is not enough that there be a momentary process suited to meeting needs and fulfilling potentials. Rather, carrying this process through over and over must reproduce the desirable conditions or even enhance them.

Evaluation requires, therefore, that we address the conditions which give rise to needs and capabilities in a society, the conditions which determine whether needs are met and capabilities developed and enlarged, and the dynamics which govern whether the situation continually reproduces in ways which increase the desirability of outcomes or, if, on the contrary, short-run positive accomplishments betoken longer-run oppressive setbacks.

In our view once we lay a set of concrete "goods" on top of this set of general insights into welfare relations, we are in a position to make evaluative judgements. The goods we seek to assess—do they emerge, are they enacted, can they prevail—are collective self-management, variety of social outcomes, and human solidarity. It seems to us, and we have argued this elsewhere, [40] that these three aims encompass most others which socialists find worthy. They arise from our understanding of human beings as innately social, historical, and beings of praxis.

Thus it is our contention that at a minimum, humans must live in a situation of collective self-management, diverse life options and outcomes, and communal solidarity if they are to meet their innate needs and elaborate their individual and collective potentials to the fullest. There is no existent proof for such an assertion, though it should certainly not be foreign for most socialists, and will be shown, as we proceed, to conform nicely with our analytic insights and political aims. That the simultaneous fulfillment of these three criteria is possible in a single social formation is a main premise of this study and will be argued throughout. That existing societies which have deemed themselves socialist have institutional forms which don't allow fulfillment of these three criteria, and which in fact militate against their fulfillment, will be another primary focus of our attention.

THREE:
POLITICS AND HISTORY

"Incapacity of the masses." What a tool for all exploiters and dominators, past, present, and future, and especially for the modern aspiring enslavers, whatever their insignia. ...This is a point on which reactionaries of all colors are in perfect agreement with the 'communists.' And this agreement is exceedingly significant.

Voline

What do we mean by "political activity"? What are the origins and functions of the state? What is the role of political activity in the reproduction and/or transformation of social relations in other social spheres, and vice versa? Was Rousseau right when he said: "The moment a people allows itself to be represented it is no longer free: it no longer exists"? When Marxists debate the "instrumental" versus the "structural" theory of the state, is either protagonist correct? Does the political sphere play a more critical role than the economy in determining the character of everyday life in the Soviet Union and Eastern Europe? Is the bureaucracy a new ruling class, or elite?[1]

These are questions we must answer in context of a broad analysis of political activity and political institutions. We will begin at the most abstract level with a discussion of political activity itself. This done, we address various orthodox Marxist theories of the state showing the differences between these views and our own. We attempt to resolve confusion concerning relations between the economic and political spheres, and briefly elaborate our own theory of the capitalist state and of its relations to the other prominant institutions of capitalist life. We analyse the social relations of democratic centralism and bureaucracy, and the relationship between the coordinator mode of production and the bureaucratic state in advanced non-capitalist societies. Finally, we will suggest a program for evaluating the Soviet, Chinese, and Cuban political experiences and for envisioning socialist political forms suitable for the United States.

A Theory of Political Activity

The difficult task of defining "political activity" is eased somewhat when we remember it is neither necessary nor even desirable to aim for exclusiveness. We have already argued that activity which is predominantly political will frequently involve other moments, and that other activity will frequently exhibit a political moment. Therefore, we want a broad definition that captures the political aspect of what the state does, what opponents of the state do, what political parties and voters do, etc., as well as the political features of other spheres.

Certainly the elaborate processes of making and enforcing laws are "political." So are the processes of formulating and winning backing for social norms, societal visions, as well as more specific social programs and "political" platforms. But the activities of law-breakers, opposition parties, and revolutionaries are also "political." The common theme pervading all these activities is social coordination—developing social coherence in the presence of opposed interests and ideas—and opposition to any particular formula for doing so.

So how do we embody all this in a single definition? Political activity is creating or implementing, obeying or resisting political regulations or programs, and reproducing or disrupting conditions suitable for this behavior. Where a political regulation defines permissable behavior to mitigate discord and provide social coordination. And a political program is a more comprehensive plan composed of a number of political regulations and might include creation of formal political institutions. Political activity is to be found wherever social coordination or cohesion would not occur without it.

Can we further delineate the components of political activity? Like most commentators, we see a legislative aspect—the determination of regulations and of the character of political programs—as well as an executive aspect concerned with their implementation. There could also be a separate judicial, or interpretive aspect, though this divorce of functions is not intrinsically necessary. There is, however, another essential though less recognized component of political activity: determination of the *type* of coordination the state is to achieve through its legislative and

executive acts—the establishment of social norms or policy aims. *
This component may occur jointly with legislative determinations,
or separately in a prior process. It could take place in the legislative
chambers, in the "policy" offices of the executive organs
themselves, in party policy meetings, or in special commissions or
"think tanks."

Defined in this way, political activity will generally embody
economic, kinship, and community moments and politics will
penetrate the whole society, but this has already been discussed.
Here we begin by looking at the network of political institutions
any society must have.

A political network is necessary because a society is not just a
conglomeration of people in one place, but a coordinated union of
their activities. Furthermore, the fully extended political network
may conceivably overlap the economic, kinship, and community
networks. For example, in different societies the political function
may have been accomplished by a tribal structure which was also the
central institution of the kinship network and perhaps of the
community and economic networks as well. This would be a stateless
society, though not an apolitical one. For "state" certainly entails
an institution whose *main function* is political, and this would be
absent in this tribal society. With Hal Draper we might say that this
society has a "protopolitical formation" serving the political
function or, more in tune with our own formulation, we could
simply say that there is a political network but its key institution is
the same as the key institution of another sphere.[2] In either
interpretation there *is* a political network and a key institution or set
of institutions which determine coordination, legislation, execution,
and perhaps interpretation. There is a political moment to activity, a
political realm of life, and a network of political institutions. **

*For a full elaboration of this idea see Paul Joseph's *Cracks in the Empire,*
South End Press, 1981.
**There is no assertion here about "tribal societies" in general nor about
the complexity of any tribal political forms. For example, in the U.S. the
Iroquois Confederacy was/is tribal but was also politically complex enough
to allow direct adaptation of its essentials by Benjamin Franklin, et al. as a
basis for the U.S. state/governmental structure. As this "new U.S. apparatus" was purportedly the most advanced of its time, one wonders about
the Iroquis who, without benefit of the "civilizing effect" of traditional

Political activity always entails an accumulation of information about society's diverse groups and their needs, about society's institutions and the constraints they impose on decisions, about individual consciousness and needs, and materials needed for execution. That is, political activity has human, social, and material components each of which enter and may be reproduced intact or altered in the political process.

Not there at first, there later, when and how does the state emerge as the key political institution? A prevalent and very plausible answer says that evolving differences between social groups at some point necessitated the elaboration of a separate institution capable of more detached and also more coercive intervention to generate coordination among hostile actors. Usually this view is proposed by Marxists urging that the roots were class differences, and that therefore the state had its roots in economic dynamics.* But of course, why couldn't the groups with contradictory interests have been men and women?** Or perhaps the state emerged as a necessary tool of inter-tribal struggle.*** Or, perhaps the state arose to mediate conflicts between those playing different roles in the pre-state political sphere itself? Couldn't tribal elders or religious leaders have hammered out such domineering *political* roles and interests that they had to elaborate the state to defend these and also to

industrial economic forms, had been using this political form's essential attributes for centuries. The critique of "mechanical materialism" implicit in these facts is worth noting.

*Engels is the prime example of this. Engels, *The Origin of Private Property, the Family, and the State,* International Publishers, p. 31. "Because the state arose from the need to hold class antagonisms in check, but because it arose at the same time in the midst of the conflict of these classes, it is, as a rule, the state of the most powerful, economically dominant class, which, through the medium of the state, becomes also the political dominant class, and thus acquires new means of holding down and exploiting the oppressed class."

**Gayle Rubin suggests this at the close of her essay, "The Traffic in Women," in Rayna Reiter, *Toward an Anthropology of Women,* Monthly Review Press, 1978.

***It seems that the Iroquois may provide a historical instance of such a process: combining tribes within cultural commonality as a defense and rationalizing male/female relations engender ever more sophisticated political structures eventually requiring a state.

mediate growing discord between themselves and other groups in their tribes? This would allow a theory of the origins of the state based on purely political dynamics. All of these "stories" represent possible explanations for the genesis of the state. Perhaps one or the other actually occurred, perhaps a combination; but the current preoccupation with resolution of the truth of this *genesis* is exaggerated. For even if the state was a product not only of political dynamics—and after all, it was necessarily partially a product of the development of the proto-political network—but also of economic, kin, or tribal dynamics, this has only limited significance. Whatever insights such knowledge might provide, it would not imply anything definitive about a permanent causal relationship running in predominantly one direction between one of these other social spheres and the political realm.

The State as an Organic Part of Society

Consider the following quotation from Hegel:

The limbs and organs of an organic body are not merely part of it: it is only in this unity that they are what they are, and they are unquestionably affected by that unity, as they also in turn affect it. These limbs and organs become mere parts only when they pass under the hand of the anatomist, whose occupation, be it remembered, is not with the living body but with the corpse.[4]

To view the state outside society as a whole is to play the role of anatomist. This need not display a concern solely for the corpse if the analyst is aware of the abstraction and its associated dangers. Study of the dissected heart contributes to knowledge of the heart in the body but only if it is undertaken in light of other studies and informed by broader knowledge than that obtained by isolated viewing. So much more so with a social organism where each "limb" does not only its own job, but contributes more or less directly to the work of all the others. The state is political, but also engages in economic activity like building roads and regulating prices. The existence of each aspect is co-extensive with the existence of others. It makes no sense to speak a priori of a permanent hierarchy between different spheres of activity. Though at a particular moment the state might play a more central role in societal changes, or the economy might at another moment; viewed over a span of time it becomes clear that all four central realms are critical to social evolution.

Engels said, "The state is a product of society at a certain stage of development, it is the admission that this society has become entangled in an insoluble contradiction with itself, that it is cleft into irreconcilable antagonisms which it is powerless to dispell."[5] In our interpretation: the society has evolved to the point where the task of coordinating conflicts between disparate groups and institutional contradictions can no longer be effectively carried out by a set of institutions whose main aim lies elsewhere, for example by tribes or families. Instead, a more politically focused institution, the state, is necessary. But even though Engels proceeds to insist that the antagonisms are class antagonisms, his statement which we endorse above does not imply that the state is solely a creation of class struggle, or that it exists simply as a class tool, mediator, enforcer, or anything else of the sort.[6]

So with the development of sufficient social antagonisms the state evolves as the key institution of the political sphere. There can be no comprehensive theory of the state across social formations for two reasons: states arise from different kinds of social conflicts, and their features depend significantly on the "social totality." Though there is a specific "political dynamic" associated with each different type of state—monarchy, electoral democracy, dictatorship, and participatory democracy—this is always textured by the character of other social spheres. "Just as the capitalist form of production does not exist for the sake of exploitation but for the sake of social production and yet represents the exploitation of the worker, so too the state is not present for the sake of political oppression but for the sake of regulating the social totality, and yet is an organ of political oppression." As Mihaly Vajda continues, the state engenders "a form of oppression quite distinct from class [kin and community] oppression"[7] but is nonetheless entwined with these. To be fully understood any particular state must therefore be studied in its interaction with other social spheres which it both influences and is influenced by. Yet for certain less comprehensive purposes different types of states, or even the "state-in-general" may be usefully studied in the abstract.

A valid general conclusion, for example, is that part of *any* state's activity is always recreating the conditions of its *own* political dominance. "The state bureaucracy which wants to maintain the existing form of political power because it is its *own* power, will suppress every movement that protests against this power."[8] One mode for accomplishing this is coercive: the state initiates penalties and backs prohibitions with judgement and coercive retribution. But this is not the only technique. State activity creates a climate of obedience, and its own legitimacy. This is accomplished by various means including subterfuge, mystification, and monopolizing knowledge, but also by "serving the people" at least well enough to "take the edge off" major shortcomings which could otherwise generate serious opposition. The state as a vehicle of social welfare is the outcome of this last function: it implies an active, positive role, though highly circumscribed to be sure.

With respect to the economy, for example, the state will mediate conflicts within and between classes, ameliorate the effects of economic dysfunctions, and clean up after economic processes insofar as their products are in part socially disruptive. Of course by the logic of accommodation we know that even if the state's hierarchy were separate from the economy's (which is not very likely), it would not significantly contradict it if the society were even minimally stable. The social normative determinations of the state will therefore, by different dynamics in different epochs and social formations, continually resolve economic contradictions to favor the "ruling economic classes"; just as, for that matter, the economic activity of these classes will help reproduce the state in ways suited to the maintenance of the social position of *its* leading elements. Specifically, under capitalism state subsidies to corporations, state spending to enhance accumulation, political strike breaking, and arresting and hounding of dissidents are all examples of such programs that reproduce the state hierarchy in tact. On the other hand, the state sometimes responds to working class anger by responding to demands for unemployment insurance, restricted workday, minimum wage, ecological regulations, and work rules reforms. The same general pattern emerges with respect to societal divisions stemming from kinship and community activity. For example, the state may institute different kinds of marriage laws, or may pass important rape, abortion reform, or equal rights laws in response to women's struggles. The state may exclude minorities from political franchise, restrict their right to property and freedom of movement, or respond to their militance with partial legal reforms and even affirmative action programs. Likewise as the state hierarchy will at least accord with the class divisions within society, so it will accord with sexual and community divisions placing men and members of dominant community groups at the top.

However, within political activity itself, and in the fulfillment of its own functions, the state elaborates not only a division between those conceiving and those executing political activity, but also divisions between people filling different roles inside state institutions. These can yield social groups who share needs and perspectives and act together in struggles within the state and struggles between the state and the rest of society. It can lead to social groups which may be important to recognize if we are to understand and try to change a particular society. For example, there can be diverse bureaucratic alignments within the state apparatus itself—the defense department, the judiciary, HEW, the energy bureau—and there may be political party allegiances, military allegiances, and the like. The importance of these demarcations is borne out by historical analyses of recent events in such countries as Chile, Peru, South Korea, Portugal, and China. The problem isn't that other analysts don't address party, faction, and military allegiances, and divisions within the state apparatuses and bureaus—practical necessity enforces such analyses—but that most Marxists don't provide us with a framework for doing this clearly and precisely. Rather than taking the initiative in this kind of political analysis, *these* Marxists must be driven to it like cows reluctant to leave their greener economic pastures.*

A* quotation from Leon Trotsky's later theoretical work makes our point graphically. Fetishizing a (misunderstood) analysis of "declining" economic relations, he is even drawn to blur the importance of a distinction between Hitler's state, and those of bourgeois democracies: "Naturally there exists a difference between the political regimes in bourgeois society just as there is a difference in comfort between various cars in a railway train. But when the whole train is plunging into an abyss [and for Trotsky and or orthodox or fatalist Marxists, it almost always is] the distinction between decaying democracy and murderous fascism

Political activity also tends to involve a very important separation of conceptual and executionary functions, the former involving design, the latter implementation. Both the social-normative and the legislative moments of political activity are largely conceptual. The executive branch is generally involved in both conceptual and executionary activity. Then of course, the population at large simply executes political directives.

The parallel to our earlier discussion of the existence of a coordinator class in capitalism and to its particularly important role in conceptual activity in advanced non-capitalist societies is quite intentional. The distinction which exists in the political sphere between conceivers and executors and in the economic sphere between coordinators and workers is quite analogous, a fact whose implications we will study further in this and the next chapter.*

The last point in this section is analytic and strategic at once. In a society where the key economic and political institutions were one, it would seem that *either* a political theory or an economic theory, a politically centered strategy or an economically centered strategy could serve as a revolutionary vehicle. But if the two key institutions weren't identical and if one were causally subordinate, wouldn't the approach centering on the dominant institutions be valid, while the other centering on the subordinate institutions would be ill-conceived?[9]

disappears in the face of the collapse of the entire capitalist system."
Trotsky and Fatalistic Marxism, Geoff Hodgson, Spokesman Books, London, 1975, p. 34.

*As we have said, in a particular society the central political and economic institutions could be the same. But under capitalism they are not. Perhaps the reason for this is that the appearance of the market and capital/labor relation as regulatory institutions diminishes (without eliminating) the importance of the mental/manual, conceptual/executionary division in the economy, thereby calling into being a special separate institution specifically geared to this division of tasks and thereby better able to coordinate the rest of social life and even the economy, as needed. Thus we have another genesis hypothesis concerning the separate state, this time rooted not solely in the existence of antagonisms, but also in the failure of the institutions of the economic sphere to be able to politically mediate these antagonisms. In any case, the idea can be pushed from uncovering the beginning of the autonomous state under capitalism to predicting the

This reasoning is false. Were the two key institutions one, it would nonetheless be false that the political and the economic had become one, that the political moment and the economic moment, the political sphere and the economic sphere, political divisions and class divisions were one. The dynamics of social reproduction and change would be encompassed not by one *or* the other, but still only by *both*. Similarly were one sphere causally more influential and dominant in a current social formation, that would not preclude transformation to a new formation in which the subordinate sphere achieved dominance. In this case, excessive emphasis on the previously dominant sphere alone could easily confuse all calculations about how a revolution was going to change the character of society. In short no matter which conditions hold empirically societies have at least four spheres critical to the nature of their social formation. Attention to all four is well advised in any attempt at understanding and influencing social change. Any partial approach entails risk of serious error by deletion. Moreover, a partial approach consigns either the "most important" economic or political network, to a weakened analysis. For no sphere can be fully understood except in context of the entire social formation where it appears.

The Political Sphere and Social Change

We have already discussed the general ideas that social change can be either evolutionary or revolutionary and that social formations involve intricate ties between different institutional networks each emblematic of a different sphere of social activity. Considering the political sphere and the state, how might social changes come about?

character of its possible demise as well. For the overthrow of the capital/labor relation and the elimination of the market as regulator could pave the way for the economic network and the political network to "rotate" anew so that once again their key institutions would overlap, precisely as the key economic institutions came to depend ever more completely upon the conceptual/executionary distinction rather than the capital/labor one and the market.

The regular operation of political institutions could lead to small difficulties or opportunities for improvement in social relations. Various laws might be amended, the CIA could be reformed, or a new department of energy created. Most of the time such changes will not involve any substantial disruption of conformity between political center and boundary, nor between the political and other spheres of society. The changes will be evolutionary, recreating the defining characteristics of society.

Occasionally however, sequences of such changes could engender severe contradictions. Politically defined groups might be subjected to new role requirements, throwing their allegiance to the whole political system into doubt. Or, the growth of a bureaucracy suited at each step to tasks elaborated by the old institutional relations, could slowly create a *new* sector with such divergent interests that they must support revolutionary changes. Often times the development of military apparatuses leading to "left" or right-wing political revolutions have such a character, and some would characterize Bolshevik "socialist bureaucratic processes" in this way as well: The new political form creates a bureaucratic elite which then bends all of society's institutions to its own purposes.[10]

Another more frequent cause of change in the political sphere, is the need for that sphere to be in conformity with economic, kinship, and community developments. This would most often be a matter of evolving with core characteristics intact. But evolutionary changes in another sphere, say the economy, could also force the economy and polity out of synchronization. Indeed, this is precisely what many people think is happening in modern advanced capitalist societies, and particularly in the United States.[11]

They argue (and we agree) that there is a contradiction within the capitalist state between its legitimation role and its role in assisting economic accumulation. Insofar as the state aims to improve and foster conditions of capitalist accumulation it may lose its ability to win the respect of the broader populace and to therefore reproduce the conditions of its own existence. On the other hand, insofar as the state engages in actions which legitimate it as a democratic vehicle serving people's needs, it may be unable to assist in the reproduction of capitalist relations, and indeed may interfere with their reproduction. We view this contradiction as one *between* electoral democracy and monopoly capitalist economic relations.[12]

Whether it is intractable and will therefore require a revolution in one sphere or the other is an unsettled question. However, there are those on both the right and left who believe this to be the case. Among the former we find certain Trilateralists like Samuel Huntington and Zbigniew Brzezinski calling for a diminution of political democracy; among the latter we find people like Tom Hayden[13] and certain economists like Sam Bowles and Herb Gintis[14] calling for a specific form of economic revolution designed precisely to allow the maintenance of electoral democracy. That is, they call for alterations to bring the economy into accord with political relations *as they are,* rather than trying with Brzezinski to move political relations to accord with the economy as it is. A final possibility is that both spheres alter, a recommendation in accord with a full socialist program and one we will investigate after we first address the problem of "socialist political institutions" as they have heretofore been understood both in Marxist theory and Leninist practice.

Problems With The Orthodox Marxist Theory Of The State

In the most prevalent version of Marxist analysis, the state is a part of the "superstructure."[15] It derives in one way or another from the requirements of the "economic base." It is the economy's reflection in political institutions.[16] It is not itself a realm of primary power, not a cause of special oppressions which may supersede class oppressions, not the seat of social divisions which may be as critical to social change as class divisions.

Society ultimately changes as a result of contradictions in its economic base. This motion is brought to social visibility and practice by economic classes. In general, social institutions of the superstructure come to conformity with the needs of the class which dominates the economy, the ruling class. Or, more precisely, they come to conformity with the requirements of the dominant class relations (in capitalism, for example, with the capital/labor relation). In any case, the state is but one of the superstructural institutions, and to understand the state it is most important to understand the economic pressures brought to bear upon it, and the economic requirements it must fulfill. There is no special need for analysis of the operations of state forms themselves and no need to examine social groups that might emerge from the operation of these forms. Certainly, above all, there is no need to think about such a thing as "political power" outside—that is, not derived from—economic power, or political oppression not reducible to the dynamics of class oppression.[17] Henchmen of Batista and Somoza and the social elements in favor of and opposed to these dictatorships can be understood in class terms alone. The role of the military in Chile in the 1960s and 1970s can be explained completely through the tool of class analysis. Finally, the evolution of the policies of the communist parties throughout Europe, and of the communist bureaucracies throughout the Soviet Bloc can be understood as class processes. The politics of all these phenomena are to be understood as a reflection of economic requirements and class struggle alone.

But this is simply myopia. When class relations, or worse, the forces and relations of production are deemed the basis of all occurrences, then the state and even the bureaucracy in socialist societies—the specifically political aspect of party, military, government, and bureaucratic activity—become but an epiphenomenon. To accept such a notion in the West where we have a state whose influence on social life is so pervasive and whose impact upon consciousness and culture so profound, is ridiculous. To accept it with respect to the Soviet Union and Eastern European societies is so foolish as to warrant an investigation to uncover the roots of the blindness afflicting the analyst. We will look first at abstract theories of the state-in-general, and then at theories of the capitalist-state-in-particular.

A Brief "Typology" of Orthodox Theories of the State-In-General

With a base/superstructure theory, no matter how refined, there are few candidates for main theme in any proposed theory of the state. In the simplest *instrumental* version the state is always a tool used by the dominant economic class. This class, enjoying the power to dispose of society's surplus largely as it wishes, creates and dominates the state as but one of many vehicles to (a) oversee the accumulation project, and (b) preserve control of this project as a right of the dominant class.

A slightly more complex, *pluralist* view allows that the state is an arena in which all of society's classes vie for power and influence over the determination of laws and the coordination of various social services and projects. However, as soon as we add the inevitable caveat that by virtue of its economic power the ruling economic class can't help but win virtually all ideological and political struggles, this second theory reduces largely to the first.

A third approach sees the influence of the economy exerted institutionally, through the state's *structure* of rule and organization. The state carries the imprint of the economic relations in a manner that compels state outcomes to reflect economic requirements. An individual in government is in an institution molded to fit the economy's image. He or she is thus constrained to choose political programs consistent with the economy's reproduction.

A final approach focusing on a mechanism by which governors might be controlled from the economic sphere sees actors in the government being able to function only insofar as the economy is viable and economic support available. These governors are thus literally held accountable by the economically dominant class from without. If the governors don't govern as the ruling class wishes, their funds will be cut and they will shortly be replaced by more compliant successors.

Problems of Orthodox Theories of the State-In-General

We are happy to grant that each of the above hypotheses does accurately describe one facet of all state behavior, but nonetheless a fixed schism between political and economic relations is introduced in all these theories where none really exists in society. Furthermore, a presumption of the dominant direction of causality is introduced where an open-minded view of mutual interaction between the economic and the political spheres is needed. For the orthodox Marxist—not for all Marxists, to be sure—the political sphere is blatantly or subtly coerced from without by the economy. The relations between the two are exterior. The causality, in the end, is fundamentally from economy to polity.

In fact, ''political relations, although entwined in manifold ways with economic relations, are not at all identical with the latter... cannot be derived from them and do not form their superstructure.''[18] Although the networks of economic and political relations are coextensive, *each* is capable of secreting social agencies, *each* is capable of engendering liberatory or oppressive outcomes, and finally there is no apriori way to discern that all these relations reduce to the dominance of either sphere over the other.

In this view the whole orthodox approach assumes an exteriority and influential hierarchy which can, at best, be true only in certain times and settings. If you repeat often enough and believe deeply enough that apple trees don't bear fruit but only provide shade, your march through even the finest orchard will be cool but dietetically fruitless. The orthodox Marxist theory of the state directs the analyst of particular governments away from the political institutions themselves, and away from any political divisions they might engender and any oppressions inherent in their own dynamics of reproduction. Instead all that is seen is the line of influence from the economy to the polity, and even this will be obscured by the fact that the communication will be seen a priori as a torrent of sound in one direction and a mere whisper in the other.

Without entering the colosseum for a full debate with orthodox Marxists, it is still useful to contrast our specific analyses of the *capitalist state* with theirs.

Orthodox Theories of the Capitalist State and Their Failings

As we have argued, there can be no theory of the capitalist state in general, only of particular states in particular societies. Economics does not determine the state. Knowing a society is capitalist does not allow us to say definitively what type of state it has. Nevertheless, knowing a society is capitalist does allow some statements concerning the most likely character of its political arena. It's in this spirit that we now address certain major Marxist theories of the "capitalist state."

The Instrumentalist Theory: Paul Sweezy at one time in his writing presented an elaboration of the first type of orthodox approach discussed above to the specifically capitalist state. He argued that the capitalist state is ''an instrument in the hands of the ruling class for enforcing and guaranteeing the stability of the class structure itself."[19] We can conceive two versions of how this general instrumentalist theory can be elaborated to understand the specifically capitalist state.

In the first, usually Leninist version of instrumentalism, the state is a tool of the capitalist class, not only in the sense of being under its control but also in the sense of having a form and organization suited especially to the ends of the capitalists. Called into being due to the division of society along class lines, the state always comes to accord with the will of the dominant class.[20] Progressively serving this bourgeois will, its institutions and social relations themselves are molded to accord. The direction of influence is from the dictates of the ruling class to the structure of the state itself.

The critical factor is that the capitalists by personally dominating state activity forge a tool reflecting capitalist hegemony. In any case, it is capitalistic to the core. To create a new society, given this analysis, it is necessary that such a state be destroyed to be replaced by one which is in accord with leadership by another class, and which will in the end also institutionally reflect the will of that other class.[21] No matter that this view doesn't help us to understand the differences between German, French, Brazilian, English, U.S., Japanese and Bolivian state activity and institutions, it does find their crucial similarity, their embodiment of capitalist norms.

In the second, usually social democratic instrumentalist view, the presence of the ruling capitalist class in the positions of highest political power is the *only* critical feature. The state itself in its own organization and by its roles does not define any particular subset of possibilities; instead it is neutral. Although dominated by capitalists under capitalism, the state could easily be dominated by representatives of another class and would bend to their dictates as easily as it worked against their wishes in the past. To change society in this view it is not necessary to destroy the capitalist state, only to seize it.[22] To say that it seems from history that reformers who enter the government invariably accommodate to the norms that preceded them is discounted by arguing that these reformers must have represented the old dominant classes or, if not, then their promotion to power must have been a fluke, insufficiently backed up by a gain in economic power accruing to the new class they represent.

The two instrumentalist views correctly perceive that insofar as the capitalist state serves class interests, it is almost without fail those of the ruling capitalists. For capitalists do move in and out of the government, and do form institutions like the Business Roundtable, the Trilateral Commission, and the Council on Foreign Relations to serve social normative purposes. But in both versions the instrumentalist view fails to address in comparable terms why the capitalist state also serves the interests of men, whites, and of its own functionaries. The second view misses entirely the importance of the specific forms state institutions take, relegating the question to irrelevance. The state is simply neutral, a good tool for governance, whoever might be governor. This is wrong and misleading for strategy in ways we will further investigate later in this chapter. For states do embody particular norms in their structural relations and roles. The first view, on the other hand, overlooks that the state is often a scene of considerable class stuggle—how could this be if it was simultaneously dominated by one class and also bent directly to serve its will? It also overlooks that the state addresses issues whose class content is obscure but whose implications for other demarcations of society's citizens are clear, and that indeed struggle ensues around these issues as well, for example, in the United States the issues of ERA or gay rights. So in sum, in both views class struggle within the state is downplayed, the structure of the state is either oversimplified or willed away as inconsequential and, though not explicitly denied, the existence of non-class issues and of a state role in community, kinship, and authority reproduction are all largely ignored.* And of course, in line with our earlier critique of the orthodox approach to understanding political activity, the state is seen as peripheral. No attention is paid to the state as *itself* a center of a network of social relations responsible for partial determination of society's contours, for oppresssions, and for social demarcations relevant to how groups of people act in daily life and in political struggle. Political authority relations themselves are not seen as central in the processes of the reproduction and change of daily life.

---

*Indeed, one can search in vein in volumes on the theory of the state even for brief treatments of these issues, as a look at the well known volumes by Miliband or Poulantzas, for example, will show.

The Pluralist Theory: Amending the second instrumentalist view to account for class struggle is accomplished by taking a pluralist approach.[23] The state remains a neutral governing apparatus. Who governs is a function of class struggle, largely in the economic realm but also in the political realm as well. The state is thus one of many seats of on-going class struggle. Those victorious, for the time, govern for that time. Or, recognizing the different types of state activity and different state institutions this view asserts that class struggle occurs on all issues and at all levels. Whether there are parties for all classes struggling for dominance in the various political institutions, or just two parties each fractured into class elements, the class struggle is pervasive. Essentially the logic of the second instrumentalist view is extended, but that is all. Indeed, insofar as instrumentalism of the second kind allows for the possibility that working class parties can seize control of a neutral state to administer society and turn it in a new direction, they must accept the possibility of a pluralist period. It is just that they view this as an exceptional period marked by crisis. On the other hand, insofar as the pluralists retain the orthodox Marxist understanding that between the capitalists and the workers the former are in position to dominate in almost all struggles due to their economic assets and control over media then they too must see the pluralist struggle almost inevitably leading to an "instrumental" control of the state by the capitalist class, even if it is continually ineffectually contested. The views are therefore not far apart and the criticisms of instrumentalism apply to pluralism with only slight modification.

The Structuralist Theory: In the structuralist view the participation of capitalists at the highest levels of state activity is an effect and not a cause.[24] The first instrumentalist approach is simply turned on its head. Where before it was the presence of capitalists in the state which caused state institutions to eventually embody capitalist norms, now it is the fact that the state embodies capitalist norms which makes capitalists so likely to habituate its corridors. Thus the state is said to come into being precisely to preserve the class structure of the society in question, to further accumulation, to reproduce the conditions of social growth, etc. As such, like a hammer is formed for the purpose of nailing, so the capitalist state is formed to insure the bourgeois order. Its very structure is conducive to this end. Forced to other purposes it would be ineffective. Its internal logic is the logic of the reproduction of society's material relations. Naturally, in most times and instances, it is the capitalist ruling class who occupies the dominant positions within the state. Yet this need not always be so. A labor party can rule, intellectuals with no property may rule, and so on. The state structure itself will insure the outcome of their activity. The material relations of society are at work. The residue of historical motion is not subject to redefinition, willy nilly, by personal intervention.

Now the structure of the state is carefully regarded but class struggle is again overlooked as are the other dimensions of social activity. Are we to believe the state is also structured to reproduce patriarchy and racism in the same way it is structured to reproduce class relations? Again the state is derivative rather than a seat of social divisions itself, though now it is the laws of motion of material economic relations that govern its form.

An improvement comes with the "condensation" theory of Poulantzas, a kind of cross between instrumentalism of type one and structuralism.[25] Here the state evolves as a structure which serves only capitalist reproductive ends as a result not of economic laws of motion, but rather of the history of class struggle. The state is a "condensation" of these struggles. Presumably this simply means that a type of pluralist class struggle which almost always ends in ruling class victory leads rather inexorably to a greater and greater incorporation of bourgeois norms and characteristics in the very institutions of the capitalist state itself. The fight may continue, but the rules are less and less in favor of the most frequent loser. A tug of war starts with one side enjoying somewhat greater strength due to the outside influence of the capital/labor relation. Each time the capitalists successfully pull the workers their way, handy knots are added to the rope on the capitalists' side while the workers' end is dabbed with grease. The struggle continues but its terms are altered due to the "condensation" within the state itself of residues of the struggle's prior results. Applied to the evolution of the capitalist state, this certainly rises above and incorporates the assets of each of the other theories mentioned. But it does little to overcome their failure to recognize the importance of the specifically political character of the state nor of social struggle from other spheres condensed in the state either.

An additional feature Claus Offe introduces is to analyze the structural features of the state as "constraining" rather than causing outcomes. They rule out anti-capitalist options, but leave plenty of room for choice among the diverse options remaining.[26] It is over these residual options only that different social groups fight. There are outcomes consistent with capitalism's reproduction that are more conducive to workers' well being and others that are less conducive, (some that are better for women and some that are worse) and outcomes that favor one fraction of the capitalist class over another, while not harming the interests of the whole capitalist class at all. So even within the constraint of excluding non-capitalist options, there remains plenty of room for serious debate and contestation for power.

A last structural notion we might call the "purse strings" theory.[27] In this view, whether neutral or not, the capitalist state must function within society as a whole. The capitalists hold the economy hostage. If the state, by whatever its dynamics, coalesces a program the capitalists do not favor, economic purse strings will be pulled tight. The resulting squeeze will cleanse the government of offenders, unless of course they mend their ways promptly to prevent such a turn-over. In either case, the capitalists get their way. This is of course a power that needn't be exercised regularly to be effective. In the wings, it can regulate as much by fear of its possible application as by continual use.

An Alternative Theory of the Capitalist State

The most critical leap necessary to creating a new theory is to understand that the state is only the central institution in an entire network of political social relationships and that this network in turn is co-extensive with at least three other "similarly" important networks. The exact nature of this co-extensive relationship can run anywhere from parallel accommodation to completely entwined co-reproduction. Thus the focus of critical attention changes. Of course the state generally yields political outcomes in tune with economic, kinship, and community requisites. This is to be expected in all even moderately stable social formulations. In capitalism specifically, as well as in all other societies, the task is to show the nature of the interrelation between different spheres that brings this about.

Likewise, the state could intervene in these other spheres to positively affect their reproduction.

Our totalist approach can help open our eyes to the symmetrical accommodation of the structures and dynamics of other realms to those of the state and vice versa without tempting us to presume that the state has only a supportive role and derivative existence or that the political realm is necessarily always somehow predominant. Therefore, in trying to understand how economic outcomes are reached, for example, an analyst pays special attention not only to the economic institutions but to the state as well. Likewise, in seeking to understand elaboration of political policies, it is necessary to go beyond assessing political institutions in and of themselves. One must also consider extra-political dynamics taking into account the pressures emanating from other spheres but impacting within political decision-making.

At the same time, the political sphere is of utmost importance for its own dynamics as well. A powerful theory of the modern capitalist state must address not only the interface between political decision-making and institutions of other spheres, but also a theory of the inner structure of the political institutions themselves. For while this inner structure must be compatible with relations elaborated elsewhere in society, it is in no way reducible to a manifestation of those other relations. Just as economic analyses must describe economic relations and show how they can cause the division of people along lines of class, and just as kinship analyses must describe socialization processes and explain their implications for how people regard themselves and one another, so political analyses must assess the social relations within the state and how these define society's different social actors.

It is necessary to develop a theory of the particular institutions of the state, their role structures, their implications for consciousness formation, and the various kinds of vested interests these institutions impose upon social actors. We have certainly not evolved such a theory, but we can point out some of the issues one would have address. We need to be able to assess the manner in which particular kinds of state organization affect both state employees and citizens at large regarding the development of personality and reproduction or dissolution of social stability. We need to be able to understand the ways in which different parts of a particular state—the defense apparatus, legal apparatus, etc.—both mesh into a single whole, and also sometimes conflict with one another causing intra-state contradictions. We need to know how the particular mentalities associated with different kinds of state structures accommodate or even co-reproduce mentalities characteristic of status-quo relations in other spheres of society. Finally, it is also critical to understand how dynamics within the state and also between the state and society's other core spheres of social life both reproduce status quo core characteristics and also cause contradictions which can potentially lead to revolutionary alterations of those characteristics.

Just as the institutions of the state are not simply manifestations of the requirements of other spheres of society within the polity, and just as they themselves have implications which in turn influence other spheres, so the evolution and potentially revolutionary alterations of the state do not necessarily always arise due to forces from other spheres in society but may instead have their roots within state institutions themselves. Obviously, as we have pointed out numerous times, to evolve a general theory of all states is impossible and even the task of developing a theory of specific types of state is problematic unless one is very sensitive to the importance of the social formation within which the particular state is to be embedded. Yet nonetheless, in context of the focus of this volume, having made these abstract comments about features we expect powerful political theories to embody, we must attempt some further analyses of particular forms that many socialist propose as viable models for socialist movements. Before this, however we'd like to make a last strategic point.

Totalist theory undermines the notion that overcoming capitalists and nationalizing property can automatically engender a superior form of society. For by its reproductive interactions with the economy, the political sphere can itself reinstitute old or changed but still class structured economic relations unless it too is altered. Likewise, a totalist analysis shows that an authoritarian strategic approach will not only tend to reinforce characteristics of the old authoritarian state but also, by the state's interactions, of other major institutions as well. Finally, it also follows that strategic approaches using the old state while not adequately contesting its structure and premises may well lead to a different society from the democratic and egalitarian one socialists seek.[26]

Leninist Political Forms

Within capitalist societies the Communist Party is discordant. An institution of political opposition, it is presumably a contradictory element of the political sphere and also presumably a challenge to the dominant characteristics of the economic, kinship, and community spheres. The party emerges naturally as a by-product of the Marxist Leninist injunction that there can be no revolutionary practice without revolutionary theory and that this theory must in turn be established and elaborated outside the working class's usual daily life institutions. But, at the same time the orthodox revolutionary theory is nearly oblivious to the social relations of communist parties themselves and to the implications of these social relations both for the party internally and for the party's relations to dynamics in other spheres. The theory is insensitive, that is, to the social, human and political outcomes that are generated by the party's own internal social relationships. Instead, emphasis has been placed on the views of party leaders, the political lines the party subscribes to, its theory and "science"—in short on what the party says rather than what the party is and does. This state of analysis has been a travesty of the spirit of Marxist social theory at the same time as it has been a bulwark of Marxism as a religion. It is tantamount to discussing the use of the state or a particular bourgeois party or trade union as a focal point of organizing and strategy without ever seriously addressing the structural implications of such a commitment.[29]

Social relations are never neutral. The social relations of democratic centralism require an inner-party hierarchy premised on centralized knowledge and experience as well as strict discipline. Moreover, the social relations of the vanguard interaction between party and all other citizens reproduces the internal hierarchy at a broader level. Now the party is at the pinnacle with advanced workers, other workers, and the rest of the population following. Both the party and societal hierarchies are highly influential in determining party and non-party members' personalities, consciousness, and behavior patterns as well as in limiting how the party will be able to influence history and social change. We begin with a revealing quotation in which Richard Wright recounts his own experience with this phenomenon:

> I had merely been called in to give my approval to a
> decision previously made. It angered me. I found myself
> arguing against the majority opinion and then I made still
> another amazing discovery. I saw that even those who
> agreed with me would not support me. At that meeting I
> learned that when a man was informed of the wish of the
> party he submitted, even though he knew with all the
> strength of his brain that the wish was not a wise one, was
> one that would ultimately harm the party's interests. I had
> heard Communists discuss discipline in the abstract, but
> when I saw it in concrete form it tore my feelings.[30]

The logic behind employing democratic centralism is straightforward. To engage in struggle for revolutionary change requires
clear lines of command; there must be military efficiency. The best
possible planning and the tightest possible coordination of all
sectors of activity are necessary. Those with the greatest insight and
experience must employ their assets on behalf of the movement as a
whole, and the movement must be organized to "exploit" the kind
of wisdom possessed by its most advanced elements as effectively
and completely as possible. Beneath the top of the party we find
many layers of membership. There is a descending hierarchy
carefully constructed to facilitate the communication of new
political lines and of associated tasks, and to allow correction of
errors, replacement of ill-suited actors, etc. Once a decision is passed
upon, obedience is mandatory. Progression up the hierarchy is
basically a function of growing capability as judged by those above.
The organization is a finely tuned mechanism, able to function
flexibly and quickly according to the best available analyses. The
unequal development of members and of people within society at
large, far from acting as a hindrance, becomes the party's chief asset.
In any case, this is the theory.

But reality is something else entirely. Sometimes the most
knowledgeable and experienced people are placed in the central
committee and politbureau of newly formed communist parties.
Certainly as time passes whatever their initial insights these
individuals accumulate more knowledge of the organization and its
history, and more experience in administering the organization and
dealing with its many intricacies. Therefore in the areas of

knowledge which determine who is to be central, the gap between leaders and other party members tends to widen. But is this necessarily a problem? If the initial leaders become more and more suited to intelligent strategic analysis and political intervention, why shouldn't they retain their positions? How else could great heights of revolutionary insight be reached other than by building upon the most advanced starting point? In other words, aren't these characteristics precisely the *assets* of democratic central-ism—exponentially cultivated wisdom disseminated with maximum efficiency, first throughout the politically most conscious, and then the entire society. But what if the monopoly the leaders hold inevitably tends to be a monopoly over mechanical theory and inadequate strategy? And what if potentially corrective imagination and insight tend to be inexorably crippled if not extirpated.

Indeed, this is in fact the result of the monopolization described above. For as the leaders must pass upon all the activities of the party and its affiliate organizations they inevitably become impressed with their own importance. Why would they be in the center were they not superior to those they order about? Isn't failing to struggle to ensure the hegemony of their own views over less well-formed ones that may occasionally rise from some other source simply shirking responsibility?   "Confronted with a new philosophical proposition a member of the elite will not get excited over its elegance or originality; he would be guilty of a lapse from duty and would be denying his entire historical role if he did not first ask: Does this proposition fit in with the accepted tenets of scientific socialism? Does it have any antecedents which might serve as a precedent for it in the corpus of safe, legitimized doctrinal theses? Is it useful from the standpoint of the interests of the ruling elite? What will party opinion say about it (meaning, of course, the frank private opinion of high-ranking party functionaries)? If I tolerate it will I be called down by my superiors for being too lenient, or reported by my subordinates?"[31] There is therefore a likelihood that the leaders' ideas and theories will become jaded, isolated, and individualist by the very way the leaders naturally impose them: teaching rather than learning, molding movement and reality alike to the contours of their ideas (and those of their superiors).[32] And yet, as if this weren't enough, there are further reasons for these sectarian phenomena to prevail.

Consider the situation for an average party member. Life goes on in the trenches, selling newspapers, organizing meetings of local workers, occasionally participating in a strike and always functioning within the strategic limits formulated above, knowing these may change momentarily. The role is literally subservient, and mimics relations in the society at large. The cadre "consumes" political directives. Political gains appear to result not from human effort but from realms "above and beyond." There is no emphasis upon the actual quality of self-activity. The cadre's self-image is judged in terms of maximizing gains and meeting imposed norms, and there is no active criteria of molding one's own immediate environment and history to attain personal fulfillment. To rise in status, of course, one must do one's job well. But "well" is preeminently well in the eyes of the immediate superior, his or her superiors, and so on. Given this dynamic and mentality, the surest route to higher status is to be reliable, efficient, and uncritical.[33] It will not do to complain about impositions from above. It will not do to make suggestions requiring extra deliberation by one's superiors when nine times out of ten nothing will come of such deliberation in any case, and the tenth time the bottom line with regard to one's personal status is resentment even if policy is changed. For the viewpoint of leaders and ordinary cadre are levels apart. Leaders are not likely to see the wisdom of subordinates' suggestions until they become the ruler's own suggestions, or orders. This is true both because of the leader's different position and outlook and because of their self-justifying need to be the only initiators of new political lines. After all, to each hierarchy there can only be one pinnacle. Perhaps, if you have a taste for risk, you might try to slightly anticipate changes coming from above and complement the new line's wisdom when it arrives, being careful to rephrase one's own ideas in the same language as the leaders themselves choose to use. In any case, in the structure of democratic centralism fealty is both personally reassuring and likely to win favor and advancement. Initiative will most often produce disfavor, less prestige and status and uncomfortable cognitive dissonance for the ordinary cadre who must continue to function, in the main, according to superiors' directives.

With these dynamics it's not likely that the ranks will become ever more imaginative and richer in their thinking, much less more sensitive to one another's needs and capacities. Rather, they will increasingly carry out orders blindly, and if they take initiative at all, it will be "on the sly" and only when required by the conditions of their situations. "Subservience to those above, severe discipline towards those below, and only in the third place competence—this is the prevailing order of selection criteria."[34] An affinity for precision, drill, and tight formation, as opposed to "cosiness," sensitivity, and creativity are the likely products.[35] The parallel with patriarchal outcomes should be evident. Similarly a world view that assumes there is always only one "correct line" to be applied across the board will rarely result in an appreciation for diverse opinions and the value of experimentation. Here, the parallel to qualities that accompany racist and otherwise oppressively skewed community relations is to be noted.*

The pamphlet *Facing Reality*, written in 1958, says "The vanguard political party substituted political theory and an internal political life for the human responses and sensitivities of its members to ordinary people. It has now become very difficult for them to go back into the stream of the community."[36] Communist hierarchy generates a dehumanization—a "political life" in the narrowest possible sense—rather than a full and sensitive approach to human relations. This also causes a divorce from the mainstream of social life. However, this latter divorce is not simply a function of the presence of a hierarchy, but of its being a *different* hierarchy than the ones "regular citizens" are entrapped in. For actually, the social relations of democratic centralism are not fundamentally different (though usually even more extreme) than the social relations of capitalist factories or of patriarchal families. Indeed this is what makes the above analysis so telling. For even a democratic centralist party sensitive to the difficulties outlined here will be unable to adequately counter them. For the membership of a vanguard party are people from capitalist society, so their dispositions start out well inclined in the same direction as the social relations of democratic centralism push.[37] In this context, even a

---

*The logical extension of this community dynamic is that the elite actually becomes culturally separate and a community unto itself in a sense, acting then as a colonizer toward the rest of society. See Alvin Gouldner, "Stalinism: A Study of Internal Colonialism," *Telos* no. 34, Winter 1977-78.

democratic centralist party cognizant of the problems outlined above, is almost doomed to failure in attempts to solve them. What is required instead are social relations that directly counter rather than enhance these authoritarian traits.

Beyond demeanor, what divorces the party from the non-party is the way its members view the non-party masses. The idea of a Vanguard is simple. The party is to the advanced workers, who are to the rest of the workers, who are to the rest of the population as the leadership of the party is to the party itself. It is just the hierarchy extended. And the discipline operates in the same direction as well. It is the party that disciplines the class and movement, rather than the reverse. And according to the logic of democratic centralism this is as it should be. For if the party leadership must dominate the party membership for the good of the party, due to its greater capabilities, then certainly this same relation should be created, to the extent possible, between the party as a whole and the rest of society. After all, the differences in knowledge and experience between party and non-party members are even more profound! The party is the repository of socialist consciousness. On the road to socialism, it must be at the helm. This is the root of the party's justification, status, and power. "Yes," says Lenin, "the dictatorship of one party we stand upon it and cannot depart from this ground, since this is the party which in the course of decades has won for itself the position of vanguard of the whole factory and industrial proletariat."[38] To even think of distinguishing the dictatorship of the party from that of the proletariat is "most incredibly and hopelessly muddled thinking."[39] As in all cases where status and power depend upon some possession, of course that possession will be well guarded. In this instance, its importance must also be constantly reiterated. So the party's knowledge and experience is called "science." It is controlled by a small circle of leaders and their "intellectual" aides. Its language is contorted until it is inaccessible to everyone else, or almost, for the ordinary cadre must retain sufficient touch with a number of main categories and catch words to facilitate communication between them and the leaders. Moreover, the simple categories which percolate through the party, "forces of production," "relations of production," and especially "proletariat," "bourgeois," "petit-bourgeois," "adventurist," "spontaneist," and "objective agent of imperialism," force reality into very convenient contours. For once the labels are affixed, real events lose all their human texture and defining features. No matter though. They are now easily striped of critical insight and efficiently discussed in the stairway world of the democratic centralist party. The mystical character of these party discussions only serves to aggravate the elitest vanguard relations between the party and everyone else. That is, the party's monopoly of "scientific" terminology distinguishes party members from outsiders in much the same way as religious terminology and rites distinguished ruling theocracies from their subjects in earlier times. Possession of the language of power is one part of the basis for differential status and privilege.

Vanguardism also serves as a basis for differential status because the single party has a total monopoly of political power. This outcome in the post-capitalist society should come as no surprise since the Leninist goal was never to generate a movement increasingly capable of taking the initiative and administering itself, but to develop a tightly disciplined movement capable of seizing power from a presumably tightly disciplined and powerful capitalist class. The justification has always been "first things first." "Win" first, and there will be time enough for diffusion of power and cultivating breadth of initiative after that. But what is more utopian than the idea that an organization with oppressive social relations quintessentially reproductive of capitalist society's main authoritarian contours could lead to liberatory outcomes!

In sum: 1) the party aggravates the authoritarian tendencies that the political (economic, kinship, and community) institutions of capitalism inculcate. 2) The vanguard notion and mentality effectively rule out autonomous third world and women's movements. 3) The division of conceptual and executionary activity within the party, the justification for this, and its percolation into personality, social relations, and values all preclude an effective attack upon similar relations in socialist economic, kinship, and community spheres. And for purposes of this chapter most important, 4) the democratic centralist and vanguard party form does not lead in the direction of socialist political institutions at all, but instead toward a centralized bureaucratic, one-party state. The usual leftist treatment of bureaucracy in socialism assumes that problems come from a tendency of the *state bureaucracy* to overwhelm the *party's* capacity to counter the bureaucracy's evil effects. We suggest that nothing could be more misleading. The party itself is the center of the problem. Bureaucracy is a product not of politics per se, but of a particular kind of political process emanating from the democratic centralist vanguard strategic orientation of the Leninist party.

Bureaucracy as a State Structure

At least when the democratic centralist vanguard party is truly concerned with overthrowing (certain of) the oppressions of capitalism, this oppositional role forces some level of resiliency into its rigid lines of authority and some level of creativity into its daily responses to changing circumstances. Furthermore, while in opposition the party can only rule over its own membership (who decide to stick it out) and the front organizations over which it retains control. But as the party literally becomes the new state, as a bureaucracy becomes entrenched and the new society stabilizes, these minimal assets and restraints begin to fade only to be replaced by a stench of complete uniformity and regulation. In power, the party is the state and can and does rule over all citizens.[40]

According to Max Weber, the bureaucracy is an institution characterized by a hierarchy of officers each of whom has a well-defined job, in turn clearly demarcated from the jobs others have. All posts (save perhaps the uppermost) are appointed, all positions are held as professions and careers and there is very strict discipline once decisions are arrived at. ''An official who receives a directive which he considers wrong can and is supposed to object to it. If his superior insists on its execution, it is his duty and even his honor to carry it out as if it corresponded to his innermost convictions and to demonstrate in this fashion that his sense of duty stands above his personal preferences.''[41]

The common reply to criticism of bureaucracy is that it is not the apparatus which is at fault, but the members of the apparatus whose behavior is faulty. The bad decision, personally motivated dismissal, and simple ineptitude are all deemed individual's mistakes. But as Marx says in a not-often-quoted passage referring to Hegel's use of just this idea of ''personal abuses'' in the latter's analyses of the state:

He   could   hardly   be   unaware   that   the   hierarchical organization is itself the *principal abuse* and that the few personal sins of the official are as nothing when compared to their necessary hierarchical sins. The hierarchy punishes the official when he sins against the hierarchy or commits a sin which is superfluous from the hierarchy's point of view, but it will come to his defense as soon as the hierarchy sins through him; moreover, it is hard to convince the hierarchy of the sinfulness of its members . . . But what protection is there against the "hierarchy?" The lesser evil is certainly eliminated by the greater in the sense that its impact is minimal by comparison.[42]

Defense of the bureaucracy through recourse to the imperfection of its agents completely misses the point. Beyond the fact that the agent's very imperfection is a result of the "self effects" of his or her activity within the bureaucracy, even if these effects could be superseded and the agents' behavior made "perfect," the bureaucracy would be an undesirable socialist political form. Bureaucracy does not inculcate a disposition and capacity for self-management. It is an institutional form which disallows rather than promotes the conditions necessary for effective self-management. It is not on the left end of the authority/participatory scale. It is far to the right. There can be no "instrumentalist" analysis of the "so-called" proletarian dictatorship. For a bureaucracy is not neutral, and it cannot be used from without like an instrument which has no impact on the ends being sought.

As Rudolf Bahro says: "The apparatus does not think, it repeats what its founders programmed into it and what circumstances have since required of it in the way of superficial adaptive reactions. The idea and strategy of a social transformation cannot even be meaningfully discussed, let alone carried through, with people who have chiefly to consider what their superiors and colleagues will say about them."[43]

The bureaucracy generates social designations for people who work within or in response to its dictates. The bureaucrat develops a bureaucratic personality, a bureaucratic way of viewing the world, and a set of bureaucratic interests including reproducing the bureaucracy and rising within it. And the citizen outside also develops traits associated with this impersonal structure: fealty before the state, generalized acquiescence to authority, and an expectation that authorities will make all decisions. The legitimacy of a bureaucracy may be historically constituted in a host of ways including God's sanction, elite theories of genetic capabilities, or electoral sanction. But most important for discussion of the state in advanced non-capitalist societies is the cult of the expert.[44]

The bureaucracy's power, in this version, is a function of its knowledge and skill. Supposedly it is its "science" that justifies the power it commands. But, remarkably enough, the "science" of the bureaucrat is a lowly science, if a science at all. The knowledge of the bureaucrat is the knowledge of how to manipulate the bureaucratic levers, how to curry favor, how to "call-in" debts, how to elicit support, and therefore, ultimately, how to get things done. Rather than possessing scientific knowledge, the bureaucrat determines what is to be considered knowledge and science, and the real intellectuals—who might be said to have "science" at their command—must then sell themselves to this definition or consign themselves to the role of isolated social critics. Under such circumstances it should come as no surprise that the intellectuals in the employ of the bureaucracy will be the most opportunistic and spineless and the least likely to challenge expected approaches.* This is, of course, hardly a prescription for a truly socialist political network. As Agnes Heller said, "when the only legitimacy is that of the 'one true science' [determined by the bureaucracy], the place of a fistful of intellectuals will be occupied by Ghengis Khans."[45]

In conclusion, it is at least amusing and perhaps quite instructive, to think of the bureaucratic apparatus as a system of social relationships in a way similar to how Marx must have approached the economy itself. There are different agents functioning according to different norms. It is more uniformly tiered than the economy, but what if we nonetheless think in terms of a kind of exchange? The order-follower obviously executes tasks

---

* "If the cultural apparatus of the Communist Parties is practically nil, the reason is not that they lack good intellectuals, but that the mode of existence of these parties paralyzes their collective effort of thought. Action and thought are not separable from the organization. One thinks as one is structured. One acts as one is organized. This is why the thought of the Communist Parties has come to be progressively ossified." Jean Paul Sartre, *Between Existentialism and Marxism,* Morrow, 1976, p. 131-132.

but in return for what? Perhaps it is for the favor that comes from above, and for the increase in status this favor brings. Why? So as to retain position in the hierarchy and so as to be able to bestow status on those below in return for their rendering of execution. Thus E-S-E^1: one's own execution of a task is exchanged for status, in turn exchanged for execution by others. There is also a parallel process of exchanging status, for the execution of a task—for what? Perhaps for the greater status that accrues to one who has overseen the accomplishment of required ends? If so, the schematic would be S-E-S^1: status is bestowed for task execution which in turn brings increased status. If we let S and E take on complex overtones representing obedience and status and also the many things that flow with them—cultural advantages, material and social benefits, etc., then the map does bear a reasonable resemblance to the bureaucratic reality. Whether this shorthand is useful for further elaboration into new insights seems problematic, but perhaps it is worth a try. One should keep in mind, however, that the Marxian schematic for the capitalist economy, $M-C-M^1$ and $C-M-C^1$ is itself flawed in disguising the existence of classes and strata of importance other than the capitalists and laborers, and also that where in the Marxist formalism each agent follows one path *or* the other, in the bureaucratic framework, most agents necessarily follow both, though with varying success and vigor and in varying balance as one goes up the hierarchy.

Summary and Theoretical Program

Our picture of the orthodox socialist political vision and process may be summarized quite succinctly. The democratic centralist party is the main agent of the revolutionary struggle. During that struggle the party's leaders monopolize not only important experience but also popular recognition for the revolution's success. The social relations of their situation foster a self-perpetuating form of elitist consciousness and practice. The economy is nationalized and comes under central control. The allegiance of many of society's middle elements is won by the image of a rationalized economy they would administer, just as the allegiance of workers is won by the vision of an increase in their own power and well being. But according to the Party neither of these groups is prepared or

organized enough to administer political or economic affairs. The
party must take command. An elite heads the new bureaucracy.
Positions are allocated on the basis of experience and "scientific
knowledge." Yet in fact the main knowledge relevant to personal
advance is knowledge of the intricacies of the bureaucracies—the
true scientists are more or less excluded. And the workers as well:

> Bolshevism enabled the intellectuals to rid themselves of
> the ideological ballast which they had been obliged to
> carry as representatives of the working class. For in treating
> the proletarian state as the sine qua non of socialism the
> Bolsheviks made an end of socialism as a political,
> economic, and social problem, simplifying it to a mere
> matter of organizing state and economy. The Bolshevik
> intellectuals did not ask in what sort of institutional order
> the associated producers would find maximum political
> and economic freedom, but only: How can state and
> economy be organized so that every decision-making
> position will be monopolized by the party's trained
> cadres, and in such a way that those power positions
> cannot be limited in scope by other kinds of legitimations
> (be it tradition, capital ownership, or political repre-
> sentation)?[46]

For the bureaucracy and the empowered political elite to make
sense as society's leadership their ideological support had to be
strengthened. If science was the legitimation decision-makers
couldn't be subject to election. Determination by scientific criteria
was supposedly objective, not a subjective social process, and only
experts should undertake this. There would be only one party in
such a society as pluralism would show that social decisions are
actually matters of personal opinion and values, and power and
interest, rather than mechanical analytic problems of determining
the single best course of action for all. Similarly, class organizations
cannot be allowed except for the planners or coordinators (to be
described next chapter), for again this would lead to social
contestation and the undermining of the principle of one right
scientific way upon which the bureaucracy is based. Thus "the
communist parties, after coming to power, quickly dissolved or
transformed every organization in which only workers participated,
from workers' councils, factory committees, and trade unions, to

workers' singing societies, theatrical groups, and sports clubs.''[47] In place of these, only corporative organizations are allowed in which representatives from all levels of economic and political hierarchies are simultaneously present. Given the differentials in social esteem, privilege, power, and skills, it is quite clear whose interests these groups will advance, and that of course is the aim.

But there are profound contradictions at work within this scenario. For the self-reproducing political elite is not the sole claimant to societal authority. In the economic realm, the coordinator class of planners, managers and other intellectual workers has a claim as well. For this class sees the revolution as a means of its own legitimation and reorganization of society. But since this class has been very weak at the outset, at least in all Bolshevist revolutionary processes to date, they begin to challenge for dominance only after the political elite is well entrenched. The resulting conflicts between "red" and "expert" can be quite tumultuous as in the Chinese Cultural Revolution. And in the long run the political elite must become more open to entry and exit from the large pool of coordinators and party members, while the economy must become more directly the province of the coordinator class. For as we will see, the daily functioning of the planned economy does progressively strengthen the coordinator class*—its exclusion from the pinnacles of economic power by a narrow political elite becomes an impossibility. In a transition to a centralized society following an anti-capitalist revolution in the industrialized West, there would likely never be any such exclusion in the first place, the coordinator class being strong enough to

*Even in the earliest stages of Bolshevik victory the process is under way in the trend toward undermining worker organization and enhancing the role of local managers. Thus as E. H. Carr says, "Those who paid most lip service to worker's control [the Bolsheviks] and purported to expand it were in fact engaged in a skillful attempt to make it orderly and innocuous by turning it into a large scale, organized, public institution." Or as Lenin put it, "large scale machine industry which is the central productive source and foundation of socialism calls for absolute and strict unity of will... How can strict unity of will be ensured? By thousands subordinating their will to the will of one"—a clear prescription for management perogatives and an impetus toward the increasing growth of the "coordinator class." (E. H. Carr, *op. cit.*)

prevent it from the outset, a point we will discuss in greater detail next chapter.

In moving to examine historical experiences in the political sphere in the Soviet Union, China, and Cuba, we must obviously seek to uncover concrete instances of the abstract processes discussed above. What were the actual political elements, how were the parties or revolution organized and fragmented, what political struggles occurred—what was the impact of democratic centralism and bureaucracy on political struggle? Moreover, how did political trends interact with and influence trends in other spheres of social life? These are among the questions we will be seeking to answer in the historical parts of the companion volume to this work. The concepts we will employ and methodology we will use will be those presented in this chapter. They include a focus on political practice, consciousness, institutional relations, and political role structures, and they pay special attention to the accommodating or co-reproducing relations between politics and other spheres of social life, and especially to the social dynamics of democratic centralism, vanguard organizational forms, and state bureaucracy. We will find that far from being subordinate to the requirements of economic relationships, politics has for the most part been the central sphere of social activity and determination in the so-called socialist revolutions that have occurred to date, at least in their initial stages of development.

With regard to presenting a new vision, we will apply the same conceptual apparatus and analytic understandings as used in our historical studies but will additionally impose certain positive norms on our search: we are seeking political institutions that can enhance collective self-management, social solidarity, and diversity of daily life situations and trends. How should citizens be organized to express their individual and collective preferences for social coordination? What should be the role and structure of political parties and movements within a truly democratic socialism? What will be the relation between politics and the other spheres of daily life? Hopefully the theoretical work in this chapter and the analytic and evaluative discussions of Soviet, Chinese, and Cuban political relations to come in volume two will provide sufficient insight to make our answers to these and other similar political questions useful in the decade ahead.

FOUR:
ECONOMICS AND HISTORY

In the individual expression of my own life I would have
brought about the immediate expression of your life, and
so in my individual activity I would have directly con-
firmed and realized my authentic nature, my human,
communal nature. Our productions would be as many
mirrors from which our natures would shine forth. This
relation would be mutual: what applies to me would also
apply to you. My labor would be the free expression and
hence the enjoyment of life.

Karl Marx

In this chapter we will discuss theoretical issues concerning
economics, social change, and socialism. We begin by presenting a
brief summary of our main economic concepts. Next there are
detailed analyses of the two most prevalent models for socialist
economic forms, central planning and markets. Each of these
allocative forms is shown to be contrary to the norms of socialism as
we understand them. Finally, we conclude with a discussion of the
concept "the coordinator mode of production and consumption" as
the tool which we find most useful for classifying and understanding
those economies which have to date called themselves socialist but
which are in fact oriented toward the interests of their ruling
coordinator classes. Unlike many other chapters of this volume, here
we will not include discussions of *general* orthodox Marxist or other
leftist economic categories per se. This is because we have done this
elsewhere in great detail and feel it is not essential to our immediate
concerns to repeat the discussion here.* Rather the critical point
here is to assess *specific* theories of socialist allocation and economic
organization, and this we will do in considerable detail. [1]

---

*Orthodox Marxist economics is *not* an economic theory of praxis, the
labor theory of value fails to be a social relations theory of value, and the
orthodox Marxist theory as a whole is permeated by "economism" in two
senses: 1) it exaggerates the lone centrality of economic relations in determining the rest of social life, and 2) it minimizes the effects of non-
economic realms back upon the very definition and character of the
economy itself. See *Unorthodox Marxism*, chapter two, op. cit. for further
discussion.

We want an economic theory that can help us achieve a detailed understanding of economic activity, including its non-economic moments, and the interrelations between the economy and other social spheres. Furthermore, our outlook calls for an economic theory suited to discovering how human characteristics are reproduced or modified in the same processes that create or appropriate the material goods necessary for life; how new needs can result from attempts to fulfill existing needs; and how different patterns of economic relationships—congealed in different systems of economic institutions—vary not only in their capacities to meet people's perceived economic needs, but also in the kinds of future needs and potentials they generate. These injunctions, betoken a theory considerably different from orthodox Marxist economics.

First, we wish to present—in somewhat abbreviated form—the main concepts of our own "economics of praxis" as it is these conceptualizations which provide the basic tools of our analysis of socialist economic models.

1. Economic Activity

Common usage says processes during which material inputs are operated on or material outputs created are "economic," and we will use the same defining criterion. We will therefore draw a conceptual "boundary " between activities aimed principally at producing or consuming material objects, and activities primarily concerned with other matters. Likewise we will often think of economic processes as self contained not only in space, being separate from other activities occurring at the same time, but also in time, having a clear beginning and end. We do this even though we recognize that all economic activities are more multi-faceted and historically pervasive than this conceptualization implies. For example, factory work in a steel plant certainly has cultural, kinship, and political features, just as kinship, cultural, and political processes have material attributes. Moreover, the production of steel today is inseparable from the evolution of the technology, social forms, and work force involved in steel production just as it is inseparable from the production of all the inputs that enter steel

production and all the uses to which the steel is put. In other words, the conceptual border lines we draw are not "naturally" present, but are mental divisions of a larger social network and of an integrated and on-going social process. We draw the boundaries to facilitate particular economic analyses, yet often, when taken too inflexibly, these boundaries have led to economism and fetishism. *
Still, with this warning, and our senses alerted, we too will employ at least this much of the usual terminology.

However, while we have set off the economic sphere by reference to the priority of material inputs and outputs as foci for attention and concern, we do not at all mean to ignore non-material objects or relations.** Quite the contrary, we focus on the multiplicity of material *and* non-material entities that enter and leave economic processes. Individual workers' personalities, skills, knowledge, and values all enter and leave these processes. The factory produces not only cars, but pollution, tired assembly workers, and women who have been pinched by foremen intermittently during the day. Work in capitalist factories produces

---

*Although our approach is very different from his, Lucio Colletti's warning in *From Rosseau to Lenin,* Monthly Review Press, 1973, p. 7, is relevant. "If we isolate, that is abstract, either the ideological alone or the material alone, the result as we can see is a dualistic separation between production as production of *things* on the one hand and production as production of *human relations* on the other. Or else a division of *production* and *distribution* (the latter understood here above all as the distribution of human labor power in the various branches and sectors of production). Or else a division between *production* and *society*. Or, finally, the separation of a relation (assumed to be) purely *material* or natural on the one hand, and a relation (assumed to be) exclusively human or better still exclusively *spiritual* on the other."

**"In production, men [and women]not only act on nature but also on one another. They produce only by co-operation in a certain way and by mutually exchanging their activities. In order to produce, they enter into definite relations with one another and only within these relations does their action on nature, does production, take place." Marx and Engels, *Selected Works, Wage Labor and Capital,* p. 81.

skills for a few workers but deskilling for most, and it produces relations among workers that vary from cooperation and friendship among some small groups, to class, racial, and sexual antagonisms between larger sectors. Similarly, the inputs and outputs of consumption processes include human characteristics and social relations as well as Skippy peanut butter and finished lunches, Ajax and clean counters. In short, economic activity involves diverse material, human, and social features and to be useful for guiding efforts at change, economic theory must not exclude any of these from analysis.

In describing economic activity and institutions we will refer to "production" and "consumption" activity and "intra-unit" and "inter-unit" institutions.

We call consumption that economic activity which has as its focused elements, inputs; and production that which has as its focused elements, outputs. Yet we must keep conscious that whether labeled production or consumption *all* economic processes necessarily have both material *and* human inputs and outputs and therefore both a production and a consumption "moment."

Certain economic institutions are primarily concerned with the actual production or consumption of goods. Others are more implicated in the determination of what will be produced and consumed, and how elements are moved about. The former we call "intra-unit" institutions of the economy, and the latter "inter-unit" institutions. The former include workplaces and families; the latter market and central planning institutions. Again, of course, care is in order since the character of intra-unit forms affects allocation, and the character of inter-unit forms in return affects production and consumption.

2. The Processor

In our view all economic activity involves a selection process. Certain inputs are chosen and processed in a particular way and, as a result, certain outputs emerge. Yet, of course, for each process inputs and outputs could have been different. We call the determinants in the selection process delimiting which inputs enter, which operations are enacted, and therefore which outputs emerge, the "processors." These usually include diverse individuals, groups, institutional relations, or natural constraints acting in a complex combination. Of the immense set of possible activities, more and more activities are eliminated while others are gradually coerced into acceptance by a combination of institutional, human, and "natural" processors. Finally, one activity, defined by its complete set of human, social, and material inputs and outputs, takes place.[4]

3. Use-Value and Exchange-Value

Virtually all economic theories distinguish economic value into two aspects—"use-value" and "exchange value."[5] A good has use-value if it is desired (or shunned)—a qualitative attribute—and also has exchange-value if it has worth in the sense of being exchangable for particular amounts of other items—a quantitative feature. This far we agree with the usual approach, but in understanding what determines use-and-exchange-values we diverge considerably.

For example, although almost all economic theorists recognize that the technical relations of production—which determine how much of every item must be used, both directly and indirectly, to produce each good—are part of what determines relative exchange values of final goods, they either exclude the social relations between actors in the economy, or permit only one economic social relation to influence relative prices. It is our emphasis on the importance of all social relations between economic agents that influence their relative bargaining strengths and not just a single class relation that distinguishes our explanation of exchange values from more traditional approaches.[*]

[*]One interesting way of characterizing and comparing neoclassical, orthodox Marxist, neo-Ricardian and unorthodox Marxist "value theory" is as follows. All four schools recognize that technical relations play a role in determining relative prices. Neoclassical theory gives the impression that these are the sole determinants of relative prices because it implicitly assumes that the relations between all actors in the economy are of complete equality. For instance, it is commonly noted that in neoclassical price theory it doesn't matter whether capital employs labor or vice versa, one gets the same outcome. Both orthodox Marxism and neo-Ricardian price theory extend the assumption of equal social relations to all actors in the economy with the single exception of the relation between capitalists and workers. In this case these is explicit recognition of an unequal relationship. For neo-Ricardians the degree of inequality is settled primarily in the political sphere and must be provided as one of the

But an even greater problem is that use-values are usually understood to be economically important only as preconditions of exchange-values: something won't fetch anything in return if no one wants it. Yet actually use-values are in part a function of exchange-value, not merely a determinant of it.[6]   Use-values, or what we desire, come about as a result of our interactions with our environments as well as due to our genetically inherited characteristics. As we discussed earlier, any change in our activities can also modify our personalities, skills, and consciousness, thereby changing our derived needs and what has use-value for us. What is and what is not a use-value therefore depends upon historical and also economic events. For example, if the process of meeting survival needs via economic activity isolates us or compels competition, this will affect our personalities and also the social needs expressed in other parts of our lives.

What distinguishes our approach is that we emphasize the direct and indirect effects economic activity and social relations can have on the formation and development of use-values. For example, later in this chapter we will go to considerable lengths in examining the kinds of use-values that participants in an economy with markets or central planning will be most likely to develop and this will be central to our critique of these economic forms as being insufficient to socialist requirements.

4. The Social Surplus

Another way our approach is unusual concerns determining a society's social surplus and understanding the ways that surplus is distributed among different economic actors. Among a variety of problems in traditional approaches, most profound is that they all reduce the calculation of surplus to a quantitative measure along a single scale.* This is a serious mistake. In the first place, since

''givens'' in order to deduce the relative price structure. For orthodox Marxists the degree of inequality in their price theory is set at its maximum by the formal device of assuming labor power will be paid its value (a subsistence wage, by definition). But beyond this single unequal social relationship, all others are presumed to be characterized by equality. Unorthodox Marxism allows for the influence of numerous kinds of unequal social relations between capital and labor in general, monopoly capitalist versus competitive capitalists, Black, female, and white workers, skilled versus unskilled workers, and coordinators versus executors. See *Unorthodox Marxism* (op. cit.) for further discussion.

exchange-values are dependent upon a host of social relationships and not simply one or two easily determinable ones, it is difficult to aggregate even the "material worths" of widely different items. More important, however, is the fact that economies produce human and social relationships as well as material objects, and use or or consume such entities and natural resources as well. In other words, not only don't economies ever exactly reproduce themselves from period to period, they also never grow (or shrink) along all their different dimensions of activity at the same rate. Since for many purposes the different components of economic activity are critical themselves, and since any effort to subsume them all into a single category is a gross abstraction in any case, to talk about an economy's surplus in a way that is useful for understanding what the economy does and for evaluating alternative economies, it is necessary to recognize this multiplicity of factors in detail. Reducing everything to one or another number is insufficient and misleading. What is the surplus of skills, of knowledge, of new personality types, of new social relations—this sort of information is lost forever by simplistic aggregating, at least insofar as the aggregation pretends to be a complete accounting. We therefore try to confine ourselves to such concepts as the "material surplus," the "skills or knowledge surplus," or the "human energy surplus," using both quantitative and qualitative measures.

5. Exploitation" and "Redistribution"

Another difficult economic problem is to address the character of the distribution of economic products among a society's

---

*This error stems from weaknesses in the Labor Theory of Value which we have addressed in detail in chapter two of *Unorthodox Marxism*, South End Press, 1978. One way to understand the error is to see that what is in reality an oppressive distortion—and in any case only partially achieved—the reduction of human labor's many qualitative facets to little account in social calculations is misunderstood to be a natural, inevitable, and even more or less reasonable "accounting procedure" imposed by inflexible economic requirements. There is a double error, therefore. First, these laws do not really exist in the form they are thought to—the reduction is also far from complete, one subject of the chapter mentioned above—and second, in any case, the laws are quite mutable and represent as abhorrent a phenomenon as exploitation itself. If Marx himself erred in population. Here, often with specifically evaluative ends in mind, Marxists generally employ the concept "exploitation," which they apply to the relationship between the capitalist and the worker because the worker's labor power, when consumed, has the peculiar attribute of creating commodities which can exchange for more

his assessment of the power of economic forces to reduce labor and even in the degree of their "disposition" to do so, he did not mistake the phenomenon as something neutral to be merely accepted at face value. Instead he recognized the horrible imposition this was: "Labor, thus measured by time, does not seem, indeed, to be the labor of different persons, but on the contrary the different working individuals seem to be mere organs *of this labor." (Contribution to the Critique of Political Economy,* p. 30.) In short, "men [and women] are effaced by their labor...the pendulum of the clock has become as accurate a measure of the relative activity of two workers as it is of the speed of two locomotives...we should not say that one man's hour is worth another man's hour, but rather than one man during an hour is worth just as much as another man during an hour. Time is everything, man is nothing; he is at most time's carcass." *The Poverty of Philosophy,* p. 54.

What is theoretically and politically debilitating, however, is that many Marxists have taken Marx's discussions and read into them an idea that 'time' is a cause itself, that it achieves its priority on its own rather than as a result of the interaction of people within the constraints of certain *mutable* social relations. It is this contemporary fetishistic error which has caused Marx's own exaggeration of the role of time as a result of his partially incorrect understanding of the *social relations* of capitalist exchange to escape serious criticism. The Labor Theory of Value, by being understood as a given and a law of economic being, rather than as Marx intended as a manifestation of human actions in certain settings, has lived a longer life then it deserved or than Marx himself would likely have desired. What is at work here, on multiple levels, is a process Marx himself described only too well: "There is a definite social relation between men [and women], that assumes in their eyes the fantastic form of a relation between things. In order, therefore, to find an analogy we must have recourse to the mist enveloped regions of the religious world. In that world the productions of the human brain appear as independent things endowed with life, and entering into relation both with one another and the human race. So it is in the world of commodities with the products of men [and women's] hands. This I call the Fetishism which attaches itself to the products of labor, as soon as they are produced as commodities, and which is therefore inseparable from the production of commodities." *Capital, Volume 1,* p. 72.

value (socially necessary labor hours) than was required to maintain the worker in the first place, thus serving as the only source of profit.[7] Our problem with this approach is that the issue is cauched and concluded on the assumption that the use of labor hours as a measure helps explicate all important sides of exchange relations. But in our view it does not. Different laboring activities are different not only by virtue of duration, but also by virtue of different *kinds* of involvement and different *effects* on personality, skills, etc. Equity therefore, is not necessarily evidenced by exchange of commodities embodying equivalent hours of labor, nor is inequality necessarily evidenced by exchange on the basis of non-labor-hour equivalents. For example, agents with equal bargaining power engaging in a completely fair, non-exploitative exchange might well "barter" products embodying quite different numbers of hours of "socially necessary labor" due to a mutual recognition that of the two kinds of work involved one was more dangerous and debilitating, and the other more rewarding in the production of desirable human skills and feelings.[8]

Nonetheless, despite this criticism, we do agree with the desire to have a concept which refers to an exchange wherein one party comes away in some sense "more benefitted" than the other—an unequal, unjust, unfair exchange, one that would not occur were both parties somehow equally able to demand fulfillment of their desires in the transaction. We believe such "exploitation" occurs whenever there is an exchange between parties of different bargaining powers (here we are talking principally about capitalism though the analysis is true for many other economic forms as well). We will confine our use of the term to direct relationships of exchange embodying on-going structural inequalities in bargaining power, though of course it will often be applicable to a whole class of exchanges as, for example, in the formula: the exchange of labor power for wages—the worker on one side and the capitalist on the other—is always exploitative under capitalism.

Beyond "exploitation," however, we would like to employ another concept to address another dynamic that is critical to the unequal distribution of any economy's economic output. Thus "redistribution" refers to a situation wherein there is an accrual of material or other advantage for one or more groups at the expense of one or more other groups, not as a result of a *direct* confrontation resulting in unequal relative exchange rates, but because of an *indirect* systemic process based on a sequence of such direct inequalities between others. General Motors may exploit a small ball bearing supplier in a specific exchange and as a result there may also be a general redistribution between unorganized workers for small firms on the one hand, and monopoly capitalists on the other. There could be redistribution between sectors of the working class (who don't directly exchange) even if UAW workers, for example, enjoyed no more power vis-a-vis General Motors than workers enjoyed vis-a-vis ball bearing manufacturers who sell to GM, but UAW workers received a consistently higher standard of living due in part to GM's exploitation of their ball bearing suppliers. Or, in a planned economy, there may be a redistributive relationship benefitting an elite which does not otherwise directly exploit the producers. In short, this new concept, "redistribution," allows us to focus on objectively unequal relations even where there is no immediate interface between the parties themselves. And "exploitation" can be retained to refer to direct relations between unequal parties.

6. Labor, Labor Power, and the Division of Labor

With respect to our understanding of the concepts labor and labor power we follow a fairly familiar Marxist approach, with a few slight adaptations. By "labor" we mean the actual work people do, the human activity expended in economic production. By "labor power" we refer to the capacity to do work that all humans possess. Labor, the actuality, and labor power, the potential, should not be confused. For example, in selling labor we agree to do whatever is necessary to accomplish some pre-agreed task or agree to guarantee the outcome of a particular production process. The skilled carpenter says I'll build that back porch for x-dollars. But notice that to do this, to sell labor per se, the seller must already have access to and control over whatever inputs besides his/her laboring capacities are necessary for accomplishing the task. The carpenter must have tools, access to materials, etc. In any economy where the workforce does not control the "means of production" members of the workforce cannot exchange labor, but must instead exchange only their labor power. In selling labor power, then, we merely agree to place our capacities within a production process for some time. How much work we then do or the actual labor that results, remains to be determined. This distinction proves critical to understanding the situation of working people in all societies and will be central to our later analyses.[9]

Though retaining the concept "division of labor" which other economists also give a central position in their economic theories, we employ it somewhat differently. By division of labor we refer to the fact that in most economies different people engage in different kinds of work requiring and generating different human attributes and receiving different incomes. Defining the precise demarcations of social labor are social processes we shall address in greater detail later. But one infrequently noticed division is worthy of special mention here. It attracts our attention precisely because we see and study both the material *and* human/social inputs and outputs of economic activity.

Many societies have included a class of individuals who do no social labor but are nonetheless guaranteed considerable power over the disposal of society's material surplus. Most analyses take note of this fact and all visions of socialism exclude any "leisure class" whether it be a priestly, slave-owning, feudal, or capitalist class. But many societies have also been characterized by a firm division between people whose work is primarily to "conceive" and organize how and to what ends labor is to be carried out, and people whose task is largely to execute the conceptualizations others have put forward. Those whose tasks are predominantly conceptual and coordinating are not outside social labor as are members of a leisure class, but instead do perform a particular action. [10] Whether this particular division of labor between coordinators and executors is a desirable one, the extent to which it is or is not inevitable, and whether the division can yield a class demarcation are all important questions we will address in considerable detail as we proceed. But even at this point, it should be clear that concepts suited to such concerns are needed for a full understanding and evaluation of socialist possibilities. The concept "division of labor" can help us to understand the structural dynamics behind emergence of different economic outcomes for different groups.

Furthermore, analyses of "divisions of labor" are also powerful tools for discerning extra class demarcations in the workplace. For example, one may search out and discover a sexual division of labor or a racial division of labor both within workplaces and job definitions and between sectors in an economy. Thus women may be relegated to nurturant and detail work within a plant, and whole sectors of work like teaching or nursing may become women's work. Or minorities may be relegated to more rote and dangerous tasks in addition to enduring differential pay and other deprivations.[11]

7. Class Relations

Perhaps the most significant difference between our approach to understanding socialist economic arrangements and those of most other analysts derive from disagreement over the definition and importance of "economic classes." For us, there are two reasons to define a group as an economic class. Either it is potentially a ruling class—a group which can attain economic dominance and use society's economic institutions to enhance its interests at the expense of those of other classes. Or its activities can influence the ease or difficulty with which other potential ruling classes attain or retain their positions of economic power. In the orthodox Marxist framework, while attention to potentials for change is a central criterion in the definition of classes, the analysis has long since settled on issues of ownership and relations to the means of allocation of society's product. Of course this is partially successful. Such classes as capitalists, workers, petty bourgeoisie, peasants and others are easily discerned with these tools and many of the relations among them well understood. However, at the same time, there is a general failure to recognize the importance of non-material relations and, as a result, most Marxists overlook the existence of classes whose character is a function more of their qualitative work situation than of significant differences in their legal means of attaining income.

Yet there are a number of analysts from many orientations who do make reference to the existence of a "new class" situated somehow between labor and capital and defined by qualitative features. Thorstein Veblin, John Kenneth Galbraith, Berle and Means, Erik Olin Wright, Simone Weyl, Alvin Gouldner, and a considerable number of East European socialists have all suggested the presence of such a group and gone to some lengths to describe certain of its characteristics and economic interests.[12] But despite the many contributions of these scholars, our own view derives more from the work of Barbara and John Ehrenreich. For us, as for them, within many economies there is a division of labor with individuals doing conceptual planning on one side, and people engaged in more physical or rote work on the other. Under certain circumstances this distinction between conceptualization and execution may become a class differentiation. Thus, rather than seeing only capitalists and workers contesting in our own society, we see capitalists, a class of coordinators, an intermediate group sharing much in common with both coordinators and with workers, and workers themselves.[13]*

This recognition proves immediately important because it allows us to better understand class conflicts within capitalism. But more important, from the perspective of this volume, the differentiation propels recognition that this new class may have interests of its own which can be elaborated into a program of economic change and even economic revolution.

The coordinator class exists because of a relatively sharp division between conceptual and executionary functions. Presumably it would attain maximum material advantages by way of its possession of dominant economic power within a society where it would be the ruling economic class. In a loose sense this class has what Gouldner terms "cultural capital," though this is not to suggest that it is somehow more enlightened, wise, or ethically motivated than other classes.[14] Its objectives, on the contrary, are to increase its share in the social product, to reproduce the divisions lying at the base of its material and institutional advantages and to gain as much control as possible over its work, and the work of others. This class exists as a result of the deskilling and subordination of the rest of society's working population.[15] It has a paternal and regulatory position vis-a-vis other workers yet is subordinate to capitalists.[16] Under capitalism it can gain by the elaboration of welfare state and planning projects.[17] But in the end, a deep and permanent advance for this class entails nationalization—so it need no longer sell its labor power to capitalists—and a generalized legitimation of the conceptual-executionary division of labor. We'll have more to say about these possibilities in greater theoretical and historical detail as we proceed.

*Recently, John Anderson's Presidential campaign was in large measure a political expression of the interests of the coordinator class and its allies in the United States.

It is worthwhile to note here, however, a possible "theoretical interest" of this class. For if the coordinators are to elaborate an economic system in which they will prevail, it is desirable that the theory guiding this endeavor hide this class's preeminence from view (and also distract attention from its extra-economic as well as economic advantages). For how else can other classes be enjoined to lend a hand in the coordinators' struggle? What might serve this purpose better than a theory which denies the possibility that this group even exists as a class? Thus arises the possibility that coordinators and many supportive intermediate elements often chose a theoretical adherence to Marxism "because they have found something in its orthodox teaching that suited them in their effort to build an apologetic ideology of state socialism, and this is precisely the assumption that class antagonism can emerge only from conflicts around ownership."[18] Or as Alvin Gouldner extends the same logic: "Marxism's stress on the role of theory and of 'scientific socialism' must inevitably invest theorists, intellectuals—in a word the new class—with great authority. For it is they and they alone who produce socialism's theory. But how can the proletariat submit itself to the tutelage of theory without also submitting to the invisible pedagogy of intellectuals—the new class? Marxism's task is to find a way of vaunting theory but concealing the new class from which it derives, concealing its paradoxical authority in a movement of proletarians and socialists.* The invention of the vanguard party was central in that manuever."[19] Actually we will

---

*Considering the situation in the United States—one that is certainly not "imminently revolutionary"—one finds the development of a slowly growing sector of Marxist intelligentsia with academic positions, writing in academic journals of the mainstream and the left, and accruing at least a semblance of legitimacy for themselves and for certain left ideology. Obviously, this has certain merits: to put it bluntly, it beats having all left theory excised from any public display of any kind. It opens the possibility of socialist academics proposing analyses and programs for political implementation in their cities, states, and even nationally. One can easily imagine, for example, centers of academic radicals competing with liberal and conservative centers like Harvard's Center for International Affairs, the Economics Department at Chicago University, or other "status quo" think tanks. At the same time, however, the existence of socialist academics also has potential pitfalls. These individuals, whatever their personal dispositions and intentions at the outset, have no choice but to

argue that the invention of the vanguard party was not so much clever as it was essential, since the coordintor class was so weak in the countries where Leninist approaches have been successfully enacted that a political vanguard had to take their place. Thus as Rudolf Bahro claims, "all in all, the soviet state, with the party at its core,

circulate amongst middle element and coordinator class colleagues. Moreover, they must deal with these people in context of appointments, preserving their positions and income, gaining some status via publication, and so on. Even further, they generally operate in an arena that has many "comforts" and is far from the daily life situations of most citizens. Indeed, it is often an arena which is almost exclusively white, male, and professional. Of course, we are not talking about leftists working at small universities or struggling with overloads at community colleges. The phenomenon we are addressing is the growth of a rather small sector of well known, highly published, university faculty of Marxist persuasion. What we worry about is the appropriation of left theory by these folks, through no malicious intent, to be sure, in ways that necessarily will largely exclude the lessons of feminism and nationalism, the insights and needs of working people, and self conscious concerns with aims and means, settling instead predominantly upon theory for theory's own sake. This is not meant as a criticism of individuals but of a process by which left theory and Marxism are appropriated from the practice of some elements into books written by others. This is not a process that is suited to the fullest possible evolution of Marxism, nor to its best dissemination, nor to the revolutionization of either intellectuals, students, activists, or those totally outside the dynamic. But it is a process with class, caste, gender, and authority roots in both consciousness and social relationships and therefore one deserving analysis and susceptable to correction. The spectre of departments or universities with high numbers of resident Marxists yet no courses on the political economy of racism or sexism, the history or social dynamics of anti-capitalist revolutions, the impact of patriarchy on history, the role of racism in social change, or even the character of "socialist societies" and the potentials for and means of winning true socialism in the United States—not to mention programs of activity on these campuses, in their communities, etc.—is truly depressing. That the resources and experiences which go to create a "socialist intellectual" should then be relatively squandered to less substantial ends than we might justifiably desire, is a serious loss. If the coallescing of numerous Marxists, for example, in a single large university is to serve the whole left and promote real educational, theoretical, and programmatic advances—rather than only statistical gains on tenure and PhD charts—the various types of phenomena addressed in this note will have to be seriously addressed in a general and public fashion.

was not the substitute for a working class too weak to exercise power, but rather a special substitute for an exploiting class,''[20] what we have termed the coordinator class. It is not a question of challenging the honesty or motives of the socialist revolutionaries in these movements but merely one of discerning the broader political and class forces that were operative. But interestingly, the fact that the coordinator class and middle strata who might align with it are much stronger in advanced capitalist countries has led to considerable resistance to vanguard Leninist strategies. For in the past, in its "temporary" role the political surrogate acquired so much economic power as to become an on-going threat to the coordinators' more general interests. The political party elite sought to entrench itself resorting to censorship, coercion, purges, and even generalized imprisonment and murder against coordinators, middle strata, and dissident workers alike. In contrast, the coordinator class is interested in creating a climate of pluralist democracy, at least for itself, and this objective is impeded by any kind of dictatorship, purges, imprisonment, etc. Thus we find the emergence of the modern phenomenon of Eurocommunism wherein the coordinator class and elements supporting it seek their economic ascendency without any sacrifice in traditional bourgeois democracy.[21] As Gouldner formulates it:

> Eurocommunism is an effort at a mini-max solution to that contradiction [opposing censorship but wanting central planning]. That is, on the one hand, Eurocommunism remains committed to the extension of the state's sway over the economy, thereby removing career blockages for the new class and, on the other, it renounces the 'dictatorship of the proletariat' and commits itself to a pluralistic democracy thus limiting the threat of censorship. For the radicalized sector of the new class, Eurocommunism is an optimum compromise and is the price that they have demanded increasingly in Western Europe for their support of the Communist Party.[22]

We shall have more to say about all of these matters in coming sections. At this point it suffices to understand that we have broadened the criteria of class demarcation to include the qualitative impact of different kinds of work on workers, and that we are quite open to hypotheses of a new kind of class capable of engendering economic transformations furthering its own interests. We must therefore be open to the hypothesis that countries calling themselves "socialist" are neither socialist nor capitalist but politically bureaucratic and economically dominated by a growing coordinator class.

8. Class Consciousness

Economic classes give rise to the existence of "class consciousness." But it is not simply what is in the head of any randomly chosen member of a class. Rather for most of history class consciousness has been a kind of abstraction—something we can deduce but which is held only approximately and diversely among real individuals. Class consciousness is a variety of awarenesses about the world which derive from the different work people do and interests they have as a result of their place in the economy. For any class, class consciousness has aspects conducive to the reproduction of the economic structure (these are generally strongest during times of relative quietude) but for the oppressed classes it also has aspects that threaten the old class structure (strongest during times of revolutionary change).

The creation of class consciousness is a complex process. In part, it arises from workplace involvement in which people develop themselves and their consciousness of the workplace and of the economy generally. In part class consciousness derives from the working of the economy's intra- and inter-unit forms, and from consumption activity. But there are also indirect dynamics which contribute to class consciousness. Class members interact outside work, in cultural and community institutions where ideas are created out of their common experience, needs, and circumstances. As E. P. Thompson asserts, class consciousnesses "arise because men and women in determinate productive relations, identify their antagonistic interests, and come to struggle, to think and to value in class ways: thus the process of class formation is a process of self-making, although under conditions which are given." And as with the dynamics of all group formation and human activity, there is a "crucial ambivalence of our human presence in our own history, part-subjects, part-objects, the voluntary agents of our own involuntary determinations."[23]

During an evolutionary period reforms in the economy generate alterations in the class's self-perception and in its perception of society as a whole, but this never alters basic suppositions and values. Or conversely, changes in a class's forms of interaction, modes of self-organization, and forms of extra-economic involvement alter its conceptions and in turn its economic relationships. In this type of steady fluctuation of consciousness and social relations the basic mesh between what the members of a class perceive, want, understand, and are capable of, and what economic institutional roles require is preserved.

Revolutionary alterations involve more drastic changes of consciousness. When a society's economic relations are revolutionized the consciousness of all actors within their sway will eventually change as well. One phase of this profound change occurs after the revolution as citizens become accustomed to new institutions. Although this transformation is likely more profound and more difficult and disorienting then gradual socialization of the citizenry to class roles in the old stable society, the dynamic is similar. People develop themselves in accord with their changing institutional environment. The main difference is that with a socialist revolution of the type we envision, this process will not be one of conforming to institutions outside their control but also one of molding those institutions. However, the alteration of class consciousness accompanying economic revolutions has another phase which precedes the creation of new institutions. This phase begins within the old society and *against its institutional requirements*. It does not result from the process by which the human center and institutional boundary usually come to confrom, but in fact subverts this process. In the first phase, therefore, class struggle is the central feature transforming consciousness.

Class struggle, in turn, results from the fact that economic modes of production and consumption pit members of different classes against one another. The very definition of classes most often reflects the fact that economic roles divide social labor in such ways that some benefit at the expense of others. Therefore classes continually find themselves in an adversary relationship. It is most often in class struggle—at work, in consumption, and also via specially formed organizations—that people evolve their class consciousness from reproductive to revolutionary premises.

In a particular society class analysis means determining the class structure, the nature of antagonisms between classes, the form these struggles take, the status of class consciousness, and the relations of this consciousness and struggle to the state of the economy. Since societal reproduction is partially a function of economic reproduction, and since social change is partially a function of economic change, classes are likely to be significant actors in historical evolution and revolution. Epistemologically this means that to understand any society we must interrogate it from a class perspective. Strategically it means that if we want to change a society we must address the problem of organizing class struggle, and coordinating it with other struggles.

What the importance of the economy and classes does *not* imply, however, is that we can focus on classes alone and expect to achieve either analytic or practical success. For there are other groups, demarcated by the social dynamics of other spheres of social activity, which are also important to social reproduction and revolution. Moreover, analysis of the economy itself will be insufficient and misleading if it is restricted to a study of classes and purely "economic" dynamics. For the existence of political, kinship, and community moments within the economic sphere imply that "economism" must be constantly guarded against.

9. Economic Dynamics

In the regular operation of any economy production and consumption lead to changes in stocks of materials and in the situation of the citizenry. There may be more things and less resources over time. Some people may have skills developed, others may be deskilled or slowly infected with industrial diseases. The relations between groups may also change slightly but only in a manner consistent with reproduction of the old core characteristics. Even the continual application of human insight to economic growth—innovations, improvements of technology and organization, variation of style and taste—is evolutionary. The changes fit the contours of what has proceeded. The system varies and yet it also remains the same. In this process society's economic classes go about their appointed chores: the members change in a variety of ways, yet the fundamental orientation of the class to the economy remains constant. The dominant classes continue to exercise control and to appropriate as much of the social surplus as they are able; the subordinate classes continue to produce most of the surplus and to survive or even "prosper" as best they can.

How do contradictions emerge which are significant enough to compel human intervention in the redefinition of the economic social relations themselves?

In the first place, people may become revolutionary by carrying out the dictates of the economy itself. That is, as evolutionary alterations accumulate, behavior which once reproduced the economy's contours may become disruptive. In some societies, economic classes may come to act in revolutionary ways by doing precisely what their economic roles propel them to do. For example in a particular capitalist society pursuit of higher real wages and shorter work hours may help cause a breakdown in reproductive dynamics, thereby disrupting society so thoroughly that only revolutionary alterations can restore stability. When this occurs, human attributes—a product of human genetic nature and the historical circumstances—develop consistently with economic dictates yet nonetheless come into contradiction with the reproduction of these same dictates. The economy works and yet it doesn't work. It is internally contradictory in a "technical way." Its very operation leads to its own dissolution. This is the sort of dynamic focused upon by orthodox Marxism.[24] And this happens, but it is not as materially determined as their accounts imply. For to the extent that such contradictory dynamics plague an economic arrangement, in the last instance it is because there is a contradiction between that arrangement's role implications and the freest possible development of human capacities. Otherwise, the contradiction could be resolved by having the economic actors act in more self-consistent ways. In the above example, were there no basic contradiction between the accumulation of capital and human nature, the former could be achieved by having workers consume only what they require never seeking more, and never struggling... they would need only be socialized to such docility.[25]

Another kind of economic contradiction, however, involves the emergence of human desires that are not propelled by the economy but antithetical to its reproduction. The contradiction is now between these extra-economic desires and the economy. Though in the previous case such a contradiction also emerged, there it was *alienated* human traits *produced by the economy* that did the damage. In this case the inability of the economy to continue producing alienated human traits, and the emergence of non-alienated alternatives cause the difficulty. For example, the increasing fulfillment of material needs may allow more qualitative desires for self-management, interpersonal solidarity, and self-esteem to be expresssed and this could propel class struggle to a revolutionary level. Or working people's self-activity, either inside or outside the workplace or market could generate similar disruptive needs and capacities. In light of all these possibilities an analysis of a particular society must uncover the depth of hegemony which produces a conformity between class behavior and economic roles, the long- and short-term trends which create economic contradictions threatening this hegemony, and the possibilities for creation of a counter-hegemony (revolutionary needs, desires, and consciousness) through the natural progression of economic activity *or* through the self-activity of oppressed classes. This is a tall order, but essential for understanding the potential for changes within a society's economy. The mechanical approaches focusing only on "material relations" and contradictions with no eye to their manifestation in class consciousness and with no eye to the implications of class activity itself over and above technical contradictions in economies, is insufficient.

But even the above plan of analysis, extensive as it is, is incomplete. It forgets that the economy is embedded in the rest of society and vice versa.

10. The Failure of the "Base/Superstructure" Theoretization and the Need for "Social Economics"

The logic of conceptualizing society in two parts, the economic base and social superstructure, is economistic.* The dual premise that makes this conceptualization attractive is that on the one hand there are a set of laws of motion which operate within the economy

*We use the word "economistic" in two senses. First, an analysis is economistic which exaggerates the importance of the economy in determining all other processes of society. Second, however, an analysis within or of economic relations themselves is economistic if it overlooks the

independent of human will and only marginally influenced by political, kin, and cultural happenings, and on the other hand that these latter happenings are ultimately products of the economic laws of motion. The distinction between ''objective'' and ''subjective'' conditions of social change is also bound up in this theoretical posture. ''Objective conditions for revolution''exist whenever the laws of motion of the mode of production are grinding toward that mode's dissolution. Subjective conditions will follow in due course.

Our analysis directly challenges the premises behind the logic of this entire orthodox orientation. Events in the political, kinship, and community spheres don't follow economic dictates any more automatically than vice versa. That is, the mixture of accommodation and autonomy is a priori as likely symmetrical as not, and can be determined only empirically for every pair of spheres in every social formation. As we noted earlier, and are about to observe further, some more flexible formulations of Marxism have accorded particular parts of the superstructure greater autonomy, implicitly recognizing the weakness of part of the dual premise we reject. But the other part of the premise, that the economy is somehow isolated rather than permeated by political, kin, and community moments, is much less frequently noted by even the most innovative Marxists. It is only economism which allows some people to infer that economic institutions are more important than any others. It is only a very narrow kind of materialism that fetishizes things that are tangible to the touch and promotes the *false* belief that institutions are more important to social change than are the ideas, needs, and dispositions of people themselves. But neither this economism nor this narrow materialism has the slightest theoretical or empirical justification once one takes off the orthodox Marxist blinders which preclude recognition of the importance of factors that orthodox Marxism does not itself conceptualize as primary. And indeed, among many Marxists these views have been largely discredited by the growing recognition that other spheres do play an important role in the way people live and organize themselves and in the ways

impact of other spheres of social involvement on economic processes and outcomes—thus, for example, claiming knowledge of a society's economic relations without having paid any attention to race or kinship or other important defining features is economistic. For a discussion of both these kinds of failings in orthodox Marxist economic analysis, see *Unorthodox Marxism*, South End Press, 1978, chapters two and three.

societies alter.

At a broad theoretical level, E.P. Thompson has recently taken a theoretical stand which bears some similarities to our own.[26] He suggests that "to thrust historical materialism [we would simply say the study of real economic and social history] back into the prison of political economy" mistakes an analysis of one part, "the circuit of capital," for the whole which may include other attributes and more important, other primary circuits, for example, "circuits of power, or the reproduction of ideology, etc.," which may "belong to a different logic and to other categories" than those of the economy.[27] By engaging in this reductionism Thompson believes "we pass on one letter—a capitalist mode of production is not capitalis*m*—from the adjectival characterization of a mode of production (a concept within Political Economy, albeit within Marxist anti-Political economy) to a noun description of a social formation in the totality of its relations."[28] The alternative, of course, is to become sensitive to the critical importance of non-economic spheres.

For example, influenced by feminism many Marxists have adopted the term "patriarchy" to refer to relations between men and women in modern societies. While some still argue that patriarchy derives from economic divisions of labor, others recognize the importance of the kinship sphere.[29] Similarly, there are Marxists who have been influenced by anarchists to address the autonomous dynamics of political institutions, and some have found that the polity may be on a par with the economy.[30] This diversity of new analyses extends as well to the study of the interplay between nationalism and class relations, and many Marxists now take seriously the weight of cultural relations in historical dynamics.[31] Still in our opinion, while all these advances are critical to the development of a new approach to analyzing social formations, each is still bound by a particularistic methodology, and also by lack of a guiding theoretical stance which is clearly different from the orthodox predecessor. As a result, while many left "scholars" can spin out elaborate arguments about the priority and inter-penetration of this cause and that effect, in practice activists are constrained to use either the orthodox formalism or their own common sense.

In our theory, however, the economic network also includes other social institutions. For example, the family is both a productive and consumptive institution. The state has an economic moment as do religious and ethnic institutions. Similarly economic institutions have a political, kinship, and community aspect. The social formation is not a hierarchy of networks separate from one another, influencing each other from without. Rather these networks are coextensive. The same people are active in each sphere and even though one aspect may be momentarily more central each individual is continually engaged in behavior which has a fourfold character. This means that class relations are affected by kin, community, and political relations as they in turn affect each other. To say a particular economy is racist or patriarchal, for example, is more than a peripheral comment. It means that the relations within this economy can be understood fully only by an approach sensitive to sexual and racial processes. It means that the evolutionary or revolutionary alteration of the economy may involve contradictions around racial and sexual as well as class dynamics. In a patriarchal and racist society to be a worker or owner is different for a man or a woman, or a black or a white. The conceptual tools we develop for economic analysis must be capable of this breadth of vision. Herbert Blumer's work on race and class relations gives evidence of the kind of unorthodox insight that can result:

> The most outstanding observation that is forced on us by empirical evidence is that the apparatus and operations introduced by industrialization almost invariably adjust and conform to the pattern of race relations in the given society. We have already touched on this observation in our earlier discussion; we wish here to develop the point in more detail. The position is essentially that the racial lines as drawn in a society are followed in the allocation of racial members inside the industrial structure. If the racial patterning in the society has assigned the races to different social positions, defining the appropriate forms of association between them, outlining the kinds of authority, prestige and power allowable to each, indicating the kinds of privilege which attend their respective social positions, and establishing clear schemes of deferential relations, this general pattern of relationship is carried over into the industrial structure. The pattern comes to define the types of occupation into which racial members may enter, the types from which they are

excluded, and those which do not befit them; it determines who is given access to training and acquisition of skills; it structures the lines of promotion, establishing ceilings or 'dead-ends' corresponding to the general social position of subordinate racial groups; it allocates positions of authority corresponding to the distribution of authority among the racial groups in the general society; it severely limits new forms of association which are not consonant with the general racial code; it exercises particular control over the managerial field, the area of representatives of industry to the outside public, and the field of entrepreneural activity.[32]

12. The Economic System and its Evaluation

An economy is a society's inter-unit and intra-unit institutions and its citizenry organized into classes with diverse needs, consciousness, and interests. And though no such economy exists in isolation from other social spheres, nonetheless it is possible to evaluate certain economic forms, in and of themselves, in terms of the implications they *will most likely* have in any society where they may be incorporated. One can ask, for example, what kinds of income distribution arise from certain types of ownership relations, or what kinds of personality structures are promoted by specific inter- or intra-unit forms. Indeed, just this sort of analysis makes up the bulk of Marxist literature about capitalism—especially if one includes the question: what tendencies for conflict and change are embedded in the particular economic forms and their operation?

But in this book we seek to evaluate socialist possibilities. First, we must understand their implications for economic actors. What are their effects on personality, need fulfillment and development, and human capacities? Second, we must have some norms against which to judge them. We seek solidarity, variety of outcomes, and self-management. Do economic relations promote these or only something else? Obviously, our evaluative program extends beyond traditional economists concerns with efficiency *and* orthodox Marxist concerns with class empowerment. But this is not because our approach neglects these more familiar concerns.

Rather, they are subsumed and integrated into a more general, and we believe more powerful and comprehensive evaluative framework.

CENTRAL PLANNING

According to orthodox Marxist analysis capitalism is an oppressive economic arrangement because it is class divided and leads to economic insecurity, immiseration, and alienation. To overcome these problems the theory says it is necessary to dispossess the capitalists and make society's means of production public and to institute a mechanism to reverse the irrational, unplanned, profit-oriented character of capitalist exchange. Thus, after nationalizing industry, the socialist revolution must also institute central planning according to the best possible assessments of productive capability and social need.[33] In this section we would like to tackle this vision in its purest form. We will show that it does not encompass socialist norms, that it does not yield an end to class division, and that far from furthering the socialist values self-management, solidarity, and diversity of outcome, it tends to restrict each.

Assume a revolution effectively dispossesses capitalists and centralizes control of an economy in a set of economic institutions which will "plan the economy's activities." What constitutes this planning? What difficulties are involved, what steps must be taken, and how might they be accomplished?

The essence of central planning is that some group attempts to generate a plan that can maximize the "society's social welfare function"—that is, one which can "best fulfill people's needs given all existent constraints." This plan must then be communicated to the various production and consumption units of the economy—what inputs are to be received, what economic processes enacted, and therefore what outputs are to be produced. Finally, there must be sufficient incentives for these units to carry out their roles.

The conditions for a successful plan are five-fold: 1) the planners must have full knowledge of what resources are available and what equipment is in place, 2) they must know the ratios in which various inputs must be combined to yield every product, 3) they must know society's assessment of the relative worths of all final goods, 4) they need sufficient computing facilities, and 5) there must be some reasons why people will carry out their assigned tasks.

To understand central planning's strengths and weaknesses, we must know how these five tasks are accomplished. But given a workable and accurate plan, there are a number of ways to both distribute final goods to the public and assign specific jobs to individuals. We will start by discussing some of these alternatives. Then we will describe procedures by which the planners can accumulate the information they need about production capabilities and social welfare, and how incentives may be evolved to promote accurate plan fulfilment. Following this survey we will offer our own criticisms showing, among other things, the intrinsically authoritarian character of the central planning approach to economic processing.

Distribution of Final Goods

There is considerable confusion, even among socialists, about what constitutes central planning: How, for example, given determination of a plan and production of all the proposed final goods, are these goods actually delivered to the populace? If it is all planned, does that mean each individual's consumption is centrally determined or is there individual choice? Similarly, when the central planning board finishes determining what jobs are to be done, for how long, and with what technologies, how is it determined who will do which tasks? How are individuals alloted to "job slots?" Again, is each person assigned by the plan, or is there personal choice?

In fact, when planners calculate they arrive only at a complete list of all the inputs that each unit will use, and the gross outputs that each unit should generate. Included among the list of inputs are the number of hours of different categories of labor services that each production center is to use, but this is not the same as a list of who will be assigned to which jobs. Similarly, when the amount of each product needed in production is subtracted from the gross output of that good called for in the plan, the net output of each good available for consumption is the result, but this is not the same as a list of what amounts of each final good will be distributed to each consumer in the society. The distribution of final goods and specific job assignments can be handled in a variety of ways. And even though the practical, political, and ethical consequences of how this is done are immense, material and allocational efficiency is preserved regardless of which of the following methods is used.

1) The plan could allocate an exactly equal portion of each final good to each member of society in each time period. Then, to make sure the final result was such that nothing better could have been attained without making at least someone worse off, people would have to be free to make all mutually beneficial private exchanges. A "white market" in final goods would have to be sanctioned. The idea is relatively simple. Though the plan presumably generates an optimal mix of final goods, it doesn't assign these to individual members of society. If we simply give equal amounts to everyone then the shuffling of goods to fit individual tastes must occur *after* this distribution. Thus arises the need for a market to bring about all mutually beneficial exchanges.

2) Another possibility is that the central planning board could introduce currency and retail outlets. For example, every member of society could be given "x" units of currency and the final goods could all be sent to retail outlets where the managers were instructed to change the prices of different goods to ensure that each good disappeared on the thirtieth day of each month, just prior to the next month's deliveries. Given efficient managers and certain technical requirements about relations between stores, this method too would attain "efficient" results.

3) It would also be possible for the planning board to hand out different allotments of currency to each individual, then use the managerial market clearing arrangement of the last scheme. This option gains in interest as soon as we begin to consider the problem of motivating individuals to fulfill their assigned tasks. For if this is accomplished politically, or by social pressure or solidarity, there is no need for differential allotments. But if such social incentives are not sufficient, then material incentives can become very important to motivate participation. Two approaches are of special interest.

The planning board could give out different amounts of currency to employees in different production units according to how closely the unit came to fulfilling its plan. Or, the board could give currency to the personnel departments of different units which would then hire workers. Each personnel department would know how many employees the plan required and would have to use its allotment of currency to hire those workers. With certain provisions about lending and uniformity of relations for similar workers in different workplaces, both these approaches would also yield "efficient" results, of course assuming that the plan was "wise" in the first place.

Job Assignment

The last method of distribution—giving currency and hiring power to production units—is one way to allocate individuals to specific jobs. Another way would be for the central planning board (CPB from now on) to send a letter to each individual in each category of work telling him or her where to report. The CPB is assumed to have complete knowledge of the amount of all different primary inputs, including the number of people capable of performing each different kind of labor service. If the CPB has a mailing address for each member of each category, they could make the assignments on any basis they wanted—randomly, alphabetically, etc.

Or, the CPB could leave the specific assignments up to associations of the individuals in each different labor category. The CPB would send the associations a list of how many of their members should report to each production unit and let the associations then decide who would go where. In turn, within any given association, this might be done by lottery, by seniority, by discussion, by voting, etc. However, if one allows for existence of different welfare effects from different jobs for different individuals, one would have to allow that after assignments or mailings people could trade positions before actually settling into job assignments. This would parallel the "white market" of the earlier distribution schemes.

These methods of distribution and job allocation are theoretically efficient even if both consumption and production have developmental effects on consumers and producers. However the planners have to have information concerning these developmental effects and must incorporate it into their determinations of societal inputs and outputs. The remaining questions, of course, revolve around the possibility of the planners effectively meeting the five requirements mentioned earlier. We must now address these matters one at a time.

Attaining Knowledge of Production Possibilities

The planning board alone can't possibly accumulate all possible knowledge of every conceivable production technique and approach in one place. Rather, this knowledge can only be held at the level of the separate firms themselves. Therefore a way must be found to incorporate these separate units into the planning process. They must provide precisely that information which is critical, at each step, to the development of a final plan. There are a number of methods by which this may be accomplished.

Historically, the first approach used was called material balances.[34] The planning authority determines a set of final demands which are communicated to all the units. They report on inputs necessary to produce these outputs. The planners add these requirements to the list of final demands and inquire again. This sequence continues, converging to a workable plan. There is not too much communication or difficult calculation called for, but the approach is quite inflexible. The demands for final goods are set at the first step, and if they are lower than what could be attained, this is never discovered. Moreover, if some trade offs in final goods would be beneficial, this too will go unnoticed. But the method will nonetheless bring knowledge of the production units' technologies to the access of the planners and will yield a workable formulation.

Another set of more complex and subtle procedures involves the planning board suggesting prices, and the producing units then developing profit-maximizing schemes given their technologies.[35] The planners then use accumulated knowledge to develop a new set of prices, the units respond, and so on. Given certain technical assumptions, this iterative mechanism will also yield a material plan of unputs and outputs, and it will communicate the technological data about the economy that the planners seek. Then, in context of knowledge of a social welfare function and other information mentioned earlier, the planners are in position to calculate other input/output schemes that are both possible and consistent with maximizing fulfillment of public desires.

Another approach reverses the roles above. Now the center proposes quantities and the units calculate associated prices.[36] But the logic is much as above. Moreover, between the extremes of the CPB using only prices and units replying with only quantities, or vice versa, there are methods wherein the CPB uses a mixture of prices and quantities and gets a mixed reply in response. The point is simply that the planners present some information and the units then use that to calculate certain optimal relations in their own situation. Repeating this a number of times slowly builds up knowledge at the center of the technical possibilities throughout the economy. So in fact, contrary to popular criticisms of central planning, the CPB can learn resource availabilities and technical possibilities throughout the economy. But it is important to note that *no more* than this is going on. That is, the units are *not* participating in any decision-making, rather they are only participating in a *communication process* by transferring their knowledge to the center. Their activity in this exchange is purely technical, the calculation of what they can or cannot do given certain assumptions, not of what they would like or not like to do given those same assumptions.

Finding the Social Welfare Function

The above iterative techniques lead to an optimal plan if the CPB knows how society values different final goods. There are three principal ways CPBs could try to learn this social welfare function.

First, it may simply be determined by an individual or agency assumed to have great insight into the public situation. Thus, a Stalin might mail the planners a social welfare function based on his own perceptions of what is good for society. Or the same role could be played by a group of individuals or even by a whole political party noted for its roots among the populace.

Second, the planning board could employ market mechanisms to acquire information about social tastes. For example, in our description of how final goods might be distributed we included the option of allocating currency and using distribution centers.[37] Were this approach used, the planning board could use the prices store managers report to determine the relative desirabilities of different goods to the general public. This would allow just as much "consumer sovereignty" as we find in western market models, and yet it would not compromise the planned character of the economy. Were the distribution technique to involve differential currency allocations—perhaps for incentive purposes—then this consumer sovereignty would be less "democratic" in the sense that some people would have more dollar votes than others, but would be no less workable for that fact.

To be sensitive to the fact that job allocations have welfare significance, it would be necessary to have a labor market too. But earlier we discussed how personnel departments could be allocated sums so as to assess wages to attract people to available jobs. This would allow just as much "producer sovereignty" as we find in Western market models.

Finally, the planning board might determine a social welfare function by allowing each citizen to have a certain number of votes or points to distribute amongst all the different products assessed by the welfare function.[38] These votes could be tallied to assess individual tastes.

Incentives for Carrying out the Plan

One might argue that in a centrally planned economy where there is no exploitation of workers by capitalists, where everyone is aware that the central plan is the way to maximize social well being, and where everyone recognizes that their productive efforts are part of the smooth operation of the economy which is seen as "one big factory," there would be no need for any incentives other than enlightened self-interest and social solidarity. We will defer discussion of why even if this might be more or less true in early stages in such an economy, it will cease to be true after a relatively brief time, to a later section of this chapter. But here simply suppose that enlightened self-interest and solidarity are not sufficient incentives to bring the plan to fruition. Are there any other means available to motivate compliance with work assignments?

There is no reason, at least in theory, that a centrally planned economy cannot use the same kind of material incentives that are presumed sufficiently motivating to elicit participation from capitalism's workers and consumers. In a centrally planned economy with markets in labor and final goods, the executors in the economy would have essentially the same material interests (assuming consumption goods are available) in performing the tasks assigned to them in the production units that workers do in capitalism. If personnel departments included some form of bonus system in the labor contract, workers in a centrally planned economy might even have material interests closely approximating those of workers in a self-managed market "socialist" enterprise. As far as the managers of individual production units are concerned, the problem of establishing incentives for them to perform in accord with the criteria of the central planning board is no different in theory from the problem of how to get capitalist managers to behave in accord with the stockholders' critera. In both cases the possibilities of material rewards—bonuses, fringe benefits, advancement in the managerial hierarchy—are all available, as are the same set of material punishments—pay cuts, elimination of perquisites, demotion, and firing. In both economies similar problems of determining whether managers are maximizing their superiors' criteria exist, but there does not seem to be anything inherent in central planning, at least in theory, to cause these problems of accountability to be any more serious.

If there is a problem with central planning, then, it does not lie in its technical impossibility, as many critics suggest, nor in a lack of mechanisms to centralize information or to motivate compliance with plans. Theoretically, this is all within reach of a capable planning board. If there is an operational impediment it must lie in the still to be discussed implications of certain social relations of this model. If there is a welfare failing, it must lie in areas invisible to traditional theories. The rest of our discussion of central planning will be devoted to uncovering some of these failings.

The Information Failings of Central Planning

What is the nature of the information consolidation and dispersion patterns that various techniques of determining the plan entail? Essentially, information concerning the production functions of the individual units is being transferred to the center, though on a kind of installment plan.[39] Issuing prices, for example, and receiving back proposed quantities, the center slowly develops a picture of production possibilities. But this is only a material insight. There is no communication of the actual human content of these material possibilities—what they would mean in terms of personality, skill, consciousness and other effects upon the workforce. Thus even the planners only develop a very partial picture of the totality of occurrences within the economy. It is only that which is most easily quantified which is communicated. Furthermore, the units themselves don't even attain a general knowledge of the material situation of the economy as a whole. Rather, they only receive trial data referring to prices or to inputs and outputs of their plant. The famous down/up process is really down-go-questions and up-come-answers ending in a list of orders from the center.[40]

Although there are differences in detail between the price guided, quantity guided, and mixed techniques, their essence is the same. A centrally planned economy fails to provide the executors of economic activity with sufficient information to exercise self-management, even if they were permitted to do so, and with none of the kind of information required for the development of empathy and solidarity between members of different units. Furthermore, the system does not even provide the central planners with the kind of information we will require all members of a socialist economy to receive. Instead the planning mechanism gives the planners a monopoly on technical information—too little to promote a full evaluation of human outcomes, but more than enough to contribute to a differentiation between those in-the-know and everyone else, a differentiation that may even take the form of a class division. Moreover, in the absence of such information about others, naturally the non-planner must act based on an estimate of their own isolated potential pleasures and pains. Ironically, the social approach of central planning reproduces the individualist role pressures of capitalism itself.

Authoritarian Role Structures

We have just seen that during the central planning iterative procedures individual units are *not* participating in generation of the economic plan. Rather, they only supply data to the central planners that they might in turn calculate an "efficient" plan and then inform the units of their role in it. The only management left to the separate units is to "manage" to fulfill the centrally planned targets using allocated inputs. Therefore, the essential character of inter-unit roles is a hierarchical relationship between the CPB and the separate units. The planners issue "marching orders" and the units obey as best they can. In Rudolf Bahro's formulation:

> The bureaucratic centralist form of planning, in which what those at the top receive from below is principally only passive factual information and 'questions,' while what they hand down are actual imperatives, stamps the mechanism by which tasks are allotted to individuals. It is a point of principle that people do not have to seek tasks for themselves, recognize and deal with problems, but they are rather assigned to tasks as duties.[41]

In essence every unit is subordinate to the planning board and superior to no other unit, and the central planning board is the superior of every individual unit and a subordinate of none. This sort of institutional structure is traditionally labelled a "command economy" to highlight that "the allocation of resources is carried out by the extensive use of orders to produce and deliver goods."[42]

But in our opinion the authoritarian character of the inter-unit roles in a centrally planned economy will likely also spread to intra-unit roles. First, an authoritarian relationship requires that the superior agent have an effective means for holding the subordinate agent accountable for carrying out central directives. This entails establishing methods of surveillance and verification as well as incentives to guide subordinates toward diminishing discrepancies between orders received and actual performance. The central planning board will quickly discern that it is much easier to hold a manager accountable for carrying out directives than to try and establish complicated methods of surveillance and verification sufficient to hold an entire democratic council accountable.* Indeed, it will become clear that an acquiescent workforce is preferrable to an informed and self-conscious one.** In turn, if the central planners choose to deal with a manager whom they appoint

---

*As Trotsky argued "[one man management] may be correct or incorrect from the point of view of the technique of administration. It would consequently be a most crying error to confuse the question as to the supremacy of the proletariet with the question of boards of workers at the head of factories. The Dictatorship of the Proletariat is expressed in the abolition of private property, in the supremacy over the whole soviet mechanism of the collective will of the workers, and not at all in the form in which individual economic enterprises are administered." Thus is the slogan "all power to the Soviets" rendered mere rhetoric and the logic of hierarchy within economic units as well as between them and the center elaborated. See *What Is To Be Undone*, Michael Albert, Porter Sargent Publisher, 1974, p. 96 for the quotation, and the chapter in general for further discussion.

**According to Konrad and Szelenyi in *The Intellectuals on the Road to Power*, Harcourt, Brace Jovanovich, 1979, p. 174: "The Communist Parties, after coming to power, quickly dissolved or transformed every organization in which only workers participated, from workers' councils, factory committees, and trade unions to workers' singing societies,

rather than a workers' council in each production unit, they must grant the manager hierarchical authority over all the other individuals in the unit.*

Furthermore, the manager's authority must be legitimized rather than appearing the result of arbitrary fiat. Insofar as a division between conceptualization and execution marks the difference between planners and managers on one side, and workers on the other, it is likely that this legitimation will be possession of certain kinds of knowledge and culture. Moreover, technologies will have to be consistent with this burgeoning apparatus of control, and the creators of such technology will also have to be permitted to join the economic "elite." In this way, even if central planning begins with a small group demarcated politically rather than economically, in time, a complete hierarchy will be established with many intervening layers of participants who are superiors to some but subordinates to others.

In addition to the need for compatibility within the institutional boundary, in this case between the inter-unit and intra-unit roles in the economy, there are strong forces pushing for compatibility between the human center and the institutional boundary. The effects of authoritarian inter-unit roles generating both passivity and individualism tend to create a human center more compatible with authoritarian intra-unit roles as well. Similarly, the elaboration of economic roles associated with conceptual activity on the one hand, and executionary activity on

theatrical groups, and sports clubs. In the socialist countries only corporative organizations exist, and workers belong to them only in company with the administrative personnel and technical intelligentsia of their enterprise or branch. Thus the general manager and the common laborer are members of the same trade union local, and it is hardly likely that the worker will have as much voice in the affairs of the local as his [or her] boss does."

*According to Lenin, for example: "It is absolutely essential that all authority in the factories should be concentrated in the hands of management—under these circumstances any direct intervention by the trade unions in the management of enterprises must be regarded as positively harmful and impermissible." Quoted in the midst of a full discussion in *What Is To Be Undone*, Michael Albert, Porter Sargent Publishers, 1974, p. 98.

the other, will give rise to different values, self-perceptions, skills, and behavioral traits among different groups of people in the economy. Obviously the inculcation of generalized acceptance of orders and lack of solidarity favors the elaboration of authoritarian role structures within separate units. It is, therefore, in the nature of central planning to divorce not only a layer of planners from other economic actors, but to also distinguish managers, foremen, and engineers responsible for technical organization from the workers themselves. For the workers have little or no power, rhetoric about their "dictatorship" aside.* More, as a division of labor between conception/coordination and execution becomes more pronounced at every level, the distinction between almost all intellectual workers and all executionary workers is likely to sharpen. As the Chinese philosopher Meng-tse asserted nearly 2500 years ago: "Some work with the mind and some with the bodily powers. Those who work with the mind rule others, and those who work with their powers are ruled by others. Those who are ruled carry others, and those who rule are carried by others."[43]

Naturally, such a hierarchy of status and power in the functioning of the economy will be accompanied by income differentials as well. In the earliest years of a centrally planned economic system, if the coordinator class is relatively small, most material inequity derives from the accrual of wealth by the political elite who, through the party, determine the economic plan. This is a directly exploitative relationship in that one group is gaining while others lose *via a direct interaction,* but it doesn't take the same form as exploitation under capitalism. Rather, the planners are simply able to manipulate the determination of the social welfare function, and of job definitions, and pay scales to their own advantage. They

---

*In fact, for all his/her alleged leading role, the Soviet worker has just as little to say in the high or low level decisions of his/her enterprise as the worker in a capitalist plant. He/she has no voice in deciding whether operations will be expanded or cut back, what will be produced, what kind of equipment will be used and what technical advances (if any) will be enacted, whether there will be piece-rates or hourly wages, how performance will be measured and production norms calculated, how worker's wages will evolve relative to increases in productivity, how the authority structure of the plant from director to foremen will operate.

are able to develop bonus prcedures, vacation plans, and especially state financed "extras" again, to their own advantage.[44]

Later, however, as the system becomes more fully elaborated and the coordinator class as a whole comes to dominate the economic apparatus, the unequal distribution of wealth becomes essentially a matter of "redistribution." This takes the form of income differentials between conceptual and executionary labor, bonuses and state favors, and of job definition, etc.* But it also derives from the planners' efforts to expand the economy in ways which always reproduce coordinator/worker class differences and elaborate the influence and power of the former groups.[45] Much work remains to be done before a full theory of these dynamics can be elaborated, but some indications will be given in a coming section of this chapter dealing with class relations in so-called socialist societies.

*"What empirical facts point to the rule of the working class under socialism? Do workers receive the highest pay? Hardly; the average intellectual's earnings are considerably higher than the average worker's, and the differential between the maximum an intellectual can earn and the maximum worker's wage is as great if not greater than in the market economies. Are the workers able to take greater advantage of state-subsidized benefits over and above wages? No; white collar people live in larger and more comfortable dwellings in pleasanter neighborhoods, and they have a far better chance than workers do of getting an apartment in a building being constructed with the aid of state subsidies. Even the right to settle in town is a class privilege: It is easier for intellectuals to get permission to settle in the cities with their superior services, and so they can live relatively close to their places of work, while a good part of the working class—in some countries as much as half—is obliged to commute to work from the ill-serviced villages where they live. The children of the intelligentsia go on to university-level studies in far higher proportion; even earlier, they gain admittance to better schools more easily than do workers' children. Only intellectuals and their dependents are admitted to the special hospitals and clinics which provide outstanding care for ranking state and party officials. The cafeterias of institutions employing mostly intellectuals offer better and more varied meals than do the factory canteens..." George Konrad and Ivan Szelenyi, *The Intellectuals on the Road to Class Power*, Harcourt, Brace, Jovanovich, 1979, pp. 171-172. The authors continue to elaborate numerous other differences of material and social situation between workers and intellectuals and to therefore simultaneously debunk certain narrow statistical studies which are blind to many non-wage differentials.

The Social Welfare Function's Bias Against Self-Management

We outlined three different approaches to finding the social welfare function: political determination, market determination, and voting. The authoritarian implications of any of the versions of political determination are obvious, yet these have historically been one of the central means employed. Insofar as a central planning approach is enacted in a society that doesn't have a wide layer of conceptual workers, it is to be expected that the task of coordinating the economy will fall upon a political elite largely credited for the success of the revolution. Still, for such a group to continue determining "what is good for society and its members" is antithetical to any conceivable notion of collective self-management. It cannot help to improve sociality, nor to spread skills and knowledge necessary to solidarity and self-management. Where one might make an argument that a group's political experience warrants granting it a prominant role in debating economic priorities, it is impossible to justifiably grant it authority to make people's choices for them.

But turning to markets as a vehicle of determining the social welfare function doesn't really improve things much. As we'll see next section, markets can't handle the problem of public goods or externalities, and markets impose behavioral and informational constraints that are destructive of socialist personality. And though some of this would be attenuated in the instance where markets were not competitive—their prices being socially determined by planners—the basic problems would remain.

So we come to voting as an alternative approach. Any serious attempt to elaborate a central planning model which pays attention to issues of democracy will focus on this alternative so we will consider it in greater detail. We will attempt to give voting every benefit of the doubt and show that it still must result in a bias against the provision of self-managed work activities in a centrally planned economy. Let's assume that everyone has the same vote, every voter is well informed, there is no gamesmanship, and there is no bias against goods with relatively great external and public effects. A problem still exists because perfect democracy is not the same as self-management.

The effects of different economic activities are not usually confined to single individuals or units in the economy, but neither are they evenly spread over all members of society. Instead, the implications of most economic choices affect a number of individuals but to different extents. In this context self-management is having decision-making input, in proportion that one will be affected by the outcome of that decision. Therefore self-management would not be the same as individual freedom except in those relatively exceptional cases where the use-value of a particular activity was confined entirely to a single individual. But more relevant to our present purpose, self-management is also not the same as perfect democratic majority rule except in those relatively exceptional cases where the use-value of a particular activity is spread equally over everyone in society, or for goods that are *pure* public goods. In other words, in most situations self-management lies somewhere on the continuum between individual freedom and majority rule. So a democratic voting procedure for determining the social welfare function, which will then be mechanically translated by the CPB into a set of production orders for members of all units in the economy, exhibits a bias against self-managed decision-making with respect to activities such as the choice of technology in a particular unit of the economy where the effects are relatively greater for those working in that unit than for people working elsewhere. Unfortunately, this is the best that a centrally planned economy can do.

The idea can be stated in a positive form as well. To achieve self-management the economy would have to provide greater decision-making authority than the social average to those working in a particular production unit over the choice of technology in their unit. As an individual, I would want this extra authority in the voting process when we come to questions about my work place, and I would be perfectly willing to grant more authority to others concerning their work place—not because of differences in information concerning the outcome, although that too might become a consideration, but simply because of differential effects that we might all know with certainty. But by giving everyone equal say in determining the social welfare function, and by arriving at an economic plan by a totally mechanical process that translates that social welfare function into a set of specific production plans for each unit in the economy, the workers in other plants have had as great a say in determining the choice of technology and organization of work in my workplace as I have, and I have had just as much say about the choice of technology and organization of work in their work places as they have. In other words, the choice of technology in a given plant has some private aspects since it affects the workers in that plant more than people elsewhere. Even the most perfectly democratic form of central planning exhibits a bias against self-managed work by treating this choice as if it were a purely public.

Although some of the bias against differential effects of different jobs can be alleviated by including the different categories of work along with the different consumption goods in the social welfare function that people may vote on, this would not solve the problem outlined in the above paragraph. To the extent that a skilled carpenter has more power to define the nature, organization, and pace of his/her work activities than a pool typist, people could record their preference for self-managed work situations by voting more points to carpentry than typing activities when determining occupational priorities in the social welfare function. But whether you are a carpenter or pool typist in a particular productive enterprise, you have no more say over the organization of work in your own unit than a carpenter or pool typist working in a unit thousands of miles away.

Individuals naturally orient their preferences toward activities that will be relatively plentiful, and away from activities that will be difficult to find. If there is a bias in the expected future supply of particular kinds of roles, people can be expected to influence their own development in a similarly biased direction. If one type of sport will be easy to participate in, all the equipment being readily available, while another will be almost impossible to enjoy, no playing fields of suitable design being accessible, people are more likely to develop skills and taste for the first type rather than the second. But we have just argued that a centrally planned economy has an inherent bias against the provision of self-managed labor activities. When we combine these insights we find that not only will there not be full producer sovereignty in any initial period, but there will be a cumulative divergence in future time periods which is increasingly disguised as people "rationally" adjust their personal characteristics to diminish their needs for self-managed work activities and increase their tolerance for labor directed by others. While it's our view that such accommodation will never be absolute, that in no way diminishes the historical implications for centrally planned societies.

A recent disconcerting talk by the Russian Marxist emigre Boris Weyl bears out some of the implications of what we have been arguing. Weyl remonstrated with the over-optimistic in his audience..."it should be said, however, that the masses in the Soviet Union have forgotten how to rise above their immediate concerns; they always weigh things on a profit and loss basis."[46] He went on to describe worker dissent as focused around almost exclusively individualistic and materialistic concerns. At the same conference Ursula Schmiederer succinctly clarified the point that "producer resistance assumes first of all the form of consumer protest" in these conditions and showed historically that this was the case for diverse uprisings throughout the 'Eastern Bloc.'"[47]

By this we do not mean to argue that there has been some sort of "end to history" in these countries, nor that there could be in a well oiled centrally planned and politically dictatorial society. That human needs of a broader and more social character are seldom expressed or keenly felt, does not mean that they have disappeared. Yet, the process of people molding their own characteristics to conform with the core characteristics of a centrally planned economy (or adjusting their desires to biased conditions of supply) is a process entailing loss of potential fulfillment and a warping of human development and desire. And as time goes on in such conditions the "warped preferences" certainly combine with the bias of the central planning mechanism to yield production programs that are increasingly further from what could maximize fulfillment and development. With complete centralization of the economy and polity our analysis does predict increasing levels of oppression, but the real world is hardly so determinant. First, these societies emerge historically and embody important elements opposing complete centralization. Second, individual consumer fulfillment can be milked only so much before the system must begin addressing more social needs—much as is now occurring in the United States. Consumer protest over poor quality, lack of diversity, or rising prices could break the hegemony of the "planning mechanism" over the workers' preferences. Then workers might begin anew to express desires regarding technology, work organization, solidarity, and freedom. Such expressions can grow at rates belying all theoretical prediction. The "revolutionary mole" can still find its way, even across borders into Soviet soil. For in a sense, it is the question of momentum that is essential. If the core characteristics of central planning are increasingly determinative of the actual conditions of work, it will be increasingly rational for people to accelerate adjustment of their preferences toward these authoritarian conditions. But if the momentum should begin to reverse, for whatever transitory and seemingly insignificant reason, then the underlying human attributes of the workforce may express themselves increasingly clearly and loudly. If, for example, groups of workers should begin to place constraints on the choices of technology available to the central planning board, perhaps only to defend their lives against the planners' acceptance of dangerous techniques, they may end by hiding more and more of their work possibilities that they would rather not have chosen by the planners. This could lead to calling into question the entire structure which imposes outcomes on them. Or alternatively, rising prices could cripple motivation and cause dissension leading to consumer and finally workplace boycotts. The break in accustomed behavior characteristic of such acts could provide a powerful impetus to the expression of long subverted desires. Yet it is also true, that in the absence of some vision of an alternative and political program, even the most widespread disruptions of this sort would likely as not eventually ebb in a reassertion of familiar norms. Were such a vision and program to exist, however, or to emerge during a series of widespread strikes or other breaks with accustomed behavior, the possibility of a working class revolution against the planning apparatus and the coordinators would certainly exist.

The Non-Socialist Character of Central Planning

We have argued that even if one grants central planning every conceivable benefit of the doubt, it remains biased against the provision of self-managed work opportunities. Even if the social welfare function is determined by a totally democratic voting procedure, even if the production units provide the central planning board with accurate information concerning their capabilities, even if the personnel of the central planning board are democratically elected, recallable, and strictly rotated and institute no criteria of their own into either the formulation of the social welfare function or the calculation of the implicit optimal plan, even should all this be true—and it never has been—the best that central planning can provide every individual is an equal say in all economic decisions. But this is not decision-making input to the degree one is affected by the outcome. It is not self-management. The popular belief that central planning represents a systemic encroachment upon the individual process to have real weight. Furthermore, there will be progressively less demand expressed for self-managed work roles in even the most democratic voting procedures as the workforce rationally adjusts its desires away from those economic activities that are accurately perceived to be under-supplied.

But if we consider the information and role biases of central planning, in addition to the snowballing apathy that it imposes upon workers regarding matters of control of production, the inherent inadequacies appear even more acute. The planning process minimizes the amount of knowledge direct producers have about how they fit into the rest of the economy, while simultaneously generating a monopoly of information in the hands of the planning board. The role structure of central planning generates a group with an established habit of playing the superior part in a command relationship. The combined result is an erosion of worker resistance to authoritarianism, and a tendency for central planners to make their own well-being a central criterion in welfare calculations.

Even should central planning have originally been combined with the intra-unit institutions of democratic workers' councils in the factories, it would not be long before the central planning bureaucracy realized that it would be easier to hold an authoritarian managerial structure within the units accountable for obeying their directives. Once authoritarian command relations spread from the inter-unit allocation process to the intra-unit determination of daily work relations, few barriers would remain to the substitution of the planners' and managers' welfare function for the society's welfare function. The process of creating a new ruling class of economic coordinators, with their own well-defined objectives including retaining their own power and authority would be complete. Moreover, as the conceptual/executionary division of labor proliferates through all social relations, the class division would be solidified and those on top would develop a monopoly of knowledge, skills and personal disposition very useful to the maintenance of their monopoly of economic power.

As executors come to recognize the extent to which coordinator interests dominate those of the mass of citizens, workers, and peasants, they will be progressively less motivated to perform their economic functions out of feelings of social solidarity. Whereas a central planning board might benefit from worker commitments to "help the revolution" so long as the workers believed their efforts were directed toward the common good and that onerous tasks were allocated fairly, as time and an on-going class struggle erode this belief, central planners will be forced to turn to either repression, material incentives, or both. In this way, the initial strength of central planning, the promotion of solidarity among the citizenry, eventually disappears along with self-management.

Market Allocation for Socialism?

Recognizing the authoritarian ills of central planning, there are a considerable number of modern day socialists who feel that while public ownership is essential, central planning is not—markets are a more desirable inter-unit mechanism.[48] For these individuals the socialist goal is an economy characterized by publicly owned, workers' self-managed enterprises and freely operating competitive markets.*

Roughly speaking, take the United States, nationalize the means of production in (at least) all major industries, amend the

*Yugoslavia is the operatiave instance of this type of "socialism," and they have indeed been quite perceptive concerning at least certain ills of central planning in boosting their own system as an alternative. It is worth quoting the Yugoslav view of what they term "Etatism" at length and noting that our view of one of the possible paths by which what we call "bureaucratic and coordinator rule" might emerge is in many essentials the same as that which they express, despite their overemphasis on similarities with capitalism.

"After the revolution, the Yugoslavs say, Socialism is endangered on two fronts, not just one. Communists have too often believed that the danger to socialism is represented *solely* by a threat of a restoration of capitalism. This is not true. The dictatorship of the proletariat must guard against *both* a capitalist constitution to include economic democracy in the workplace—workers are organized into councils where they are free to democratically administer their efforts however they see fit with only a few restrictions to guard the public interest—and strengthen the national government to effectively intervene to overcome prior monopoly centralization and other deformities of the free market.* Within the workplace councils each worker gets one vote, and majority rules. Profits are divided among workers and all decisions from the length of the work day and the division of tasks, to the purchase of new equipment, are subject to vote. Finally, workers are free to seek employment in the council of their choice.

What would be the strengths and weaknesses of such an arrangement? Obviously nationalization eliminates the largest cause of inequality in material wealth under capitalism. Likewise, the use

> restoration and monopolistic tendencies which result from the total power which the state exercises. To battle the first threat while ignoring the second can be fatal to socialism. An uncontrolled Socialist state can easily transform itself into a matter of society instead of its servant, and become a fetter on the development of Socialist Democracy.... When a centralised Socialist state is allowed to concentrate in its hands enormous and unrivalled strength in society, a new stratum of bureaucrats emerges at its helm which in all respects resembles the capitalist class of old. While claiming to rule in the name of the working class, this group actually transforms itself into 'a privileged caste which lives at the expense of society as a whole.' '' (Milovan Djilas, On New Roads of Socialism, Belgrade, 1950, pp. 9-10) ''If the state insists upon controlling the means of production centrally, then the position of the workers remains identical to that which they held under capitalism. State management of the economy perpetuates the alienation of the worker from the means of production, for he has no more control over them than he ever did.'' (Blumberg, p. 177.)

*Actually, in practice, given the competitive market arrangement, this problem must prove nearly intractable. The Yugoslav experience provides a case in point:

> ''Monopolistic practices in the best tradition of Western capitalism have blossomed under workers' management. Borba, the Belgrade party newspaper, accused firms which were the exclusive producer of some goods of using their economic power irresponsibly. These firms often 'blackmailed' their customers

of markets eliminates the presence of an all powerful central planning board. Let's assume that the government is effective in preventing monopolies, keeping markets competitive, and moving them quickly to forced equillibrium. Then the question becomes whether even giving markets every benefit of the doubt, they lead to the most socially fulfilling economic outcomes and generate the development of self-management, solidarity, and diversity among participants in the economy. If so, markets would be an effective corrective to central planning and we could settle on them as the mainstay of truly socialist economic allocation. But if not, *we will have no choice but to initiate a creative search for an alternative to both markets and central planning,* however difficult such a search might be.

Cybernetic Miracle or Commodity Fetishism?

In any economy production and consumption are both part of an encompassing network and process. Each seemingly individual act of production or consumption is actually connected to countless others in ways establishing relationships not only between things, but also between people. To abstract from this whole network is to ignore important aspects of each act. Moreover, every act of production and consumption occurs as a flow through time and each

> into paying high prices and accepting inferior quality goods and/ or more goods than they actually needed. (Blumberg, p. 212)

We largely abstract from the issue not because it is unimportant, but to spend more energy on issues which will prove more instructive for our positive aspirations to describe new economic relations. But to give further flavor of the magnitude of the problem—and thus also of the role of markets rather than private ownership as its cause—consider:

> "The big producers are competing with us unfairly. No matter which customer we contacted the answer was that others were selling more cheaply. Our collective accordingly decided that we should sell at any price provided it would cover our costs. The representatives of the big oil factories then threatened to sell their products at a discount in the areas supplied by the small factory and were told that the small factory would not accept an ultimatum and if necessary would cut its own price still further." (from above cited UN publication, p. 92)

"separate" flow is part of a still larger flow which is the motion of the whole economy from period to period. In a particular social setting individuals may or may not be aware of these complex features of their actions and this can have considerable impact upon the extent to which they can intelligently assess and benefit from them.

The market is one possible institution for coordinating economic activities of disparate groups of people. Markets coordinate activities by providing all individual units the opportunity to offer the material outputs of their activities in exchange for the material outputs of other units' activities, with a general assumption of non-coercion. This exchange between different economic units is an expression of the fact that people in those separate groups are actually engaged in social activity with one another. Although the two units involved in exchange are separated by distance and lack of information about the nature of each other's roles in their shared activity, neither of their processes makes sense, or could continue without the other. The exchanged outputs of one group's activity would have no purpose were they not destined to be inputs of the other group's activity, just as the activity of the second group would be impossible without the inputs received from the first. We have no difficulty understanding that the workers at the beginning and end of a General Motors assembly line are engaged in the social activity of making automobiles. And even though the workers in the blast furnace divisions are not connected by a physical assembly line to the workers in the rolling mills in a Bethlehem Steel plant, we also easily see their activities as integrated and part of one process. But we frequently fail to understand that workers in Bethlehem and workers at G.M. are similarly involved in a shared activity. The reason for our blindness is that *within* local units the activities of different individuals are consciously coordinated to achieve a known goal. However, in market economies the individual activities of *different* economic units are *not* consciously coordinated by anyone. For those working on the G.M. assembly line do not appear to be engaged in a social activity with the steel workers, or bound by a specific set of production relations with those other workers. Instead it appears that they are engaged in isolated productive activity and have relations only with other things, i.e., the sheet metal they utilize as inputs in their labor process and the automobiles they create as outputs.

In other words, in commodity producing societies people see individuals (or small isolated groups of people) consuming material inputs, producing material outputs, or exchanging money in markets for commodities—we see relationships between people and things. Relations between people and other people either disappear from sight or are confined to recognition of relations between people within the same economic unit. By focusing on this surface appearance we lose sight of the fact that in social economic activity people must have relations with other people and that it is precisely these human relations that are disguised as relationships between commodities in exchange. This information disguising character of markets which causes people to attribute to things the creative power that actually resides only in themselves, is called "commodity fetishism."[49]

But the information-disguising character of markets goes further. For the G.M. workers to really evaluate their work in human terms they would have to know the human/social as well as material factors that went into the items they need to work with, as well as the human/social outputs of their work, the uses to which their cars will be put, the human contribution they will make, the needs met or aggravated, and the human and social characteristics produced. Suppose, for example, that G.M. workers overcome the misinterpretation of economic reality called commodity fetishism and set out to discover the nature of their productive relations with steel workers or coal miners or any other group. Let's say the auto workers have complete information on the social relations of production within their unit and want to extend their understanding to their unit's relations with other groups' economic activities. The only information the market provides about the relations between auto workers, steel workers, coal miners, etc., is a price that accompanies the physical commodities that are exchanged. Even if these prices accurately represent the total human costs and benefits that have occurred in the various processes that have utilized this commodity as input or output—and we will argue shortly that this is *not* the case even when markets operate ideally—this information is totally insufficient to allow the auto workers to themselves understand and evaluate their relations with the steel workers and miners. The price leaves us in ignorance concerning what went into a commodity's production, what needs were met or left unsatisfied, and what human characteristics were simultaneously produced. Prices someone will pay for goods we are producing don't let us know what concrete pleasures and character development they will promote. Market institutions hide all this information about the concrete human relations that are necessary for morale and empathy, and they thereby preclude the development of solidarity based on each unit's concern with the well-being of all others.

Markets make it almost impossible to think relationally and historically about one's involvements with other productive processes. Assuming that a group of workers "sees" its own possible activities with all their alternative possible material and human inputs and outputs, what they need to expand their understanding fully is a vivid picture of the same details for other units in the economy where the *human* inputs and outputs of the other processes are particularly crucial to understand. The so-called "cybernetic miracle" of markets is actually the *suppression* of all these information flows. Based on the prices of material inputs and outputs alone, economic actors are totally unable to think in terms of network and process and therefore unsuited to themselves judge whether a change in their own productive activity, shifting the relative amounts of material inputs and/or outputs, eases others' conditions or makes their situations more difficult. The very absence of information about the concrete effects of one's own activities on others leaves little choice but to consult one's own situation exclusively.* More, this calculation, as we'll see, becomes a rather perfunctory and uninteresting, technical one.

Market Roles: The War of Each Against All

Markets simultaneously require competive behavior and prohibit cooperation as irrational. For markets create a direct

*This affects not only consciousness and personality, undermining tendencies to solidarity and inducing narrow egotism—it also distorts outcomes. In Yugoslavia, for example, workers firms turned to the production of luxury oriented goods for which their was high demand at the expense of providing basic necessities and long-run investment goods necessary for economic development. One case often cited is that of two canning factories in Croatia suddenly adding equipment to produce the popular sweet, 'Turkish Delight.' (Fred Warner Neal, *Titoism in Action*, Univ of California Press, 1958.) And in the remainder of this book, Neal catalogs a whole series of such "excessive self-interest at the expense of the wider community," to use Gerry Hunnius's words (*Workers' Control* Hunnius, G. David Garson, and John Case, Vintage, 1973) opposition of interests between the role of seller and the role of buyer. The interest of the seller is sale at the highest possible price. The interest of the buyer is purchase at the lowest possible price. Neither participant is concerned with the human situation of the other as such concern would undermine the functioning of the market mechanism between them. The essence of every market exchange is an act whereby each party tries to take maximum advantage of the other. As an economic agency, markets establish an institutional setting of the war of each against all. As Marx put it, those who want markets under socialism "want competition without the pernicious effects of competition. They all want the impossible, namely the conditions of bourgeois existence without the necessary consequences of those conditions."[50]

More recently Gar Alperovitz pointed out that "as long as the social and economic security of any economic unit is not guaranteed, it is likely to function to protect (and out of insecurity, to extend) its own special status-quo interests—even when they run counter to the broader interests of society."[51] But this is the situation a market system creates. Workers in a plant generating pollution have an interest in hiding the weakness if paying a pollution tax or using more ecological technology would lower their average income. Workers in a plan creating useless or dangerous products have an interest in advertising to generate market demand, even knowing that consumers are being duped. And workers in an auto factory would, under Market Socialism, be tempted to oppose desirable changes in the nation's overall transportation system, since the market system would not ensure their continuing employment, secure income, or dignity in their work.

To put it most generally, markets systematically establish divergences between individual and societal well-being. They embody the incentive to pursue individual well-being at the expense of the rest of society because they guarantee that the rest of society cannot be relied on to safeguard one's individual welfare.* Markets generate a lowest common denominator consciousness in individual

*This actually extends to the relation between the employed and the "job seeking" as well. "Some firms have artificially reduced the size of their work force to increase profit shares for the remaining workers. This helped to lead to a fairly serious unemployment situation during the early 1950s" (Blumberg, p. 213). Workers are pushed in the direction of making anti-

groups. "Under market conditions a minority of the workers in an industry—perhaps even one enterprise—can impose its preferences on all the rest." If one firm chooses to use deceptive advertising or lower the quality of the product in imperceptible ways, for example, "all the other firms must follow suit—or find themselves driven out of business."[52]**

In sum, the information markets delete, as well as the roles they define and incentives they imply, all combine to generate traits of individualism and competition. And what is perhaps even worse, these tendencies create a context in which it makes little sense for the workers' councils to function socialistically in their internal relations as well. The councils *can* meet, but why should they? The workers *can* exert their authority over all decisions, but what is gained by taking the time to do so? Under market "socialism" decisions within firms are rendered effectively technical; there is increasingly only quantitative data to examine and employ to calculate the "bottom line." There are two different reasons for this tendency for all human and social criteria inside the workers' council to be subordinated to a single bottom line calculation. In the first place, although production units are ultimately in competition with one another to attract and retain workers, a populace made increasingly more individualistic and materialistic by their participation in market determined production and consumption activities means that appeals to greater work enjoyment, work solidarity, and sociality will increasingly lose out to appeals to higher

solidaritous decisions with respect to fellow workers in their employment decisions by the institutional structure of market socialism. What the level of Yugoslavia's already troubling unemployment rates would have been over the past thirty years had a substantial part of its labor force not been employed abroad and in central and northern Europe is not a pretty picture no matter how you calculate it.

**We have not found any extensive studies of either advertising or pollution in Yugoslavia, but one of the author's impressions during a visit to Yugoslavia during the summer of 1973 was that both problems were even more out-of-control there than in the United States. Of course, in our view to criticize individual workers' firms for behavior that the structure of the economy compels them toward is pointless, and that the appearance of such behavior is not a "reversion" to a petty-bourgeois mentality but the emergence of precisely the individualistic mentality one should expect from market "socialism."

income per employee. In the second place, to the extent that competition for survival is most effectively pursued by growth and expanding one's production unit's share of the market, maximization of re-invested profits will tend to replace even maximization of income per worker as the guiding criterion. But in both cases, "social" decision-making is increasingly replaced by "technical" decision-making that can be effectively delegated. As workers come to have less desire for, disposition toward, and skills essential to collective decision-making, a manager will be hired who will function in an instrumentalist framework. He will sign on engineers and administrative staff who will transform workplace design and job roles according to the same kinds of criteria, theories, and techniques taught in the business engineering schools curricula of Western capitalist societies.* And a process that began at the will of the workers themselves as the delegation of "technical" decisions reducible to a bottom line, will increase the division between conceptual and executionary work, enlarge the powers of the managerial strata who will increasingly monopolize important knowledge, skills, and decision-making experience, and end by substituting the managers' own bottom line aims for that of the workers within the "workers' self-managed" firms. The new managerial class' bottom line, of course, can be nothing other than maximizing the size of the economy's surplus earmarked for them, and defending and enlarging their social power to preserve such a result.

And so finally, far from being an appropriate institution for socialism—one that embodies cooperation, diversity, and solidarity as core characteristics—markets are instead an inter unit form embodying individualism, greed, and competition, and suited not to the enhancement of the power of the direct producers over their own workplace activity and its product, but to the development of economic hegemony by a new class of managers and other intellectual workers or coordinators. The argument above is valid or

*When one of the authors inquired at a Yugoslav hotel about the criteria for hiring a manager, he was informed that the workers' council would, of course, like to get someone who had graduated Cornel's School of Hotel Management, but would in all probability be unable to since only the biggest and newest hotels for foreign tourists were able to attract the small number of Yugoslavians with such high credentials.

invalid irrespective of whether or not the prices generated by competitive markets accurately reflect the relative social costs and benefits of different commodities. But now we will argue that, in fact, markets do not deserve a good score by this criterion either.

The Inefficiency of Markets

The common view of markets is that their prices lead to efficient use of society's resources. That is, markets are like good trucks. If you want to move goods, then trucks are efficient instruments. If you want to coordinate economic activity, markets, or at least the relative prices that would result from competitive markets, are efficient instruments for doing this. If this were true, there would be some sense in trying to rescue the parametric function of market generated prices from the informational, role, and incentive problems which we have found inherent in the use of competitive markets in a "socialist economy." But when we examine the efficiency properties of market generated relative prices in light of a radical view of human beings and human societies we discover that this parametric quality, of even the most perfectly competitive market structure, is illusory.

In market transactions the balancing of costs and benefits goes on only between buyer and seller. If people beyond the buyer and seller are affected, for example, if there is more than one "consumer," then market exchange which *treats* commodities as if there were only one consumer, that is, as if the use of commodities were equally as "alienable" as their ownership, cannot be expected to generate an accurate evaluation of goods. The reason for this is quite simple: In a market system one economic agent pays for a commodity, and therefore will evaluate the worth of that commodity only in terms of its effect on him/herself, paying the price if its effect is deemed worth more than the loss of other commodities that the purchase out of a limited income implies. Therefore, the weighing and evaluating that takes place is only in terms of the effects on one agent. If the "consumption" of the commodity by one agent also produces effects on other individuals or firms, then these are ignored and there can be no claim to "efficiency" by the process involved. In other words, the market process misestimates the human worth of commodities whose "consumption" has use-value for more than one economic agent because it does not provide means for joint, or social expression of desires.

But why can't a number of effected agents ban together and become a joint buyer of any goods whose consumption has extended effects? The answer is that they can and will whenever the result or failure to do so is so grossly inadequate to drive them to forge a make-shift social structure outside the institutional structures provided by the market. But the problem is that the situation of the individuals who join such a group is no longer characterized by the structural conditions of a competitive market. And when economists analyze the expected outcome for individuals assumed to behave like homo-economi (which is indeed how we are compelled to behave by markets) in this new structure they are forced to conclude that the resulting allocation of payment shares among members as well as the sum total payment agreed to by the group need not reflect the relative and total benefits of consumption, and therefore need not lead to an efficient use of resources.

To summarize the traditional assessment of the source of the problem, whenever the consumption of a commodity has effects on more than one agent and they attempt to ban together to express their desires jointly, they are plagued by the problem of not being able to effectively challenge individual's deliberate misrepresentation of preferences. This can be due either to the impossibility of excluding an individual without the rest of the group having to cut off their noses to spite their faces, or because the group is so small as to make rational the strategies and tactics of gamesmanship. In the case of a flood-control project, a sanitary campaign, national defense, or cleaning up pollution, the problem is clearly that the group cannot effectively challenge an individual's underestimation of benefit without being willing to do without the benefit themselves. In the case of a park, a bridge, or a lighthouse where only one ship passes at a time "exclusion is perfectly possible...but there would be only one buyer (each individual user) and one seller (the manager of the public good)" and there is no reason to believe the two would arrive at an optimum outcome since there are "no competitive equillibrium."[53]

In any case, the important point for our purposes is that voluntary associations of effected agents, precisely because of these problems, can be expected to express demands for "public goods" and goods with positive "externalities" that *underestimate* the true social benefit, and demands for "public bads" and goods with negative "externalities" that *underestimate* the true social cost. The market will overprice public goods and underprice goods which have negative social impacts not felt directly by their buyers. This much is agreed *by all economic analysts*.

At this point, however, we diverge from most other commentators. As Kenneth Arrow points out, "There is one deep problem in the interpretation of externalities which can only be signalled here. What aspects of others' behavior do we consider as affecting a utility function?"[54] That is, what goods involve external impacts such that when consumed by one person or institution, their buyer, they affect other persons or institutions not responsible for their purchase? Most economists feel that there are relatively few goods of this type (and few public goods with generalized social effects) and that they can be readily catalogued so a government can intervene to correct market failures in their allocation by tax policies, penalty payments, and the like.[55] But we consider that *all aspects of others' behavior* affects "a utility function," our potential well-being and development and even our preferences, until proven otherwise.

This is not to say that any individual's well-being is affected to an equal extent by all human activities irrespective of which individuals are directly involved in performing the acts and how distant they may be in time and space. We expect that individuals will be more affected by activities that they and their closer aquaintances are involved in, and by activities closer to them in both time and space. But our social view of human behavior entails a denial of the notion that there are impermiable borders around economic acts. As individual personalities, skills, consciousness, and needs are all "inputs" and "outputs" of every economic act, and as we are all social beings affected by the situations of our fellow citizens (their personalities, skills, consciousness and needs) and as social relationships are also often "produced" along with commodities—naturally economic acts combine to affect one another and all citizens, as they combine into a vast single network and process. In this perspective externalities and public goods become the social norm, and market mispricing due to externalities and public goods becomes more than a peripheral flaw.

The vision of economies as millions of isolated Robinson Crusoes connected to one another only through the material goods they interchange is precisely the view we have criticized as commodity fetishism. Although in a market economy it is only material outputs that are exchanged, in fact what are *shared* are all the various economic activities that in combination produce the joint economic outcome, that is, the environment in which we all live and the changes in human characteristics and levels of need fulfillment that it allows. Moreover the processes that produce material outputs are the same ones that generate human outputs. Instead of seeing only the physical objects we should relate to them as proxies or "social hieroglyphics" to use Marx's phrase, for the human activities that stand behind them. Viewed in this light, the public character of goods is more discernable. It is clear that the human outputs embodied in others are of primary importance to ourselves as well. As proxies for human outputs material commodities must therefore assume a public nature as well. In this context market prices are not like good trucks.

Snow-Balling Individualism

When we combine the inherent deficiencies of markets with respect to the external and public aspects of all commodities with a view of people as having needs and desires which are a product, in part, of their economic activities, we find that not only will market economies be "anti-socially" biased at any point in time, but that within limits the degree of bias will increase or snowball as time goes on.

Needs, preferences, or use values—the terms are effectively synonomous—are affected by economic acts because people can, to some extent, orient their future needs towards goods and activities that will be relatively available and away from goods and activities that will be relatively scarce. Therefore, if there is a bias in the expected conditions of future supply of particular goods or roles, people will likely influence their own development in accord. But we have argued that markets promote the expression of individual needs and dampen the expression of social needs thereby leading to a relative over-abundance of private and scarcity of public goods. With markets, given initial human potentials, too much of society's resources will be allocated to the production of private goods, goods with negative external effects, and public disutility, and too little of society's resources will be allocated to production of public goods and goods with positive externalities. Over time, people will rationally adjust their personalities and consciousness to dampen their needs for public goods, diminish their aversion to public bads, and increase their needs for private goods that the structural bias of market allocation ensures will be in over-supply. But this process of people molding their desires to biased conditions of supply is a process entailing loss of potential fulfillment and development and warping of the optimal human development pattern. Markets therefore not only lead to generally inefficient allocations in an interconnected human world, they also form an institutional boundary that prevents people from effectively exercising their social qualities and developing their social potentials and propels people toward materialistic individualism in a snowballing way that leads to a cumulative divergence from maximum fulfillment."

Markets: If Not Socialist, Then What?

Markets delete concrete information about the human consequences of economic decisions. They define roles which require people to take maximum advantage of one another. They promote a divergence between individual and social well-being and establish a bias against the provision of public goods as well as against the development of sociality in the populace. Thus if markets are used to coordinate the activites of different enterprises and individual consumers they will promote ever-increasing individualism and desires for private as opposed to public goods. In their roles as consumers the citizens of a market economy, even with social ownership of the means of production, will steadily progress toward individualistic materialist values which in turn place a high premium on having even greater levels of personal income for individual buying. Thus, in their positions as workers, we can expect the citizens of this market economy to be pushed toward greater emphasis on increasing their income and less on "humanizing work" whenever there is a trade-off between the two.

There is of course another factor pushing in the same direction, competition. If a particular workers' council were to opt for a shorter work day while its competitors didn't, naturally it would risk losing a share of the market and eventually perhaps even its existence. The pressure of market competition which forces capitalists to "accumulate," lest they be out-competed, is hardly mitigated by social ownership, though now it exerts itself on the workers themselves rather than the capitalist owners.

Between the pressures of competition and the growing desire for private spending money, an increasing dominance of mercantile values would express itself in each workplace even in the absense of a growing stratum of managers within workers' self-managed firms in a market economy. But a shift in workers' values toward more emphasis on income and less on quality of work—and their recognition of market competitive pressure—would simultaneously tend to lead each workers' council to hire a managerial staff to guarantee "economically efficient outcomes" even if these managers would have to be granted steadily more authority over the work place as a result.

Of course once such a strata of managers exists, there is no longer a single criterion within the workers' self-managed workplace. One criterion is still the well-being of the workers (citizens at large never had a direct input). The other criterion is the well-being of the managers. The first prerequisite for enhancing the well-being of the managers is that there continue to be managers. The precondition for this is that workers be excluded from what makes a manager a manager, his (mostly his) monopoly on knowledge of the work process, on certain organizational skills, and even on a managerial "personality type." This is best accomplished by insuring that the control of the organization of the work process is always delegated to a very small group of coordinators—the

*Although in the foregoing discussion we have "deduced" aspects of market effects on workers' consciousness from theory, there is also a body of empirical evidence deriving from Yugoslav sociological studies and questionaires. Josip Obradovic's study covering 537 workers in twenty enterprises, conducted in 1967 found that "workers list wages, working conditions, and possibilities for advancement highest in their list of desired job characteristics. Participation in self-management bodies came fifth for participants and sixth for non-participants." (Hunnius, p. 303). In a survey article summarizing the results of several studies done in different years, Veljko Rus concludes that whereas in the early years "workers tend

division between conceptual and executionary labor must be continually enforced. Since the workers' attitudes regarding the trade-off between income and "quality of work experience" is the primary factor influencing the degree to which control over the work process will be transferred to managerial strata, the managers have a vested interest in further biasing the development of those values, beyond the bias introduced by the market mechanism itself, in the direction of placing greatest priority on "profits per workers." If the process should continue long-enough, it is likely that people who began as managers chosen by the workers to serve their interests would become a well-defined class, different from the rest of the work-force and managing the work process and the workers as well in their own interests. *

The dynamics of market allocation coupled with expropriation

to favor an increase in the influence of all groups other than top management...these aspirations seem to have weakened somewhat by 1968. Latest studies show that workers' desires still place the workers' council at the top, but the desired influence of managers is now almost equal to that of the workers' council." (Rus, "Influence Structure in Yugoslav Enterprises," *Industrail Relations*, Vol. IX, No. 2, 1970, p. 150.) It seems to us there are only two possible interpretations of these findings. Either workers are more concerned with material gain and less with participating in "self-management bodies," and becoming more so. Or, the answers to these questioners do not reflect a shift in workers' values from self-management to material consumption, but rather a perception on their part that worker participation in the various committees and councils of seif-management is a farce since effective control is excercized by the managerial staff in any case.Although the interpretations are quite different, each fits part of our theory about the expected results of market "socialism." If the answers reflect a combination of the two perceptions, so much the better for our theory, and so much the worse for Yugoslavian "socialism."

*If we look at the patterns of participation of the work force in Yugoslav institutions of workers' management, and the pattern of wage differentials, the picture is not encouraging from a perspective emphasizing solidarity.

"With regard to the composition of the organs of workers' management...the highly skilled and skilled workers predominate; semi-skilled and unskilled workers are few in proportion to their of capitalist property prove not to be socialist at all, or so it seems by this analysis. Disenfranchising capitalists, but relegating workers to continuing apathy, relative ignorance of economic functions, and isolation, while promoting conceptual workers and coordinators into the dominant position in the economy all seems more compatible with the elaboration of the coordinators as a new ruling class than with workers' self-management, even if the latter phrase adorns the doorway of each factory. As with our study of central planning as an allocation tool, we have been pushed toward a new kind of analysis of so-called socialist economic relations wherein workers don't really exercise power nor develop their fullest capacities. But if these societies are not capitalist—and as capitalists have ceased to exist that seems a reasonable assertion—and not socialist, then what are they? How does our assessment of these models contrast with the views of more orthodox socialists?

> numbers in the work force. Although the highly skilled and skilled workers constituted less than half of the Yugoslav labour force in 1960, they comprised nearly three-quarters of the members of the workers' councils and 80 percent of the members of the management boards. At the same time, while semi-skilled and unskilled workers made up about half the labour force, they comprised only about one-quarter of the members of the workers' councils and one-fifth the members of the management boards.'' (Blumberg, p. 217)

Among white collar workers there was a similar pattern of overly proportional representation of the relatively more skilled white collar workers in workers' management bodies. And finally,

> ''Women do not serve on workers' management in the same proportions as they participate in the labour force. Although women comprised more than a quarter of the labour force in 1958 they had only 16 percent of the seats on the councils and 10 percent on the boards. Furthermore, only 5 percent of the presidents of councils and the boards were women.'' (Blumberg, pp. 219-20)

Although Blumberg noticed a slight increase in women's representation in later years, he admitted that it might all be accounted for by a similar small rise in women's participation in the work force. Wachtel discerned a negative trend, if any, in all the above participation ratios on the basis of later studies. (Wachtel, Howard, *Workers' Management and Workers' Wages in Yugoslavia*, Cornell Univ Press, 1973).

To be brief, interskill, inter-republic, and inter-industry wage differ-

The Coordinator Mode of Production and Consumption

To this point we have found both markets and central planning institutions seriously wanting as economic forms for building a socialist society. But we would like to ask whether there is a different kind of economy for which these institutions are appropriate. Or, put differently, do markets and central planning tend to propel post-capitalist society toward economic outcomes different from those of socialism, toward an economic arrangement dominated by, and organized to promote the interests of a class different from both the working class and the capitalist class?

Shortly after the publication of the first volume of Charles Bettleheim's trilogy on the Soviet Union there began a sequence of articles in *Monthly Review* magazine dealing with the problem of the mode of production in the Soviet Union. It opened with a piece by Paul Sweezy reviewing Bettleheim's volume and presenting some of Sweezy's own ideas on the subject.

Early on Sweezy asserts, "With respect to class relations the primary distortion of Marxism is to treat them as juridicially defined and determined. This not only permits but necessitates the conclusion that the abolition of private property in the means of production does away with the bourgeoisie.... Furthermore, this view of classes and class relations as being essentially an emanation of the property system, means that, short of the restoration of private property in the means of production, no new exploiting class can arise."[56] In short, this view a priori closes the discussion of the existence or non-existence of an exploiting ruling economic class in the Soviet Union—yet that is the question we want to address. Sweezy goes on to describe how one can explain the absense of desirable socialist outcomes in the Soviet Union and yet hold to the mechanical view of classes. This is the Trotskyist approach which

entials all increased throughout the '50s and up into the mid-sixties leveling off thereafter. To give some feel for the degree of inter-republic income differentials, the per capita gross republic product of Slovenia was approximately three times that of Montenegro in the early '60s and has not declined significantly since that time.

In sum, it seems to us that the data we have seen corroborates rather than contradicts the accounts of visitors to Yugoslavia, namely that there is a level of individualism, materialism, and apathy toward the work process among Yugoslavians very similar to that among citizens in capitalist societies.

argues that though the economic revolution was successful, the need for development was paramount and in context of the small size and strength of the working class a political bureaucracy arose to disfigure the revolution. Yet whatever truth there might be to the existence of a non-socialist political regime and institutional form, Sweezy quotes Bettleheim concerning the just as obvious reality of failure in the economic realm: "The factories are managed by directors whose relations with their workers are those of command and who are responsible only to their superiors. Agricultural enterprises are run in practically the same way. Generally speaking, the producers themselves have no say in what happens, or rather they are consulted only when they are asked to give their ritualistic approval to proposals worked out elsewhere, in the 'higher spheres' of the state and the party."[57]

But then, if the economy is not socialist, isn't the most likely choice that it has returned to capitalism? If property alone isn't the basis for the existence of a class, then why not suppose that the capitalist class has regained its economic dominance, simply in a new form? In the next article of the *MR* sequence, Bernard Chavance makes just such an assertion: "The Soviet Union is clearly a society in which the capitalist mode of production predominates. Consequently, the dominant class is in fact a capitalist class, a bourgeoisie."[58] He argues that profit has become a motive in the Soviet Union and that there is a combination of competition and monopoly in the Soviet economy, as one might expect in the most centralized kind of state monopoly capitalism.

Sweezy is mercilous and compelling in response. To plan investments using prices along with other economic indicies while making efforts to minimize costs is a far cry from letting profit rule. The allocation of output between sectors is different, the determinants of the distribution of product among consumers are different, the economy is under the direction of conscious human agents, not the blind interplay of discordant human desires which are compelled by market pressures.[59] Finally, Sweezy asks, without really answering his own question, why should some analysts be so intent upon fitting the Soviet system into a mold from which it so obviously diverges?[60] The fact that this would be a shortcut to understanding—we could apply our knowledge of capitalism gleaned over a long period of study without further ado—seems a pitiful

explanation. Perhaps more important is the attractiveness to many
Marxists of the notion that if the Soviet Union were capitalist, it
would betoken a simple kind of failure on the part of the Bolshevik
revolution. They did not successfully overcome their opponent.
Next time, we must simply struggle harder and more effectively.
But if one asserts that the Soviet economy is neither capitalist nor
socialist, then the Bolshevik revolution didn't fail to overthrow the
old system, but its "success" led to something other than what had
been sought. This would call for rethinking the entire revolutionary
process. When Sweezy closes his reply to Chavance by suggesting
that in the Soviet form of society we must "entertain the
possibility" that "the superstructure, and in particular the
ideological factor, has regained some of the relative potency
characteristic of pre-capitalist social formations,"[61] is he moving
toward this recognition, or is he moving away to a new kind of excuse for the revolutionary program? Where the Trotskyists blame
the political apparatus for disfiguring a successful economic revolution, now Sweezy in his Maoist turn may blame an overbearing
ideology—old consciousness?

But then in the very next installment to the debate, Sweezy is
adamant. "I shall argue in favor of the thesis that there is a ruling
class in the USSR and that it is of a new type."[62] He demolishes
Trotskyist apologetics and yet asserts finally, at the very end of the
article, that the new class which dominates the Soviet mode of
production is a product of the revolution itself. He quotes Trotsky
for irony: "If the Stalin regime is the first stage of a new exploiting
society...then, of course, the bureaucracy will become the new
exploiting class."[63] And he goes on to say, "The new exploiting
class develops out of the conditions created by the revolution itself."[64] And looking at the Soviet Union this seems plausible. But
isn't it a varient of Trotsky's view? Doesn't it again pass the buck
from an economic analysis to a political one? Granted, it does call
the revolutionary process of the Bolsheviks into question, at least at
the level of political forms. And of course it is quite understandable
as a partial analysis in context of our earlier discussion of the
dynamics of political bureaucracy and of the struggles of the
political elite to dominate all sides of the new society. But it jumps
over the issue of *specifically economic institutions* and their
relationship to the elaboration of a new ruling class. It fails to

foresee any possibility of a struggle between a political elite, a politically elaborated bureaucracy *and* an economic class elaborated in the economy itself; a class which whether present previously under capitalism or not, has certainly grown to a high level of coherence and power in the new society. It is our view that the whole discussion of socialist economics put forward by analysts like Bettleheim and Sweezy is flawed by an unwillingness to entertain the basic economic questions of the relation of certain economic institutions to class relations, and also by an unwillingness to entertain the possibility that the new economic ruling class was present even in the prior capitalist society. Perhaps the hesitancy on this last point derives in the following way—if Marxism Leninism is consistent with the rise to power of a class elaborated under capitalism, yet not the proletariat, then might it not be the theory of that class and therefore not the proper tool of people seeking socialist revolution? In an article in *Critique*, a journal devoted to Soviet studies, Ivan Szelenyi suggests that "the Soviet ideologues chose Marxism because they found something in its orthodox teaching that suited them in their efforts to build an apologetic ideology of state socialism, and this is precisely the assumption that class antagonism can emerge only from conflicts around ownership."[65] Whatever we may think of the analysis of motive implied here, Szelenyi brings us back to the initial point of the *MR* sequence of articles, but with a new orientation to the matter. If class is not a function solely of property, from what other possible institutional relations could it derive? Rather than begging off the question of identifying the class structure of the Soviet system as too difficult at this time, save for the hypothesis that maybe it is just a bureaucratic phenomenon with roots in cultural or political dynamics, the real task is to seek to locate economic definitions for class outside of simple ownership dynamics.

We have already argued that there exists a class other than workers and capitalists, which within capitalism is at odds with each, and within post-capitalist societies has the potential of elaborating a position of dominance for itself as the new ruling class. We see the existence of this class in terms of the social relationships of economic activity—principally the division of labor between conceptual and executionary tasks and in the effect of this division on the distribution of knowledge, power, skills, and personality among economic agents. In industrialized capitalist societies we believe that the coordinator class is of sufficient size and organization to constitute an immediate threat as a new ruling class, and that there are also very substantial numbers of intermediate strata who could be expected, under certain circumstances, to align with the coordinators and increase their strength still further. In peasant-based economies, however, these elements are often much smaller and weaker. Their ability to attain a position of dominance within a revolutionized economy is severely compromised—more likely, they will grow as the new economy grows, organizing in tune with their positions within new economic institutions and challenging for greater power and economic dominance as this process proceeds. That is, the new ruling class, though existent in a fledgling form at the outset of the anti-capitalist revolution, may only develop the coherence and clarity of purpose to dominate the new economy as a result of that economy's elaboration and growth. For this to occur, however, the economic institutions of the new economy must foster the growth and power of this coordinator class. If this analysis is correct we should expect that in developing countries which have extricated themselves from capitalism there will be a complex struggle involving one or more political elites, the coordinator class, the workers, and the peasants where each group may have rather different interests. In developed countries, on the other hand, the impact of the more powerful coordinator class should be expected to have considerable effects on how the struggle against capitalism is itself redefined to prevent emergence of a political elite who might dominate all but a coopted fraction of the coordinators. We have already theorized about both these phenomena in brief discussions of the interrelation between political and economic struggles on the one hand, and in criticisms of Eurocommunism as little but a coordinator strategy on the other.[66] In the second volume of this work we will look at the history of economic developments in the Soviet Union, China, and Cuba to see if our theoretical expectations about central planning, markets, and the coordinator class are borne out. Furthermore, we will describe an alternative approach to economic organization which does not create a new class division but which instead allows for a dissolution of classes and the emergence of collective self-management on the part of all economic actors. We will call this system ''decentralized socialist planning'' and describe it in considerable detail addressing the structure of production, consumption, and allocation. Finally, we will also examine this economic apparatus in social context—what will be its relations with socialist political, kinship, and community spheres?

The general conceptual orienation outlined in chapters one and two of this book, and the specific economic concepts developed throughout this chapter provide the main tools for these historical and visionary tasks. The most crucial guiding themes will be recognition of the non-neutrality of economic institutions vis-a-vis the development of workers' and consumers' personalities. This recognition will be put to the test as we try to envision institutions whose implications are to advance human potentials for diversity, self-management, and interpersonal solidarity.

FIVE:
KINSHIP AND HISTORY

Behind us lies the patriarchal system; the private house, with its nullity, its immorality, its hypocrisy, its servility. Before us lies the public world, the professional system, with its possessiveness, its jealousy, its pugnacity, its greed. The one shuts us up like slaves in a harem; the other forces us to circle, like caterpillars head to tail, round and round the mulberry tree, the sacred tree, of property. It is a choice of evils. Each is bad. [And so]...Break the ring, the vicious circle, the dance round and round the mulberry tree, the poison tree of intellectual harlotry.

Virginia Woolf

We are born children but grow up to be adult men or women. This is a biological and social process. Moreover, some of us become husbands, wives, fathers or mothers, uncles, aunts, grandfathers or grandmothers. These changes in our lives are not the same as changes from being twenty to thirty years old and later from being fifty to sixty. Aging is biologically inevitable, but the changes in our kin roles and the associated ways we behave and view ourselves are socially variable. These can differ from society to society, and within any particular society for different groups, and from epoch to epoch. In contrast, aging is inevitable and universal, though its social meaning may alter markedly. This process of young children becoming boys and girls, women and men, and mothers and fathers is socialization. Along with courtship, sexual interaction, nurturance, and child rearing, socialization constitutes the central feature of what we mean by kinship activity. Kinship institutions, therefore, are those conglomerations of social roles most central to accomplishing these same ends.

In this chapter we will discuss gender formation, kinship activity, and the paradigm contemporary kinship institution, the nuclear family. Our aim is to critically evaluate traditional Marxist and feminist theories and present certain socialist feminist ideas that can help people critique "existing socialist" practice and formulate new feminist/socialist alternatives.[1]

Some Preliminary Comments
Concerning A New Theory of Kinship Activity

Kinship activity refers to the transition from the relatively amorphous sexuality of babies, to the more precise and distinct sexual needs and dispositions of women and men. Kinship activity is what determines how children acquire adult demeanor, personality, and capabilities in ways that distinguish between men and women and bear upon processes of socialization and sexual interaction. Examples of kin institutions include different kinds of tribes, clans, nuclear families, extended families, schools, and daycare centers—and, at a still greater distance, the kin-penetrated moments of the institutions of the political, economic, and community spheres.

What enters kin processes is an undifferentiated baby; what leaves is a highly differentiated and socialized adult man or woman. Historically, certain features have appeared universal. Women mother the young and this includes not only giving birth and nurturing them, but also providing emotional sustenance essential to early human development. On the other hand, men will generally fulfill the protecting role. Furthermore, even if they have not carried out most familial tasks, men have almost universally determined the norms of socialization and administered the life of the family. Men most often initiate in sexual matters, garner greater benefits from sexual divisions of labor, and control the bodies of children and women. However abhorrent these features may be, they are empirically undeniable and testify to the overwhelming predominance of patriarchal male dominance to date.

Yet these sexual characteristics are products of human interaction and therefore may be made to disappear in future social formations. In short, though the *existence* of kinship relations is a given in human history—"the existence of *some* web of durable generational-spanning primary group bonds is a matter on which our humanness itself depends"[2]—the forms these relations can take are historically contingent. Though evidence suggests that to date the vast preponderance if not all of these forms have been patriarchal, this does not mean they have all been identical, only that whatever features may have varied, male dominance was universal.

After the obvious critical question—how do we overcome patriarchal divisions in the future?—perhaps the most interesting question is what are the *differences* between alternative patriarchal kinship networks. For just as the preponderance of human history has involved economies that are class divided and we can nonetheless ask about important differences between these economies, so the fact of the prevalence of patriarchy needn't deter us from asking about *different* patriarchal organizations of kinship. Finding such differences—comparable to the differences between feudal, capitalist, and coordinator class relations—we would be in position to categorize different kinship systems and to appreciate the complexity of their specific internal attributes.

The Traffic in Women

An attempt to provide concepts suitable to this task is the theory of the "exchange of women," or, as Gayle Rubin says, "the traffic in women." In this view, kinship activity principally involves the exchange of women as gifts and conduits of communication between groups of socially organized males. According to this approach we can distinguish different (patriarchal) kinship systems according to which offspring are socialized into the role of giving women, and which women are given to whom. For example, do fathers, uncles, or grandfathers pass the woman along, and is she passed directly to a future husband or to another "handler" on her way to becoming a mate? By following the "tracks" and treatment of women we might discover how the relations between adults and children and between men and women are organized to facilitate the exchanges.[3]

However, in Rubin's opinion this anthropological orientation lays too much burden on a single feature, the exchange of women, while largely ignoring that conditions of sexual access, status, and identity also flow in the intricate processes of kinship activity, and that they do so as more than mere incidental accompaniments to the "flow" of women. This is not to say that the primary focus on women is unmotivated, for women have generally had the fewest rights in these transactions. Indeed, as Levi Strauss, the originator of the more elaborate analyses along these lines has suggested, in kinship exchange women have been little more than gifts. However, by centering almost exclusively on the primacy of the flow of women rather than also paying central attention to the other phenomena associated with kinship interaction, this theory sacrifices any claim to generality.

Perhaps most important, this narrow focus may ignore the interpersonal and psychological dynamics by which personality structures, consciousness, and specific skills of socialized women and men are constructed. For even if the idea of women being exchanged could allow us to develop broad categories for distinguishing different kinship networks and even if a full elaboration of the roles defining kinship exchanges could be developed, this still wouldn't explain *how* these systems inculcate their norms in the human center. To understand this it is necessary to refocus the analysis away from the stage of the whole social scheme "down" to the individual stage of people's personal interactions within specific kinship institutions. Furthermore, it is necessary to study this personal level to understand how patriarchal kinship relations might be *changed*. For certainly, to address the consciousness that reproduces patriarchal features, and to uproot it and develop alternatives in its place it will be necessary to understand why patriarchal views are held, why they persist, what needs they address, and what needs they suppress. In short, as Rubin argues, "anthropology and descriptions of kinship systems do not explain the mechanisms by which children are engraved with the conventions of sex and gender. Psychoanalysis, on the other hand, is a theory about the reproduction of kinship. Psychoanalysis describes the residue left within individuals by their confrontation with the rules and regulations of sexuality of the societies to which they are born."[4]

Psychology and Kinship

Psychology is therefore the conceptual orientation best suited to analysis at the interpersonal level and to a surprising extent, within psychology many feminists are now pointing toward the theories of Freud. For it was Freud who first addressed the question of the transformation of biological sex into social sex. And however sexist his perceptions of these dynamics were, and however uncritical he was of their implications for the subjugation of women, his work is still, in the view of many feminists, the best *starting place* for the creation of new theory relevant to these issues.[5]

In the Freudian view—unamended—the process of sexual differentiation revolves around the Oedipus complex and its Electra counterpart. Traditional theorists interpret these complexes biologically by arguing that they derive from organic differences between little boys and little girls. Other theorists emphasize the *social context* at the time when the child discovers/becomes/or is coerced to acclimate to its own sex.* It seems to us that the social rather than biological interpretations can be of greater use in developing a theory of the "laws of motion" of socialization and kinship activity.

How do girls become women and mothers? How do boys become men and fathers? How much is the dynamic a function of emotional ties interpreted in light of different sexual anatomy? Or, alternatively, to what degree is gender differentiation a function of power relationships, dependency, and the struggle to fulfill needs and achieve a self-identity in particular hierarchical kin institutions? Whether the traditional focus on emotional ties and physical attributes or the modern approach centering on role structures and institutional relationships offers a more promising start is irrelevant to the abiding need for basic psychological understanding. For in either view, the inculcation of male and female attributes occurs by way of personality development in a social context, and this is preeminently a psychological issue. Moreover, in either view, a critical factor in early sex role differentiation is the almost universal fact that *it is women who "mother."* Women provide nurturance, emotional support, and comfort, and men are largely removed from these types of activity. This affects not only the communication of notions about proper social roles for women and men, but also norms of interpersonal bonding: how little girls and boys will conceive of the proper emotional responses to female and male individuals. As Nancy Chodorow argues, "The sexual and familial division of labor in which women mother and are more involved in interpersonal, affective relationships then men produces in daughters and sons a division of psychological capacities which leads them to reproduce this sexual and familial division of labor."[6]

*This is only for the traditional Freudian theory. Neo- and post Freudians differ substantially. A forthcoming volume from South End Press on mental illness by Sandy Carter not only clarifies these points, but also provides a powerful study of the interaction between psychological theorizing, the definition of mental health and illness, and the problems of achieving social change in modern social settings.

Homosexuality

In any case it is important to notice that the patriarchal division of the sexes in child rearing roles (and/or as exchanger or exchanged) necessitates *a clear differentiation of male and female sexuality*. Any breakdown in demarcation of men from women threatens to reveal that what it means to be a "man" or a "woman" is a social outcome and a mutable one at that. This would in turn threaten the legitimacy of what otherwise appears as a natural kinship system. Thus the legitimacy requirements of patriarchal kinship systems provide a sufficient explanation for the predominance of heterosexuality because respect for homosexuality would be subversive of patriarchy. That is, people's biological homosexual dispositions are socially negated in patriarchal societies as an intrinsic part of the kinship activity of socializing boys and girls to fit as "proper men" and "proper women." Bisexuals in such societies have somehow escaped the repression of either side of their sexuality. Homosexuals may have had the heterosexual aspect socially repressed, may have consciously or unconsciously self-repressed their heterosexuality, or may simply have chosen to act on the basis of their homosexual impulse alone. Although this approach does not imply that *all* homosexuality and bisexuality is freer than *all* heterosexuality, nor that *all* non-heterosexuality is indicative of things to come under socialism, it does suggest that at least some homosexuals and bisexuals have a lot to teach the rest of us about what socialist sexuality will be like.

Moreover, this analysis of the link between heterosexuality and the maintenance of patriarchal role definitions for men and women also provides a sound basis for explaining the repression of homosexuals in many past and present societies. The isolation of homosexuals, their degradation, and their reduction to a subhuman status becomes but one more violent means of upholding patriarchy especially when other means to the same end are temporarily inoperative. In the case of anti-capitalist third world revolutions that remain strongly patriarchal, the necessity of opening many "male" roles in the military and economy to women in order to win the struggles against imperialism and underdevelopment is already seriously threatening to the reproduction of a clear division between what is "male" and "female." In this context the presence of even a few men adopting women's personality traits and sexual preferences—and vice versa—becomes even more threatening to the reproduction of patriarchy than homosexual manifestations under more "regular" patriarchal circumstances. This provides a plausible explanation for reports that homosexuality is a serious crime in some post-capitalist societies, even reportedly punishable by death in China.[7]

In any case, one welcome by-product of our analysis is that interpretations of homosexuality as "biologically unnatural," a "warped outgrowth of restrictive circumstances," or "a bourgeois disease" all become mere ideology. For these demeaning analyses, backed up by pitifully uncompelling evidence, are best explained not as being a serious response to real circumstances, but as being a reflection of the insecurities of their purveyors.*

Similarly, the requirement of a clear demarcation between "what is a woman" and "what is a man" has implications with regard to parenting. We already brought attention to the feminist claim that the exclusive assignment of women to mothering was a critical factor in the reproduction of patriarchy. By "mothering" we mean a whole constellation of activities including nurturing, dressing, watching-out-for, teaching, disciplining, comforting, cleaning...and more important, a *mindset* that sees these tasks as a priority and is continually alert to their organization and accomplishment. "Fathering," on the other hand, generally involves another constellation of activities with perhaps some overlap but very little as fathering generally requires an average of only a few minutes of primary child care a day—*and almost no primary responsibility* as well as no mindset of attentiveness to childcare tasks. One person *is* a mother, as a being, the other merely acts fatherly, *being* something else which earns money. Indeed, even when the mother works, she is, of course, a working *mother*. The fact of primary intimate relationships for all children forming

---

*It is certainly worth noting, as an apparently counter instance of the common presence of homophobia, that the Cheyenne and Lakota "draw no apparent negative connotations from the existence of homosexuals. To the contrary, the Lakota seem to have considered them as *waken* or spiritually powerful and unique." (Private communication from Ward Churchill). If there were no homophobia in these cases, given our analysis of homophobia's roots, this would certainly be consistent with the views of many Native Americans that these tribes were/are not patriarchal.

only with mothers and therefore, in patriarchal societies, only with women, is perhaps the main pillar of the "reproduction of mothering" argument. But less subtly, it is also true that the idea that women are organically and inevitably mothers—or frustrated mothers if childless—while men *choose* to do more or less fathering as they wish, is an immense support for the clear differentiation of gender definitions. Women *are* mothers and men choose what they will, and there appears to be nothing contingent or alterable about this. It seems likely to follow, therefore, that really shared parenting would be doubly subversive of patriarchal kin definitions. It would involve an enactment of intimate relations between children of both sexes and men to parallel those with women, and also a disproof of the notion that sexual divisions of labor are biologically rooted in what it means to be of a particular sex. It also follows, however, that as long as women alone take primary responsibility for affective and thoughtful parenting—mothering—women and men will bear very different proportions of all kinds of "housework" and therefore have different roles throughout society, and also that children will experience this differentiation first-hand at every emotional and perceptual level, thereby helping to ensure its reproduction from generation to generation.[8]

Preliminary Lessons

One immediate implication of this general discussion of sexuality, parenting, and kinship is that we need to do our social analyses with tools sensitive to kin. We need to use kin categories, not only class or political categories. For insofar as kinship activity has different requirements for different actors, and insofar as the resulting variations in behavior, position, and power translate into different personality, people occupying different roles in the kinship network will react differently to historical situations, opportunities for change, and organizing efforts. It is important not only that a person is a worker or capitalist, a party member, or non-member, but also that the person is a mother or father, brother or sister, uncle, aunt, wife, husband, homo- or heterosexual.

But there is another important step we must take in an expanded socialist-feminist analysis of kinship activity and institutions. We must extend our understanding of the kinship network throughout society, recognizing the kinship "moment" in activity conceptualized primarily as occurring in other spheres. We addressed this idea in general in chapter one. Socialization is not confined to the family (which is most often the central kinship institution), nor even to the family and immediately obvious extensions such as daycare centers, schools, and the T.V. Instead, since people affect their self-development and consciousness by all their activity, there is socialization occurring in all spheres of daily life. That is, each form of human activity has a socialization and/or sexual/procreational moment, and the kinship network, when fully extended, is coextensive with the other networks.

This means: a) kinship relations may vary, perhaps substantially, for different classes, races, or political groups. b) All institutional hierarchies, to be stable, will have to largely accord with the role differentiations between men, women, and children generated in the processes of kin activity. And c) beyond this simple accommodation, activity in other spheres may actively reproduce kinship norms and be reproduced and affected by them as well.

The kinship network is socially embedded. It exists only in context of accompanying economic, political, and community relations. One can't fully understand kinship networks in the abstract; they do not exist in isolation from the rest of society. A typology of kinship networks, like a typology of economic or political networks, has only limited applicability and explanatory power. Though such a typology would be useful to many ends, it could not even explain kinship activity of the most basic sort a) when it occurs in institutions other than those central to the kin network, and b) when the kinship sphere performs political, economic, and community functions as well.

Perhaps the clearest illustration of these points is the family, which, in addition to being the central kinship institution in most known societies, has sometimes been the central economic and community institution as well. Even in capitalism where functional differentiation is exceptionally elaborate, the family remains a very important economic, political, and community institution. The position of individuals in the family can only be understood in light of this fact. Psychological theory focusing on familial roles is necessary, to be sure, but a psychological theory which abstracts from spheres of social life other than socialization and reproduction will be inadequate. Consider trying to understand the different pressures, possibilities, and responsibilities which attend to being a mother *or* a father. Without taking into account the different situation of women and men (assuming women "mother" and men "father" in contemporary patriarchal families) in the broader economy and polity, and paying scant attention to the class and race or ethnic affiliations of the people involved, a psychologist will at best gain only a partial insight with very limited explanatory or theraputic power. Therefore, however sketchy, when Mao Tsetung did a class analysis of his family, it was not in fun.[9] Insofar as the family engages in economic activity, and insofar as all activity that it engages in has an economic moment, there will be economic features and characteristics of family activity and thus family activity will have to at least accommodate to economic class relations. What Mao, and most socialists have been oblivious to, however, is the reverse logic. As the family has an economic aspect—production and consumption occur—so the workplace has a kinship aspect—gender socialization takes place. As one can usefuly study the influence of economic requisites within the family, so one should study the impact of kinship requirements in the workplace.[10]

The point is that women of different class, race, and political positions endure different degrees and forms of patriarchal oppression, and men of these different backgrounds enjoy different patriarchal advantages, just as women and men in the *same class* nonetheless occupy somewhat *different* economic positions due to gender effects.

To conclude our overview, despite the need for further analysis of the dynamics of socialization, all socialist feminist theories point to certain general conclusions. 1) An extensive sexual division of activity and especially the fact that women are primary nurturers is critical to the reproduction of patriarchy 2) The existence of patriarchal kinship networks severely restricts human fulfillment and development. In conjunction with other social networks it establishes restrictions which oppress women and children, and men to a lesser extent. 3) The creation of a society in which biological gender differences are not translated into non-biological social role differences requires a revolution in kinship systems. 4) Advance in other spheres is likely to hinge on a kin-revolution as well, for kinship activity molds the individuals who enter the work place, the polity, and the community, and if these individuals are psychologically maimed upon arrival, the hope for liberatory outcomes in other spheres is utopian. 5) On the other hand, the co-extension of the kinship network with the other major social networks implies that a feminist revolution cannot succeed without revolutionary change in other spheres as well.

Alternative Theories of the Situation of Women

Orthodox Marxism

The orthodox Marxist approach to the "woman question" is relatively straightforward. The class division of labor and the sexual division of labor derived from it are together responsible for the situation of women in different historical formations. The family is a superstructural institution. It is molded by economic requisites including the accumulation process and the reproduction of class relations. In any particular society men and women may certainly experience different social situations and pressures associated with these superstructural phenomena. But these differences are not fundamental to problems of major social change. They do not require a separate analysis to determine their roots as these roots are known to be economic. They do not require a separate non-class defined movement to eliminate their effects. A revolutionary change in the economy will be sufficient for achieving equity between men and women at the superstructural level, and this revolution can only come from the activity of a class defined movement.[11]*

*Of course this is an all too brief presentation ignoring many insights and fine distinctions. Still, it is descriptively representative of the more orthodox approaches and their influence on many creative Marxist thinkers. A volume devoted to the intricate relations between Marxist and feminist thought is *Women and Revolution*, edited by Lydia Sargent, South End Press, 1981. It is important to be absolutely clear that until a new socialist theoretical framework is well established the effects of orthodox priorities and habits of thinking will necessarily continue to plague Marxist efforts to

As Batya Weinbaum asserts, "Marxist class analysis abstracts from differences based on sex and age, as if incidental to the economic order, and socialists have no plan to overcome the resulting problems."[12] Or as Heidi Hartmann says, "Most Marxist analyses of women's position take as their question the relationship of women to the economic system, rather than that of women to men, apparently assuming the latter will be explained in their discussion of the former."[13] Explaining how the oppression of women is useful in reproducing capitalism is not the same as explaining the basis of women's oppression, its tenacity, nor the means by which it may be overcome. Analyses of economic relations do not explain foot-binding, rape, chastity belts, nor the full contours of more "normal" family relations and their impact upon women's lives.

In many non-capitalist societies the family was the central institution of the economy, but this does not mean it wasn't also the central institution of the kinship network.[14] Furthermore, this duality of function cannot serve as an argument that the contours of sexism are governed solely by economic requisites—it can only serve as evidence that there may be a co-defining relationship between kin and economic arrangements. The original orthodox Marxist thesis that the advent of private property and the ensuing need for fathers to know which children were their own together engendered the birth of patriarchy is the kind of hypothesis that comes from trying to overburden economics with responsibility for extra-economic results.[15] It is not even in accurate historical order, much less logically compelling.[16]

A better basis for a theory of the origins of patriarchy is that in early societies there was a sexual division of labor, the men more often the hunters, the women more frequently gatherers.[17] The biological need for the mother to be within easy reach of young infants could explain the practical origin of such a sexual division of tasks, and the "by-product" implications for the assymetrical development of the sexes might well have been profound. We are

understand and affect kinship relations. Moreover, insofar as new theory and aims are broached from within a Marxist orientation, however modified as for example in our own work in this volume, they should rightfully remain suspect until proved successful in on-going political experience.

certainly not in agreement with some superficial analyses that suggest the gathering was mindless, stunting women's evolution, while hunting provoked the further genetic or social development of men. But it does seem plausible to us that hunting could have produced personality traits and skills *emphasizing more aggressive facets of human potential,* thus leading to a situation where the hunters—men—could successfully physically coerce the gatherers—women. Certainly gathering required as much ingenuity and creativity as hunting, including the discovery of the single greatest technical innovation in human history to date—the development of agriculture. But insofar as physical prowess and aggressive psychologies conferred great power, the activity of men and women might have been conducive to the social domination of the former by the latter. In any case, regardless of its origin, patriarchy predates the birth of capitalism (just as class divisions predate the specific kinship forms of modern societies), and its causes are social rather than solely biological. But it is patriarchy's reproduction in specific personality types in the human center through their reproduction in specific kinship networks which must concern us now.

As Gayle Rubin argues, "hunger is hunger, but what counts as food is culturally determined and obtained. Every society has some form of organized economic activity. Sex is sex, but what counts as sex is equally culturally determined and obtained. Every society also has a sex/gender system—a set of arrangements by which the biological raw material of human sex and procreation is shaped by human, social intervention and satisfied in a conventional manner, no matter how bizarre some of those conventions may be."[18] The problem with the orthodox Marxist approach is that it is economically reductionist. Instead of recognizing the existence of a kinship sphere that has implications of its own for human development and organization, the orthodox Marxist view seeks to relegate this sphere to a secondary status and derivative position. Orthodox Marxism forgets that the worker came from a particular kind of family, and that the worker sees the world through eyes which first grew accustomed to seeing social relations in that same family.[19]

Zillah Eisenstein offers another critical observation: "The mutual dependence of patriarchy and capitalism not only assumes the malleability of patriarchy to the needs of capitalism [which is what allows the orthodox analysis to yield many fruitful insights] but assumes the malleability of capitalism to the needs of patriarchy.''[20] Therefore by its reductionism, which ignores half of this "dialectic," the orthodox Marxist analysis of the factory as well as the family, is crippled. For within the factory not only are the social relations, the relative wages, and the relative burdens of work determined by class, but they are also determined by the kinship moment of factory activity and the complex accommodation and/or co-reproduction between the economic and kinship spheres. This is overlooked by the orthodox analysis and so the essential failure of orthodox Marxism—economism—even has repercussions on one's ability to analyze the focused economic network as well as rendering one helpless to fully explain the general relations and struggles between men, women, and children.[21]

In addition to these central failures of the orthodox Marxist approach to "the woman question," we find that other Marxist theories which attempt to more concretely address capitalism, the family, and male-female relations are also lacking. For example, in Engels' classic formulation, the oppression of women under capitalism is due to their exclusion from the realm of work and their restrictive handling by husbands concerned about the amenities of passing on property.[22] Those few women who do work are deemed for the most part free from these oppressions.* But according to orthodox Marxism the dynamics of the capitalist mode of production tend to attract women into the workplace and thereby undermine the basis for any special oppression of women that might have been inherited from pre-capitalist societies. However, since it is evident that capitalism has not eliminated patriarchy, new orthodox theories have had to account for this. The facts that working women in the U.S. today earn about 65 percent of what their male peers earn, that they are clustered in low income and degrading jobs, that there is still such a thing as "women's work," and that working women suffer no less in the family for their involvement in public work, have propelled many Marxists beyond Engels' analysis of the "women question."[23] For obviously working women are oppressed

---

*"Then it will be plain that the first condition for the liberation of the wife is to bring the whole female sex back into public industry." Engels, op. cit. p. 138-139.

as women *and* as workers. Work is not free of sexism. Capitalism has not ended patriarchy and has in some ways even intensified it. Engels must be surpassed, at least on this question.

The "Public" Versus "Private" Conceptualization

To overcome these weaknesses the author of one popular Marxist work, Eli Zaretsky, argues that social life under capitalism is divided into a public and a private sphere.[24] The former, the world of wage labor and politics, is largely inhabited by men. The latter, the world of the household, is primarily the domain of women (though it isn't explained *why* women have a monopoly *here*). This split between public and private has occurred because the wage labor force must be procreated, nurtured, and socialized, and for the most part this cannot be done effectively in the profit-oriented public domain. It is therefore relegated to the household where the task may be efficiently accomplished by women. In Zaretsky's view this household work is doubly privatized in that it is separated from wage labor and because each woman must carry out her tasks individually and in isolation from other women. Moreover, since they are primarily caring for and dependent on particular men, women necessarily become more or less beholden to these same men and oriented to their needs. The private is therefore a subservient sphere whose characteristics are derived from the requirements of the public. So, in Zaretsky's theory, yes, there is a sexual division of labor. Yes, women endure a special oppression. And no, capitalism does not have a built in tendency to diminish this oppression.

But at the same time as it yields these truths which Engels' theory had obscured, Zaretsky's approach also has a number of fundamental weaknesses. First, Zaretsky offers no compelling reason why it must be women who are relegated to the "household sphere." Why isn't it men? Or why not men and women equally? Second, the framework excludes analysis of the effects of the patriarchal relations of the private sphere on the structure of relations in the public sphere. Zaretsky's flow of influences all run in the opposite direction, from public to private. So in Zaretsky's scheme, women are actually working for the capitalist, reproducing his labor force. The solution is for women to withold this labor and enter the public domain instead. Engels is revived at the last minute, resuscitated by a clever new theoretical twist, and Zaretsky side-steps the central feminist issue of the relations between men and women. For again entry to the workforce is women's critical need. Struggle with men is misguided and patriarchy disappears as the primary opponent. In the end, Zaretsky's contemporary analysis is just an improved application of the more general orthodox theory.

"Wages for Housework"

The theory that women in the home work for capitalists and not for their husbands and that this is the crux of their situation is also held by another school of Marxist feminists. But where Zaretsky sees private and public spheres they conceptualize the situation in terms of a "household mode of production" and a "capitalist mode of production" existing simultaneously and in the same social formation.[25] Yet as compared to Zaretsky and Engels, for these Marxist feminists the solution to women's oppression is reversed. For by reproducing the workforce, women in fact create surplus value. They are important to capitalism because of their effect on profits as well as through molding the workforce. So instead of entering the workplace, women should demand recognition and power within their current milieu. "Wages for housework" is the specific demand suggested by one proponent of this analysis, Mariosa Dalla Costa.[26] But despite its sensitivity to the importance of women's work, in addition to confusions about the determination of profits, this view still focuses principally on economic relations and treats the specific kinship relations between women, men, and children only derivatively. Like Zaretsky's approach, Dalla Costa's analysis certainly contributes ideas that can help anyone already sensitive to the dynamics of both capitalist economic relations and the present form of patriarchal kinship relations, especially in seeing how the former sometimes influences the latter and vice versa. But her view cannot substantially help one understand the core causes and dynamics of sexism in modern societies since for the most part these are not even addressed.

Segmented Labor Markets

The last modern variation on the orthodox Marxist analysis

we'll address focuses on what is called "women's work" and the "women's labor market." Adherents note that the previous approaches ignore that almost 50 percent of women in the United States are employed in the wage labor force at any given time. Why aren't these women markedly different from "isolated housewives" if women's greatest oppression and the major determinant of "female personality traits" is the exclusion of women from the public work force? The point is obviously well-taken. The answer comes in the form of an "epicycle" correction tacked onto Marxist theory. There are jobs which are "women's work" and women workers compete only with one another in a labor market that channels them into these jobs. This powerful idea introduces the possibility that life in the factory doing women's work can reproduce sexism rather than eliminate it. It destroys the notion that women's entry into the workforce guarantees their liberation from specifically female oppressions. Indeed, the process of orthodox Marxists introducing the idea of a sexual division among otherwise united workers, and then of a sexual division of factory labor is similar to the process of radical feminists introducing the idea of a class division among otherwise united women and then of an economic factor in the determination of kinship relations. Each advance is a major improvement, which, if it is to be fully elaborated, undermines the single-realm-is-dominant-approach it is appended to. However, perhaps since this theory threatens to make a shambles of traditional orthodox Marxist economic analysis, it has received little attention from orthodox theorists. Because activists find these ideas useful—especially women activists organizing women workers—while orthdox theorists who have more say over what gets attention in the radical media find the ideas disruptive to their paradigm, the theory tends to blow in the wind.

Marxist Strategies

All of these theories with the possible exception of the last, yield similar strategies. There must be a class revolution. Of course it is important that women be involved in fighting for socialism. The rupture of the mode of production will overcome the material basis of sexism by bringing women equal positions in the workforce. This in turn will give women economic independence, opportunity for social advance, and access to culture and skills.

In the course of struggle women may be appealed to by entreaties to their working class interests or by reference to their special oppressions (depending on the variant). However, since there is little focus upon the special relations between men and women, little analysis of kinship structures, little discussion of what constitutes "male approaches to organizing and organizations," and little recognition of the need to develop new approaches to socialization and sexuality as they will exist under socialism, there is usually only opportunistic support for womens' efforts to organize themselves autonomously. For even when forthcoming, this support is only part of a general strategy for recruiting women into "socialist" organizations.[27] In the Bolshevik case, for example, in the early years of their existence there was no emphasis on the need for womens' organizations, but as women became more militant and a potential source of energy it was important both to tap their resources and to prevent their entry into non-Bolshevik inspired organizations. Yet at no time did the resulting womens' organizations constitute really autonomous movements which were self-directed and which took responsibility not only for "the women question" but also for politics in general. And further, whenever womens' movements conflict with male dominated socialist organizations, given an orthodox understanding they must be denounced for splitting the working class and being petty bourgeois or bourgeois. Again using the Bolshevik experience as an example and quoting from Anne Bobroff's study we find that "in late 1913 the Bolsheviks decided to publish as an organ of the Central Committee, a journal Rabotnitsa, working women, specifically for working women." The following quotation from an editorial in the first issue is indicative of the "anti-splitting mentality" that surfaces in practice which is guided by narrow class-centered theoretical analyses of the situation of women:

> Politically conscious women see that contemporary society is divided into classes.... The bourgeoisie is one, the working class the other. [peasants? coordinators?] Their interests are counterposed. The division into men and women in their eyes has no great significance.... The woman question for working men and women—this question is about how to involve the backward masses of working women in organization, how better to make clear

to them their interests, how to make them comrades in the common struggle quickly. The solidarity between working men and women, the common cause, the common goals, and the common path to those goals. Such is the settlement of the womens' question in the workers' midst....[28]

In this view organizations of women are not meant to improve the quality of the whole socialist left by taking leadership in all aspects of political struggle, nor are they even meant to take leadership around the problem of dealing with oppressive relationships between men and women within society, nor are they even supposed to somehow act as a corrective against sexism within the left—rather, they are nothing but an auxiliary for the "backward" but nonetheless needed masses of women. And remarkably, the sacrifice of feminism isn't even made for workers' gains as touted—for in fact a feminist revolution in kinship would be necessary for a full liberation of workers and even for an economic revolution to sucessfully put workers in command of the economy—but for gains by a male party bureaucracy and a predominantly male coordinator class and intellegentsia.

Finally, in looking at so-called "socialist" societies through orthodox-tinted theoretical sunglasses, the light falls heavily on women's participation in the workforce but more dimly on equalization of housework and the *qualitative character* of the jobs women hold. What remains in the shadows, however, are the sexual relations of teenagers, who controls childbirth processes, the character of early child-rearing relations, the situation of gays and lesbians, the nature of dominance/submission patterns in dialogue and interaction between men and women, sexual anxiety, the nature of the division of labor in the household, the "traffic in women,"—in short, the kinship sphere and its impact upon daily life possibilities. Yet this kinship sphere is critical, both to the situation of the sexes and for its impact on the definition and reproduction of economic, political, and community activity.

Robin Morgan has recently interviewed four women, all exiles from the Soviet Union and all feminist, regarding the plight of women in "already existing socialist society."[29] Although some of the discussion is vague the overall impressions are stark. Talking about the invasion of Afghanistan one woman says: "We must get rid of the myth that Afgan women are getting freedom while sitting on Russian tanks. Look at the fate or women in the Soviet Eastern and Southeastern regions. They were 'freed' long ago and got rid of their veils but they work out in the cotton fields 14 hours a day, and then, in the evenings go home to their husbands who have bought them—and if such a woman does get some education by the Soviet government, it means only that her bride price goes up. Carrying the Red Banner is really no different than wearing the veil.'' And another says, ''The Soviet woman is emancipated as far as education itself is concerned. She can get her education but she cannot use it.'' In general they report a situation in which women are still subordinate, work in jobs that are defined as inferior and accorded less pay and status, still primarily responsible for the home and certainly for child rearing, still subject to severe physical and mental abuse—''One of the most idiotic ways of terror the KGB uses is faking a sexual attack,'' as Robin Morgan explains, ''letting the woman escape at the last minute but leaving her terrorized''—and yet quite fully incorporated into the workforce. Traditional socialist strategy of the Bolshevik kind is, as we have already argued, unsuited to the creation of a socialist economy due to its coordinator orientation and political authoritarianism. At the same time, it is also easy to see that simplistic ideas about an end to patriarchy being possible simply on the basis of changes in women's supposed positions in the economy—stemming in turn from nationalization and the institution of planning—are also flawed. Bolshevik strategy did not yield a feminist society. Similarly, traditional Marxist approaches to understanding modern societies, including those that call themselves socialist, are insufficient to understanding the situation of women or men regarding kinship relations, and thus regarding all sides of social life affected by kinship—to varying degrees, everything. They are likewise insufficient to the task of elaborating a feminist vision for any sphere of social life, and will therefore be unable to win and sustain allegiance of women or men who develop ''feminist needs.'' As Heidi Hartmann asserts: ''A struggle aimed only at capitalist relations of oppression will fail, since their underlying supports in patriarchal relations of oppression will be overlooked. And the analysis of patriarchy is essential to a definition of the kind of socialism that would destroy patriarchy, the only kind of socialism useful to women.''[30] Given this, what then is there to say about the various feminist theories which aim to replace the economism and class-centeredness of orthodox Marxism with something more psychologically self-conscious?

Radical Feminism

In the radical feminist's perspective one or another theory of kin and gender relations is elevated to being a theory of society in general. As with the orthodox Marxist school, the character of all social relations is seen as the outgrowth of a single primary dynamic, this time born of the kinship rather than the economic sphere of daily life. Kinship relations are basic (one is tempted to say "in the last instance") and others merely derivative. Kinship must be revolutionized as a basis for change in all aspects of life. From one reductionism we move to another. In speaking of the two polar conceptions Zillah Eisenstein says, "One either sees the social relations of production or the social relations of reproduction, domestic or wage labor, the private or the public realms, the family or the economy, ideology or material conditions, the sexual division of labor or capitalist class relations as oppressive."[31] But as Eisenstein argues and as our approach attempts to clarify, this is a false dichotomy. One does not have to accept either one pole or the other.

Shulamith Firestone's work is an excellent example of this inversion from orthodox Marxism to radical feminism.[32] Firestone's approach seeks the *origins* of on-going male/female social polarities almost exclusively in innate male/female biological differences and their social interplay, and tries to explain the current reproduction of patriarchy as well as class in these terms as well. Firestone treats the problem of socialization via the Oedipus dynamic primarily in power terms, which is a definite improvement on the psychologism of those Freudians who ahistorically abstract from social relations and hierarchies of power to analyse the Oedipus Complex only in terms of genetic biological and psychological structures. One might say that where the orthodox Marxists often carry a justifiable concern for "material relations" to the unreasonable lengths of denying the critical importance of biological and ideological relations, many Freudians and radical feminists allow their psychological and biological insights to blind them to the parallel importance of history and social structure. But what was critical about Firestone's work was her effort to tackle questions of sexuality, psychology and the relations of men and women head on without subordinating them to some other dynamics, while also seeking to preserve a social and historical orientation. In this, her work can be seen as a precursor to the socialist feminist approaches other women would create shortly thereafter.

Another radical feminist approach with closer ties to Marxism has emphasized the concept: "mode of reproduction."[33] The point is to focus on the reproduction of the species as a form of production necessary to society's existence. This is reasonable, but regrettably most attempts to combine the concepts "mode of reproduction" and "mode of production" have led to serious confusion. Radical feminists who use the concepts insist that the "mode of reproduction" must be prior and primary, but Marxist feminists employing the ideas insist just the opposite. The ensuing fruitless debate obscures the fundamental realization that the two spheres are co-extensive and must either accommodate or reproduce one another's structures in any stable social formation. The fact that one sphere might be more important at a certain moment—either for its social impact or for the importance of its agents in bringing about historical change—does not mean there is a generalizable hierarchy of relations between the two spheres. Moreover, labelling the spheres "levels" as the Althusserians do, is also an invitation to reaching this same dead-end, since about levels one habitually almost immediately asks, "which is higher and which lower?" Juliet Mitchell, for example, seems to be following this Althusserian route having now concluded that economic relations are more basic, and kinship relations essentially ideological and therefore, however important at certain times, derivative.[34]

The second problem with the concepts "mode of reproduction" and "mode of production" is that their use masks the extent to which the economy is involved in socialization and reproduction, and the family in production and consumption. In sum, the problem is a familiar one. Theoretical constructs that attempt to introduce an a priori hierarchy between the spheres of social life or that blind users to the functional mixing between institutional networks of the different spheres, are all conceptually debilitating. We end up emphasizing only one dynamic and ignoring important features of interaction. Although the idea "mode of reproduction" needn't have led users down this path, in context of being employed alongside more traditional Marxist categories, it certainly has.

The concept "patriarchy," as Gayle Rubin points out, also contains a possible trap which helps illustrate another weakness of radical feminism.[35] Using the term patriarchy to refer to kinship networks in particular societies obscures the fact that these networks undergo substantial changes. China was and remains patriarchal, and the same term applies to relations in the United States today. Yet the kinship networks of Mandarin China, Communist China, and the United States today are different from one another in very important ways. If the only name we had for economies was "class system"—if we didn't have the concepts of slavery, feudalism, capitalism, and the coordinator mode of production and consumption—we would have similar problems in our economic analysis. Labelling Mandarin China and Communist China and the United States today simply "class societies" we would lose track of great differences, even while successfully pursuing a worthy effort to emphasize an aspect of continuity that has been historically ever-present, class division. Similarly, confusing patriarchy with what should be a number of terms applicable to *different* kinship networks can cause two kinds of errors. On the one hand, analysts can become cynical about the possibilities of change—male dominance appears permanent. On the other hand, real changes that have occurred may be continually minimized: the eye flies instead only to those features which recur.

Radical feminism's main contribution is to draw attention directly to the relations between men, women, and children. Everything from mannerisms and morality, to forms of language and ways of thinking is scrutinized for "male supremacist" aspects that will render them dysfunctional to the species, albeit temporarily advantageous to men. And then extrapolating to a strategic level, radical feminists add a critical sensitivity to how male supremacy can be embodied in organizational forms, political styles, and social theories, thereby helping to explain how attempts at changing society often fall prey to the inner dynamics of their own sexist modes of behavior. In short, a sexist movement, organization, and conception of social discourse can only give rise to a patriarchal "socialism," one that women would have little reason to look forward to.

But while these insights of radical feminism must certainly be incorporated in any socialist analysis and strategy that would hope to overcome patriarchy, the weaknesses of radical feminism will also have to be corrected. Radical feminism is largely insensitive to differences in the experience of patriarchy that exist for women of different classes and races, and for that matter to the importance of different class and community effects on men and women, as well.* Eisenstein pointed out in an earlier quotation that capital conforms to patriarchy and so does patriarchy conform to capital. Since the same holds true for polity and community as well, radical feminists' insensitivity to these other spheres of social life even diminishes their ability to understand the kinship sphere insofar as it necessarily contains economic, political, and community moments. Thus 1) radical feminists mis-specify the complex relations between sexual activity and economic, political and community relations. 2) They often lapse into an ahistorical mode of analysis rendering certain of their judgements about the possibility of social change cynical. And 3) they do not criticize the economism of Marxism *as an economic theory* since they themselves ignore the impact of kinship relations on economic institutions. These weaknesses often cause critics to apply the labels "bourgeois" or "petty bourgeois" and "racist" to feminism and this has roughly the same legitimacy as when feminists label Marxism or nationalism "sexist" and reflects a similar kind of insight.

Totalist Socialist Feminism

The alternative we prefer is a totalist approach which underestimates neither the importance of economic nor kinship activity. While separating the spheres, this "totalist analysis" does not lose sight of the economic moment of activity in the kinship sphere (nor its political or community moments) nor the kin moment of

*For further discussion see Gloria Joseph's article, "The Incompatible Menage A Trois: Marxism, Feminism and Racism," in *Women and Revolution*, edited by Lydia Sargent, South End Press, Boston, 1981.

activity in the economic sphere. Our view is quite compatible with the work of many socialist feminists. For example, Nancy Harstock argues, "...we are led to see that each of the interlocking institutions of capitalism, patriarchy, and white supremacy conditions the others, but each can also be understood as a different expression of the same relations."[36] Or as Gayle Rubin asserts:

> A full-bodied analysis of women in a single society, or throughout history, must take *everything* into account: the evolution of commodity forms in women, systems of land tenure, political arrangements, subsistence techno-logy, etc. Equally important, economic and political anal-yses are incomplete if they do not consider women, mar-riage, and sexuality.[37]

We begin with a commitment to see kinship both in historical evolution and as it relates to other major social activities. Moreover, the analysis must extend to center and boundary, to both the characteristics within people and to role relationships. The concepts we use to forge such an approach are the methodological tools of thinking in terms of process and network, the general social concepts of human center, institutional boundary and core characteristics, and the identification of the four major spheres of social life each penetrated by moments from all others.

We do not yet have the capacity to distinguish one patriarchy from another, as we distinguish, for example, one class system from another. But because of greater familiarity, we do have further insights into the workings of the particular patriarchal kinship system operative in the U.S. today. The sexism that exists as a core characteristic here is not confined to the realms of sexuality and socialization. Sexism has its roots in these areas, to be sure, but sexism in our society pervades all that is "male" and "female." In the kinship process which takes children and creates modern men and women in the U.S., it is not only the orientation of the sexes to one another and to their offspring which is narrowed. Rather, a male and female "mode" are produced, which in turn govern how men and women perceive and interact with the world, the character and extent to which we relate to our own emotions and thought processes, and even our carriage, gait, and language. What it is to be a man is different from what it is to be a woman, and both are skewed away from what it should/could be to be human. There is not, however, a simple symmetry—you go your way and I'll go mine, both the same distance off the main track. Instead sexism skews male and female development asymmetrically so that "male" dominates "female."

This means that as a core characteristic sexism is not confined to the family. Our analysis also suggests that sexism is co-defining with other core characteristics in our society and thus centrally active in all major social spheres. In the economy we see social roles which are kin defined as well as class defined. Men and women have different tasks. The work day is a very different thing for each. Yes, there is women's work and men's work, but this is no longer understood as only a designation of jobs that preserves a power hierarchy created in an external kinship sphere. Instead, the differences in work, pay, and more especially *in expected behavior and workday attitudes* all tend to reproduce male and female attributes and are part of what defines the male and female modes that pervade our society.[38] There is reciprocal causation. And a similar analysis can be made of the co-definitional presence of a kinship moment with community and political relations. For example, one need only think about the dynamic interrelation between white supremacy and male supremacy involved in the sexual relations and norms which hold between Blacks and whites. White women are not to be looked at by Black men—lynching was at one time the penalty for real or imagined transgressions—while Black women are legitimate objects of lust and rape for white men. The underlying dynamic between fears of other communities and fears of sexual impropriety and impurity is obviously quite strong through history.[39] In general, the male supremacist product of kinship activity peculiar to our society is part of a totality of relations including racism, classism, and authoritarianism, and to be fully understood it must be analysed in this totality.

Sexism does not affect women of different races or classes identically, even if it does affect *all* women. And regrettably, a sensitivity to sexual oppression no more insures an anti-racist sensitivity than a sensitivity to race or class oppression, for example, necessarily assure an anti-sexist sensitivity. Indeed, quite the contrary. It seems to us that in our society, using an orientation that *does see* one or more spheres as primary, *neglecting* one or more as well, almost insures objectively oppressive results. Feminists and socialist feminists, for example, use the word "women" in a way which really connotes "white women," much as Marxists use "worker" in a way which connotes "white male worker." So, to understand kinship phenomena in full requires a totalist theoretical framework lest we not only fail to perceive intimate ties between kinship and other activities, but also the different meaning of sexism for different men and women, implicitly (or explicitly) being racist or classist in the process.

The family is the central institution in the U.S. kinship network. Sexism is produced first in the family by the interaction of actors with unequal power facing different constraints and each seeking security, a positive self-image and various other fulfillments. And while the need to investigate male-female and parent-child emotional, sexual, and power relations to determine how familial psychological processes produce sexist outcomes is apparent, we must also develop a full understanding of the political, economic, and community moments of familial activity if we are to gain a full picture. How do the non-kin moments constrain and mold the operation of kinship activity in the family and visa-versa? How is the sexual maturation of people of different classes and races different, and how is it the same?

Certainly the socialization processes in bourgeois or working class families and in black or white families, are different. Sex role differentiation is necessarily communicated in all cases, but its specific features, and therefore the effects upon men, women, and children of different backgrounds, certainly varies. And this goes beyond the important matters of access to birth control and frequency and type of female labor outside the home and its impact on home life. We refer to the full implications of "producing a Black" or "producing a worker" as compared to "producing a white" or "producing a capitalist," and the effects these differences necessarily have on early socialization, the roles of the parents, and the general content of familial interactions.

In other words, kin activity in the United States not only pushes outward to effect relations in other spheres but also reproduces the features of other spheres within the day-to-day production of male and female adults in socialization. Thus economic requisites ensure that children discover within the family the "rights of property holders'' and ''the value of a dollar.'' The dynamics of upbringing teach acquisitiveness and a work and consumption ethic suitable to capitalist work and market conditions. The relations between families with different class allegiance as competing antagonists with different power in the market place powerfully molds family activity.

Similarly, the family must respect the community divisions which exist within society at large. Community hierarchies and norms operative without, must also be recreated within. The Black or white child must grow up to fit his/her community. The cultural aspects of kinship vary in accord.

The family is also a ''production unit'' for authoritarian/submissive personalities. The kind of personalities and consciousness necessary for acceptance of racial, class, and political hierarchical relations are neither innate nor easily produced in the human species. They are a product of long periods of special kinds of socialization necessarily starting in the family.[39] The father is usually the first authority figure we are taught to respect, fear, and obey. He is the first of many patriarchs—the teacher, the boss, the ''man'' (meaning both white-man and police-man)—who we will obey. The mother is usually the first servant we will disdain. Thus the essential features of authoritarianism—respect for authority and power and willingness to obey orders from above, combined with disdain for subordinates and insistence on obedience from below— are all built into and first encountered in the essential structure of patriarchal familial relations. Of course the authoritarian patterns and lessons must be—and are—different for young boys and girls, Blacks and whites, members of different religious and ethnic communities, and for children from the working, coordinator, and capitalist classes. But authoritarian characteristics must be indelibly stamped in all, which is precisely the result of an early socialization geared toward molding a child to fit given social roles, rather than freeing a child to become what he or she will; a socialization in which the use and threat of both physical and psychological coercion is ever present; in short, a socialization that is preeminently a manipulative affair.

The individual as produced in the family, and it is different for families whose parents are of different status in various social hierarchies, is generally eminently qualified to enter modern life as a ''productive and accommodating'' participant. There are contradictions, as we will discuss below, to be sure, but to the extent that the family and kinship network as a whole operate "successfully" they produce fragmented men and women, each partially "de-sexed" and also inclined to be workers, coordinators, or capitalists, members of different cultural communities, and people with authoritarian personalities and consciousnesses. Likewise, though we can't possibly address the actual dynamics here, the diverse types of *non-nuclear family* one can find in the U.S. (when they function within the general bounds of system reproduction) also produce people to fit. In short, in its usual operation the kinship network as a whole generally reproduces the core social differentiations and hierarchies —in consciousness and in material relations—characteristic of all the central spheres of social life.

Kinship Change

However, as mentioned above the kinship sphere does not develop without "internal" contradiction, and other spheres can also create considerable disruption of kin relations. Divorce rates surpassing marriage rates, children from "broken homes" outnumbering children from "stable families" in average classrooms, and majorities of new wives experiencing pre-marital intercourse are neither unknown phenomena among segments of U.S. society nor insignificant ripples in kinship activity. And the reasons for the crisis that has been brewing in U.S. kinship relations are to be found both within the "internal" dynamics of kinship activity, and also in disruptive pressures from external other spheres. Advances in knowledge about psychology, sexuality, and birth control techniques, for example, and the spread of that knowledge to large numbers of women, men, and adolescents, bears a major responsibility for the "crisis of the American family." These changes might usefully be thought of by socialist feminists as developments of *kinship knowledge* that disrupt the established "social relations of kinship" leading to intensified gender struggles, in much the same way orthodox Marxists see the development of new economic knowledge as sometimes disruptive enough of established social relations of production to intensify class struggles. In part, therefore, the crisis is a result of the *internal dynamics* of kinship activity "throwing up" obstacles to the reproduction of its own previous patterns: principally the changed consciousness and hopes of women. But this is not to say that the crisis has not also been fueled from "without." The pressure since World War II to rush greater numbers of women into the wage labor force and the commercialization of housework and health care that came about principally from competitive dynamics within the economic sphere are only two examples of changes within an external sphere, the economy, that have had a profound impact on kin relations.[40] Another more voluntarist influence was the emergence of the civil rights movement in the community sphere, challenging not only community norms around race, but also the very ideas of dominance and submission in a way that "percolated" across spheres to help catalyze the early development of women's consciousness and the formation of the women's movement of the 1960s.[41]

The idea is that contradictions within a kinship institution like the family, or between it and developments occurring in some other sphere of daily life can lead in diverse directions. After a time of disruption, there can be a return to old forms, an evolutionary reformist alteration which causes certain changes but leaves defining relations intact, or in some instances a revolutionary alteration which redefines basic contours of institutional and consciousness relations. A powerful understanding of the emergence of the women's movement (and of the new right) as well as insights into the different meaning of kinship relations for different classes, ethnic groups, and races would, for example, depend upon recognitions of these kinds of contradictions and dynamics.

Many socialist feminists and radical feminists have already gone far toward building an analysis of the reproductive and disruptive forces impacting on the U.S. kinship sphere. We suggest that a totalist framework that neither subordinates kinship dynamics to others nor neglects the impact of economic, political, and community forces on the kinship sphere, offers a comfortable and suggestive environment for furthering this path breaking work already initiated by feminist activists and scholars. Moreover, such a framework may serve to break down barriers to the use of insightful concepts developed by modern feminists in the work of analysts focusing instead first on the economy, polity, or community.

Less ambitiously, if we have said enough to undermine the notions a) that socialists need concern themselves only with "material economic relations" in faith that kinship alterations are second-ary, and b) that as a part of a "superstructure" kinship relations will automatically follow socialist transformations in the economy, then we have accomplished our priority purpose. For we will have communicated that the fact of the penetration of kinship norms into all spheres of daily life belies these orthodox myths. Certainly, the same old family will tend to reproduce "familiar adults," and cer-tainly these familiar adults will not fit comfortably into dramatically altered economic, political, or community structures unless those changed structures have only replaced old forms of subservience with new ones. Certainly the economy can as easily be constrained (or forced to change) by dormancy (or alterations) in kinship relations, as kinship relations can be constrained (or forced to change) by dormancy (or alterations) in economic relations.

Therefore the strategic implications of our approach to analyz-ing kinship relations are significant. As one pillar upon which patri-archal, racist, capitalist society rests, as one core characteristic that penetrates all spheres of social life, male supremacy is one of the fea-tures that must be eliminated by any revolution that truly seeks to enrich human possibilities. This can be effectively accomplished only if it is taken as a conscious programmatic priority. Further-more, sexism must be overcome as a necessary condition of revolu-tionizing other spheres of life activity. And finally, in developing organizations and elaborating organizational techniques, it is neces-sary to fight against the reproduction of "male" and "female" modes and their hierarchical relations to one another. "Male linear thinking" and "female intuition" must not continue to be divorced from one another, much less segregated by sex and fixed in a hierarchy.

This implies an additional critique of the traditional demo-cratic centralist approach to organization and of the vanguard approach to relations of organizers to "organized."[43] For these approaches are impregnated with male norms—objectivity to the exclusion of intuition and emotion, single-minded focus versus totalism, and an ends versus means rather than holistic mentality. Therefore, even if it has sometimes attenuated extreme manifesta-tions of woman-hating, traditional democratic centralist organizing has nonetheless contributed to the reproduction of male supremacy, rather than to its overthrow. The very notion of the "vanguard" is antithetical to the possibility of women organizing with real autonomy and power over the direction of the whole movement.[44] We are not suggesting that men and women face the sky, proclaim themselves degenderized, and thereby begin functioning as perfect socialists and feminists in all ways. This is impossible. It may take generations to completely undo all the negative effects of historic kinship divisions on men and women. But this is no excuse for continuing to actively reproduce the oppressive and debilitating status quo. What is required is a practice which poses organizational norms and techniques that *counter sexist modes of conduct, rather than ones which reinforce them.* Women have already argued quite convincingly the need for autonomy of their organizations, for the importance of intuition in analysis, for the need to overcome "male rationality," macho-behavioral norms, and hierarchy.[45] We suggest that these ends can only be achieved if autonomous women's movements form part of a larger all-sided socialist movement, and if women participate fully at the total level while they also *lead* in the definition and development of programs addressing the creation of socialist kinship relations. The aim must be solidarity *and* particularity, collectivity *and* autonomy, complementarity within a framework of totality. Most existing theory and practice, especially that which yielded those societies which now call themselves "socialist," could not be further from these goals.

As a result we must embark on a program of critique of "socialist" kinship experiences, and also formulate a new kinship vision of our own suited to the potentials and realities of modern kinship requirements. These are tasks to be undertaken in the companion volume of this study, *Socialism Today and Tomorrow.* We will show how the Soviet, Chinese, and Cuban experiences embody patriarchal failings to different degrees and in different ways, and how their history simultaneously bears out our theoretical expectations and also teaches many lessons relevant to social change under modern conditions. We will also use our general theory to address questions of what kinship relations might or could be like under a new form of socialism in our own hopefully not too distant future. We will speak to questions of family organization, communal living, sexual preference, sexuality in general, socialization, schooling, and of course the changes in the roles of men and women regarding child rearing and other aspects of kinship activity. We will also enumerate the impacts these changes can be reasonably expected to have on the quality of socialist daily life and even hypothesize about some of the more subtle alterations of personality and desire which might accompany a socialist transformation of kinship relations. Last, we will discuss the interrelations between kinship and the three other primary spheres of social life arguing how it is that transformations in those spheres both foster and are fostered by kinship alterations. Now, however, the next step is to address an area which socialist theory has been most lax in attending, despite obvious historical evidence of its centrality: the dynamics of community definition and struggle.

SIX:

COMMUNITY AND HISTORY

Walk on water, walk on a leaf,
hardest of all is to walk on grief.

Anonymous Black

Community is the last of the four critical spheres of social life addressed in this book, and in many ways it is the most difficult to theoretically comprehend. It is as difficult to define succinctly as was politics. Identifying the common element uniting different kinds of community activity such as religion, nationalism, art, and racism is not always easy. The community sphere is frequently more diffuse than other spheres of social life because it is often not centered around one key institution. And finally, the actual character of any particular society's community sphere is as likely to be determined by the nature of the interface between that community and others as from the operation of internal forces.

In light of all these additional complications, perhaps it is not so surprising that formalized leftist ideologies such as orthodox Marxism, feminism, and anarchism have so consistently underestimated the importance of community issues.[1] To make the point bluntly: If one were asked to cast all ideological predispositions aside and draw the single most important lesson from the raw data of history of the twentieth century to date, that lesson might easily be the power of nationalism, racism, and cultural identification as motivating forces in human affairs. An inadequate appreciation of the nature and power of these forces is perhaps the single largest blind spot in formal left theory.

The Inadequacy of the Base/Superstructure Framework for Understanding Culture

As we have seen, in the orthodox Marxist analysis economic relations are basic and cultural relations derivative. Of course their "derivation" may be more or less direct and the derived cultural realm can feedback on material relationships. But in the final analysis it is material interests stemming from economic relations that determine cultural norms and habits, however imperfect or delayed the translation from economics to culture may sometimes be.[2]

231

Though this orthodox view is largely discredited among many neo-Marxists, it nonetheless hangs on tenaciously in a variety of ways.[3] Most debilitating, many Marxists are inflexibly unwilling to ask whether non-economic factors can have an important impact on cultural forms. Underestimations of non-material human needs have seriously constrained most Marxist treatments of subjects such as what constitutes good art and the source of nationalism's power.* But we should take this discussion one step at a time.

Marx himself said, "Certain periods of highest development of art stand in no direct connection with the general development of society, nor with the material basis and the skeleton structure of its organization."[4] That is, these "periods of highest development of art" escape the base/superstructure logic of the Marxist orthodoxy. One might argue that such moments of "high" art are infrequent enough so that the orthodox position can be preserved, in the main, even against its originator's protest. But if one claims that art—merely one facet of a people's complete culture which embodies not only artifacts, but language, customs, and norms of intercourse—is essentially a reflection of material relations, how does one explain the enduring beauty that a Greek play or vase has for modern admirers?[5] We certainly live within a very different web of material relations than did the Greeks responsible for this object of our pleasure. Moreover, most of us know nothing of the social relations of production reigning in the times of Greek tragedy and certainly have never experienced those relations. Nor is our interest entirely due to curiousity concerning our historical roots.[6] The explanation is less "materialist": all art has an "aesthetic" which

*An interesting passage from a recent Marxist volume which forebodes many concerns we will raise—though the author avoids addressing the issues in any detail at all—is found in Melvin Rader, *Marx's Interpretation of History*, Oxford University Press, 1979, p. 82: "We are confronted by a whole nest of questions. Can we explain religious beliefs and practices by simply paying attention to the way in which people make their living? If we were given enough information about feudal economy would we see that a certain form of religion (Catholicism) must ensue? If so, is this a logical as well as a causal entailment? Are the religion and the economy united in a larger organic configuration? Is the economy the more basic causally at all times and places? If not, what accounts for the difference? Until a Marxist can answer these questions he or she has not solved the puzzles of historical explanation, but perhaps neither has anyone else."

speaks to humanity across time and across modes of production and consumption. Artifacts from prehistoric or unfamiliar modern cultures that have appeal here in the United States today offer graphic evidence of the point we're making. As Herbert Marcuse expressed it: "However correctly one has analyzed a poem, play, or novel in terms of its social content, the questions as to whether the particular work is good, beautiful, and true are still unanswered."[7] And if art transcends economic determination, might not the broader sphere of culture as a whole do so as well?

It is true that art appeals in *historical* context, often resonating with feelings arising from our current economic or social situation. But art also appeals to our species being and our innate aesthetic sense which, however it may be socially and historically molded, also has an element of permanence. We can distinguish art from factual reporting. We can appreciate art across great spans of time and social organization. Marcuse says, "it seems that art expresses a truth, an experience, a necessity which, although not in the domain of radical praxis, are nevertheless essential components of revolution."[8] Brecht says, "a work which does not exhibit its sovereignty vis-a-vis reality and which does not bestow sovereignty upon the public vis-a-vis reality is not a work of art."[9] That is, for Brecht the very character of escaping determination by another aspect of society—principally the economy—is a prerequisite for terming a particular production art.

Simplifying for the present purpose, we can identify three "sensitivities" of artistic communication. First, and this is what orthodox Marxists recognize, there is a historic/social sensitivity. That is, we relate to the content of art which addresses our historical predicament. This could be the art's spirit or tone—militant or somber—or its actual meaning, for example, a poetic clarification of the essence of human alienation. Second, there is a universal *social* sensitivity. There are existential feelings, moods, and textures that are simply a part of being human in society. These relate, for example, to the phenomena of birth, death, friendship, love, aging, learning, loneliness, etc. Though of course these are socially mediated, when considered in the abstract, they are more "universal" than "historical." Art that resonates with this social sensibility speaks across time, space, language, custom, and experience. Finally, there is what we might call a biological sensibility attuned to shape, rhythm, tone, color, pace, texture, etc.

This too expresses itself only historically: we develop a greater or lesser taste for jazz, rock and roll, or classical music and for one tonal scale or another depending on many social and historical factors. But the genetic substratum which recognizes and reacts to lines, curves, tones, colors, and rhythms is innate and gives human continuity to this aspect of aesthetics. Surely these three sensibilities often work together: consider audience response to a Shakespearean play, a Picasso painting, or a Bruce Springsteen concert. There is identification in all three cases with historical, human, and physical sensibilities.

So certainly there are intimate relations between art—as one part of culture—and the economic relations of the society within which it is created. But once one assumes that this relation operates predominantly in one direction—from the economy to art (or to culture as a whole)—there is little reason to investigate artistic processes themselves as autonomously important forms of human activity. If art is an economic reflection, we need not search for its roots other than in the economy. If culture is but an ideological deposit of material relations, we needn't ask if it arises from non-economic needs and has attributes "of its own." But however this assumption may benefit the economist, whose science is thereby elevated to great heights, it does little to shed light upon the real dynamics of cultural creativity and activity. And though these general problems concerning art and culture arise from assuming a reflective base/superstructure theory, they do not disappear as soon as one becomes sophisticated enough to allow for "mutual causality" or for a moment of "relative autonomy" for culture.*

---

*It is important to note that beyond crippling one's understanding of culture, the base/superstructure conceptualization also embodies an implicit Euro-centric racism. For if one says that history is fundamentally a function of economic (read: "forces of production") development, then one can naturally equate "primitive" technology with backwardness in all other social realms as well. If the tools are close to "stone age" so must the culture, polity, kin patterns, and other social life characteristics be barbaric. There is no capacity in this orthodox Marxist, materialist approach for understanding that a culture might consciously opt against "technological advance," nor that there can be cultural, political, and ethical wisdom alongside what western science might call "technological ignorance," nor even that this so-called ignorance may be ecologically enlightened in a way our own atomic awareness is not.

Rather, to transcend the orthodoxy's inability to understand the reasons why people create, defend, live and die for cultures, it will be necessary to make more than "reformist adjustments" in the central concepts and categories of orthodox analysis. One way to develop a further understanding of the radical kinds of changes required is to move from the problems of art to the dynamics of another cultural instance, race.

The Failure of Orthodox Understandings of Race

In one orthodox analysis racism is a tool the capitalist class employs to divide workers. In this view, the dynamics of capital accumulation tend to unify all wage laborers. As this is potentially threatening to capitalists, they must find ways to counteract the tendency.* One way is to play diverse groups of workers off against one another: use one group to supervise the work of another; allow one group better accommodations, wages and services; reserve higher status occupations for one group; use one group as strikebreakers against another. In general, produce mistrust and antagonism where there would otherwise be a dangerous threat of unity. Create super-exploitation on one side and coopted allies on the other by making it appear to the favored group that they have something worth protecting in the capitalist order.[10] In this view racism is only a subterfuge. The real issue is working class solidarity. It is therefore imperative for the left to appeal to commonalities rather than confront differences. "If racism was simply a device by the capitalist class to divide the workers, then it followed that the workers could be expected to join forces to oppose racism."[11]

*In a still prior view which is however not uncommon even today, racism is seen as not that important a problem, period. For the logic of capitalist accumulation itself is expected to continually overcome racist spillovers from earlier periods. This idea of capitalism's logic being independent of and counter to racial divisions—in turn seen as feudal residues—and of this logic eventually blurring all but class distinctions derives from the classics. For example, it is clearly expressed in *The Communist Manifesto* and in the *German Ideology* about which Horace Davis writes: "Marx here speaks as if the working class already dissolves the several nationalities within itself in the existing society, and the constant efforts of Marxists like Lenin was to make this asperation an actuality."

This view that racism divides the working class and that class analysis fostering class solidarity is central doesn't deny the impact racism can have, nor suggest ignoring it tactically or even strategically. But it does preclude asking whether there are seeds of racism other than those planted by capitalists. It does fail to explain why, though capitalists exploit all differences among workers, racism is particularly enduring and incendiary. It doesn't explain why, though Black people demand social equality and the right to live and move about freely, when given the choice they generally prefer to live and marry in Black communities. It doesn't fully explain the ways whites benefit from racism and why they often display racist attitudes that go well beyond anything capitalists seek to inculcate. Nor does it explain the wide variety of cultural differences that make whites, Blacks, and Chicanos different from and "strange" to one another. These differences make communication difficult and often suspicious and fearful. We talk, eat, dance, move, and celebrate differently. Is it realistic to speak and act as if "unite and fight" is an obvious and achievable aim? The orthodox approach precludes examining any strategy for overcoming racism other than integration. It relegates racism to a tactical and strategic concern, rather than treating it as a matter of highest principle.[12] The orthodox approach ignores Amilcar Cabral's injunctions that cultural differences between social communities may have fundamental impact on their receptivity to socialism and on the energy with which they will struggle for it.*

In a similar vein, Marx and Engels often spoke of the benefits that imperial expansion could bring "backward" peoples, for example "energetic yankees" could aid "lazy Mexicans." As Horace Davis sums up, "the idea that the 'backward peoples' might get farther if they resisted the encroachments of Saint Bourgeois and made their own selections of the blessings of civilization in their own time, was indeed slow in penetrating Marxism." *Nationalism and Socialism: Marxist and Labor Theories of Nationalism to 1917*, Monthly Review Press, New York, 1967, p. 61.

*"In the thorough analysis of social structure which every liberation movement should be capable of making in relation to the imperative of the struggle, the cultural characteristics of each group in society have a place of prime importance. For, while the culture has a mass character, it is not equally developed in all sectors of society. The attitude of each social group toward the liberation struggle is dictated by its economic interests,

The highest orthodox principle is class unity. Racism is a problem primarily because it is a division of that unity. Once racial division is overcome class struggle can resume with the working class significantly strengthened. Logically, "no matter how vocal the Communists were, for example, on 'Negro rights,' in the final analysis they looked upon the white labor movement as the dominant factor and considered the 'Negro' as the most oppressed worker and therefore the paradigm proletarian: when integration is achieved it will be the Black workers who lead the class struggles, as workers to be sure."[13] Regarding racism, this vision recognizes an economic dynamic, but no independent cultural one.

Abstracting from issues of motivation or underlying analysis, integrationist strategies have both positive and negative aspects. On the one hand there is an assertion of equal humanity and political rights. But on the other there is a loss of dignity and self-respect and a denial of legitimate separate history and culture that accompanies being integrated from below. Widespread Marxist support for integration as the main aim for Negroes was largely insensitive to this duality. In this light frequent Marxist hostility to Black nationalism—a movement sensitive to the positive aspects of Black history and culture—should come as no surprise. "What the Marxists called 'Negro-white unity' within their organizations was, in reality, white domination."[14] For it was at best an assimilationist unity which presumed the superiority of white norms and the expendability of "Blackness."

As we will continue to argue, the economistic analysis of the roots and dynamics of racism was totally insufficient to the task of addressing both Black needs and aims as well as the receptivity of white workers to the manipulative tactics of their bosses. Certainly the capitalists, as one among many tactics, played upon racism, but

but is also influenced profoundly by its culture. It may even be admitted that these differences in cultural level explain differences in behavior toward the liberation movement on the part of individuals who belong to the same socio-economic group. It is at this point that culture reaches its full significance for each individual: understanding and integration into his [or her] environment, identification with fundamental problems and aspirations of the society, acceptance of the possibility of change in the direction of progress." Amilcar Cabral, *Return to the Source*, Monthly Review Press, New York, 1973, p. 44.

why were these endeavors so successful? Why did working people often respond to nationalist, racist, and religious appeals so forcefully? As was the case in our discussion of orthodox analyses of sexual dynamics, the fact that there must be some form of accommodation between economic and other relations, means that an economistic analysis of racism will necessarily embody partial truth and yield some understanding. Thus, explanations of racism based on the idea of "white skin privilege" —that is, based on material advantage—do explain part of what goes on. But the roots and tenacity of the non-economic racial (or patriarchal) phenomena are invisible to such an approach. The influence of neighborhood and family life, and the role of image, psychology and culture are all ignored. When Harold Cruse wrote, in 1969, "The coming coalition of Negro organizations will contain national elements in roles of conspicuous leadership. It cannot and will not be subordinate to any white groups with which it is allied. There is no longer room for the revolutionary paternalism that has been the hallmarks of organizations such as the C.P.,"[15] the part of the left infected with orthodox Marxist ideas was incapable of hearing what he was saying. The problem was *a misunderstanding of Black nationalism*, another side to the failure of orthodox Marxist analyses of race.

Nationalism Is Neither Bourgeois Nor Proletarian

If one sees culture as an embodiment of the implications of economic relations and racism as a product of ruling class manipulation, it makes some sense to speak of a "common or international culture of the proletarian movement,"[16] and to work towards it. But this orientation insures that "desiring to see the Negro group as an appendage to the main body of white workers, the Marxists have been unable, theoretically and practically, *to set the Negro off and see him in terms of his own national minority group existence and identity inclusive of his class, caste, and ideological stratifications.*"[17] Communist Party historians would examine Negro history in a way to glorify what they liked and obscure what they did not like (in particular, nationalist heroes and aspirations). Herbert Aptheker, for example, fails to even acknowledge the existence of Marcus Garvey and the nationalist Garvey movement even while analyzing Negro activities during the period of Garvey's heyday. As Harold Cruse says of this, "The causes for these omissions are, of course, apparent: orthodox western Marxism cannot incorporate nationalism into its scheme."[18] Similarly, according to Robert Allen, Communists study Black history and the history of racial oppression but they do not address the history of white supremacy as a cultural formation. The point is that the orthodox intellectual framework steers the analyst away from examining Blacks and whites as communities with different cultures, and only toward class relations as they cut across community lines. Frantz Fanon makes a similar point though perhaps implicitly accepting more of the orthodox approach than we do: "In the colonies the economic substructure is also a superstructure. The cause is the consequence: you are rich because you are white; you are white because you are rich. This is why Marxist analysis should always be slightly stretched every time we have to do with the colonial problem."[19]

Cruse says that the Marxists "use their method of analysis not to understand the Negro but to make some outstanding Black leadership symbol fit the political line of their own preconceptions."[20] But why does such behavior occur? For the orthodox Marxist, Black nationalism is seen as a product of Negro false consciousness. The Black nationalist takes the superficial appearance for reality just as the racist white worker is deceived into taking a superficial appearance (hostility between communities) for reality. The issue underneath these appearances is class structure and the consciousness that must replace black nationalist aspirations as well as white supremacist notions, is class consciousness. In this view class struggle confronts the real enemy and race struggle is a misplaced diversion. It follows that Leninists should seek to use Black organizations primarily as recruiting grounds for the "working class party."[21]

Naturally the definition of the "national question" (and the "woman question") is couched in class terms. Eugene Genovese makes the point well in *In Red and Black: Marxian Explorations in Afro-American and Southern History*:

Until recently, American Marxists like many others viewed racism as simply a class question. They regarded racial discrimination as a 'mask for privilege'—a technique by which the ruling class exploits minorities and divides the working class. According to this view, capitalism generated slavery, and slavery generated racism; but the destruction of slavery did not end the economic exploitation of black people that racism justified and perpetuated. As an oppressed proletariat, the blacks had class interests identical with those of the white working class and a clear duty to join with their white brothers in bringing down the capitalist system: 'Black and white, unite and fight!'[22]

Naturally the well-read Trotskyist will argue that Black (and women's) organizations which form at a time of relative class quietude are progressive, having the potential to spur class struggle. But once class struggle deepens and once the working class becomes militant, anti-racist (and anti-sexist) demands must be pursued in context of a class movement and subject to the discipline of a class-based party. Separate attempts to address these issues by racially (or sexually) defined organizations will only be construed as peripheral if not hostile to socialist struggle. They will be diversionary. They will not promote working class solidarity—the goal, after all—but impede it. As such, they will finally be either bourgeois or petty bourgeois. For movements can only represent class interests, and movements outside the working class movement must therefore express the interests of other classes.[23] So as far as a program for Black people, and as far as a vision of something other than white supremacy, the orthodox Marxists of the Communist Party and many other Leninist organizations offer little more than the integrationist program of the NAACP, save that these "revolutionaries" attach a call for "socialism" which is, however, defined only economically.[24] True, some will be prodded by the activism of Black movements to modify their orientation adopting slightly altered views and acceding to some nationalist demands, but as long as the orthodox Marxist retains a guiding theory which has no place for analysis of non-economic bases for racial divisions and aspirations, any race sensitivity inspired by struggle will be tenuous. It will prove opportunist and disappear every time the working class and its production-based organizations give even the slightest sign of growing militance.

Harold Cruse relates a passage put to him by a white Communist Party organizer in Harlem: "You are for consolidating the Harlem ghetto as if it were a 'nation.' That is wrong. The Party is for breaking up the ghetto and integrating the Negro people all over New York City."[25] The cadre's view is propelled by a desire for integration as a means to end racism. The view attributed by the cadre to Cruse is propelled by a nationalist desire for autonomous culture and heritage. Can the two be reconciled? Is there a single theoretical perspective which can embody the positive attributes of each orientation? Obviously this must be the goal of a truly revolutionary understanding but before going further into the theoretical requisites for such an advance, more should be said about practical experiences within the United States.

Weakness of White Leninist "Community Practice" in the U.S.

In his brilliant book, *Reluctant Reformers*, Robert Allen chronicles major portions of the history of racial struggle in the United States. It is a story of racist depravity on the one hand and of profound resistance on the other. But it is also a story of multi-faceted alliances between whites and Blacks, based upon the United advance of both groups, in which in the end the Blacks are left behind. It is a story of paternalistic anti-racism wherein white groups fight for general Black interests and yet simultaneously exclude and otherwise oppress more accessible local Blacks.

For example, Allen tells of the abolitionist movement's attempts to widen its base of support by excluding Blacks from meetings and general membership. "Those white abolitionists who sought to deny membership to blacks were calculating that by excluding Blacks they could gain wider support for the cause..."[26] But what exactly was "the cause"? Certainly not an end to white supremacy. Rather, for these abolitionists the issue was getting rid of slavery and the associated mentality that Blacks were simply animals deserving no rights whatsoever, and adopting more benign forms of stratification in its place—segregation—and a moderated consciousness that Blacks are indeed people, but inferior people requiring aid and administration if they are to accomplish all they can for themselves and for society. "As late as 1826," Allen reports, "some 143 white controlled anti-slavery societies excluded Blacks and women from membership."[27]

Considering post bellum organizing efforts among farmers and workers in the South and throughout the country, Allen notes that two pressures affected the possibilities. On the one hand workers and farmers were pushed by a shared class perception toward some sort of unity against big capital. On the other hand, however, the requirements of maintaining white supremacy propelled white farmers and workers to oppose the Blacks in pursuit of equality. As Allen documents, there was more at work than the simple divide-and-conquer machinations of some bosses. Even when movement leaders actively pursued alliances, pressure from the rank-and-file propelled racist outcomes and molded the leaders in turn. Allen goes to lengths we can't repeat here in addressing the history of populist and women's suffrage experiences to demonstrate these points.

And when analyzing the development of the labor movement in the U.S., Allen shows the shallowness of pointing to the use of Blacks as strikebreakers as a fundamental cause of racism among whites. In fact, argues Allen, it is the other way around. Widespread racism allows the boss to employ Blacks in such ways as to break strikes, but only because the mental disposition called racism is present among whites in the first place. "Race prejudice causes the Black strikebreaker, even though he may be only a few among hundreds of white scabs, to be singled out for special slander and violence."[28] The press and racist commentators of all kinds inflate the impact of Black scabs all out of proportion and make little mention of their white counterparts. Certainly this creates a climate of violence and division that is beneficial to the boss. But the workers are on the scene. Why do they believe the inflammatory rhetoric? Scare stories about their own tactics are not so effective in disrupting their perceptions. Regrettably white workers have a disposition to believe the lies in the first place, even before they are told. And when in some instances solidarity becomes so powerful that no such fragmenting can work, of course the movement is stronger and the demands more often won. But does racism disappear as a result? Not at all. Once the strike ends white workers return to relatively better work at relatively better pay and go home to relatively more comfortable environs and better schools, and the momentary solidarity begins to erode once more. Blacks have been used—even if they were the most militant fighters and leaders of the workers' struggle. The division of communities that lies at the basis of racism in the U.S. is more substantial and abiding than any "capitalist trick" could ever be.

In his review of the history of CIO organizing drives, Allen argues that local white resistance to racial equality forced union leaders to a steadily more racist position: "In Illinois white workers even went on strike to maintain segregated toilets. CIO leadership opposed these strikes but the leadership itself was becoming less militant on the question of racial superiority"[29] as the desire of national union leadership to organize the South increased. For instead of viewing the rabid cries of Southern industrialists (and the threatened AFL) that they were "nigger lovers," "communists," "jew-boys," "carpet baggers," and the like as evidence of their strength, the CIO leaders appointed local anti-communists and racists as organizers and relegated Blacks to segregated locals. The point of Allen's analysis, it seems to us, was not to belittle the importance of class forces and capitalist machinations but to show that racism had independent roots among whites as well, and that it is critical to understand the non-economic roots of racism. What Allen's work points to is that racism is interwoven into every aspect of our existence—into cultural but also economic, kin, and political relations of all kinds—so that a partial approach to overcoming racism will always be insufficient. Even the anti-racists held their views only very tenuously. Pressures of various sorts could reduce their principles much more rapidly since they had no analysis of the desirability of Black cultural development. But what is the orthodox Marxist response to all this, for neither we nor Allen are the first to voice such complaints.

That communists were among the most staunchly anti-racist in their demands and programs during the thirties and forties cannot be denied for a minute, at least at the first level of analysis—at the same level of analysis that portrayed white abolitionists as paragons of anti-racism. But just as the abolitionist had a different agenda than the complete elimination of "white supremacy" and would even adopt racist policies to attract white support, so too Leninist organizations wanted to increase working class strength above all else, and fought racism only to achieve this end, dropping the fight whenever other means became more effective. This, at least, is the historical picture Black analysts like Allen and Cruse paint.

"Protestations to the contrary, the party's practices in fact reduced black people to the role of passive objects to be manipulated in accordance with priorities that had little or nothing to do with the economic or political objectives of black workers themselves."[30] The Communist Party, according to Allen and substantiated by a variety of historical lessons he brings to bear, had but one strategy: "to gain control of the Black movement and bring it in line with the current policy of the Communist International."[31] The case of the National Negro Congress is indicative. Proposed in 1935 at a conference at Howard University, the Congress was to be an on-going organization bringing "unity to the Black movement by embracing Black labor unions, religious, reform, fraternal and civic groups."[32] The Congress "adopted a long list of resolutions covering a wide range of problems affecting Black people."[33] Communists were members from the outset, and very concerned that the Congress also adopt an anti-fascist plank, as unifying anti-fascists was the main Communist Party aim at the time. And indeed such a plank was adopted, meeting with the "wholehearted approval of the Communists." The Congress was successful in setting up local and regional councils throughout the country and it rapidly became "one of the more important Black organizations of national stature."[34] But then came the Russo-German pact of 1939 and a change in line by the Communist International: anti-facism was out, now the U.S. must be kept out of the war at all costs. The Party sought to convince Blacks that they had no stake in the "European war." The Negro National Congress had to be brought into line. The ensuing chaos succeeded in "decimating the ranks of this once promising organization."[35] But the critical thing to realize is that this was no cost at all, at least in the eyes of the Communists. Their class line was the basis for all programs. If a Black organization usefully fit in, that was good and beneficial. If such an organization did not comply, it was useless or worse.

With no understanding of the basis for Black nationalism, save for grossly asymmetrical analogies between Blacks and national groups in the Soviet Union few had ever heard of, orthodox U.S. Marxists couldn't possibly understand the importance of autonomous Black organizations, much less their analyses and programs, especially as these were sometimes even contrary to the immediate desires of white working people. Richard Wright's career and autobiography, *American Hunger*, testifies powerfully to the tensions between communism and nationalism in the U.S. Wright portrays the communists as seeing Black workers as paradigm proletarians all ready to lead an American revolution, when the truth was anything but. "The speakers claimed the Negroes were angry, that they were about to rise and join their fellow white workers to make a revolution. I was in and out of many Negro homes each day and I knew that the Negroes were lost, ignorant, sick in mind and body. I saw that a vast distance separated the agitators from the masses, a distance so vast that the agitators did not know how to appeal to the people they sought to lead."[36] Wright's account of his own efforts to diminish this gap and of the resistance from orthodox thinkers (including Blacks) to his thoughts and writing, is a testimony to the power of such a narrow vision to cloud and mystify the minds of even the most devoted fighters against oppression, as many of the Communists were.

But beyond offering a graphic illustration of how maintenance of views that fly in the face of obvious facts could only be accomplished by a tortuous mutilation of the critical consciousness of many Black communist activists, Wright demonstrates that party members were subject to the same defensive dynamics that plague all "communities" that have developed a hostile "we versus they" ideology:

> While engaged in conversation, they stuck their thumbs in their suspenders or put their left hands into their shirt bosoms or hooked their thumbs into their back pockets as they had seen Lenin and Stalin do in photographs. Though they did not know it, they were naively practicing magic; they thought that if they acted like the men who had overthrown the czar, then surely they ought to be able to win their freedom in America.

> In speaking they rolled their "*r*'s" in Continental style, pronouncing "party" as "parrrtee," stressing the last syllable, having picked up the habit from white Communists. "Comrades" became "cumrrrades," and "distribute," which they had known how to pronounce all their lives, was twisted into "distrrribuuute," with the accent on the last instead of the second syllable, a

mannerism which they copied from the Polish Communist immigrants who did not know how to pronounce the word...

An hour's listening disclosed the fanatical intolerance of minds sealed against new ideas, new facts, new feelings, new attitudes, new hints at ways to live. They denounced books they had never read, people they had never known, ideas they could never understand, and doctrines whose names they could not pronounce. Communism, instead of making them leap forward with fire in their hearts to become masters of ideas and life, had frozen them at an even lower level of ignorance than had been theirs before they met Communism.[37]

Obviously American Communists themselves were subject to a negative community dynamic involving artificial cultural uniformity and demeaning views of others, and ideological defense mechanisms against contrary notions. If it is far fetched to argue that *this* whole phenomenon can be reduced to the product of economic forces or the manipulative powers of the ruling class, we would suggest that a similar reductionist analysis of racism between the larger Black and white communities is far fetched as well. Morever, if the Communist Party was ever to have been able to address the situation of Blacks in the U.S., if it was to have had real social equality rather than only assimilationist racism within its own organizations, if it was to have been open to growth rather than continually defensively ruling out threatening ideas of all sorts; then, at a minimum, it would have had to have had a theoretical orientation sufficient to understand the broader roots of racism, nationalism, and sectarian community formation and activity in general.

Allen summarizes this point as follows: "The party responded to racism organizationally, (but never with caucuses) instead of ideologically. Individuals were purged but the virus of white chauvinism —an ideological phenomenon—was not attacked."[38] The party was against racism because it saw racism as a barrier to working class solidarity. That logically implied that racism should only be fought in ways promoting class solidarity. Blacks and whites would be urged to "unite and fight" so that class struggle could be heightened. But to support Blacks against whites, to fight racism in ways that temporarily aggravated tensions, or to recognize the merits of strengthening an autonomous Black culture and community, were all considerations beyond the party's orthodox orientation. "The racism and sexism of American society found curious reflections in the social behavior of the party members."[39] And this curious fact, along with certain others also stemming from the narrowness of their theory and practice, eventually consigned the orthodox thinkers to the mechanical and defensive sectarianism Wright railed against.

Contemporary History

While we cannot present here any detailed analysis of the various organizational trends and experiences concerning relations between white and Black movements in the sixties and seventies, a few comments on one prevalent phenomenon might be revealing. For the sixties did see the emergence of a powerful Black organization that was both nationalist and committed to a Leninist formulation of socialist aims and imperatives: the Black Panther Party. On the one hand, many more white leftists and white left organizations tolerated Panther nationalism than would have been likely in the 30s and 40s. But could this have been in part—however unconsciously—because the Panthers were useful as "victims" to expose the oppression of American capitalism? Or was there a feeling among members of white communist groups that the Panthers' disciplined cadre organization could act as a spur to the formation of (real?) white Leninist organizations? In any case, where the Black community was astute enough to realize that the revolution had not yet arrived, and that white people were not nearly ready to defend Black militants when push came to shove, the Black Panther Party was not so astute. And whether or not the failure of the Panthers to read the level of their actual support—not just the sympathy for their aims and great courage—in the Black community was partially due to their blind adherence to revolutionary models that had little to do with the situation or mindset of their natural constituents, they found themselves out on a limb as a result of an underlying societal racism that was easily focused into repression because of the party's overt militance and espousal of violence. The Panthers were sacrificed, literally, to the forces of the state.

The sixties were a profound moment in U.S. history replete

with courage and insight not often attained before or since. Yet the subservient behavior of many white leftists toward the Panthers—uncritical, blind support of an idealized reflection of what one wishes oneself to be, all experienced in relative safety—was a testimony to both the diversity of forms racism can take, and to the need for movements which address racism in *all* its cultural forms, head on. When the Panthers were unceremoniously moved off center stage, the white left developed a similar temporary infatuation with the American Indian Movement. But who now remains concerned over the fate of Means, Banks, and Camp? Who any longer spends a thought on the membership and constituency of AIM, much less on the plight of Native Americans?

The attention some white Leninist organizations continue to give to issues of racism is much like the adulation many whites had for the Panthers and Native American Indians. It doesn't stem from or necessarily grow into a serious understanding of cultural and community relations. It is not oriented toward a clearly enunciated goal which will protect and further develop diverse cultures. Almost always it is tactical. For it is built into Leninist analysis—the honest Leninist shouldn't really even be upset by the accusation—that support for "national democratic rights" is a means toward class solidarity and socialist revolution behind the vanguard party of the working class. We are not contesting that many Leninists are actively anti-racist, both in their personal behavior and in their political commitments. Rather we are saying that the orthodox, class focused theoretical approach, coupled with the vanguard and democratic centralist approach to strategy, consign even the most responsibly anti-racist individuals to a group dynamic which undercuts the basis, depth, and insight of their anti-racism. The primary lesson of this whole section on white and Leninist practice seems clear enough: we need a movement sensitive to the complicated relation between racial and class dynamics that does not relegate *either* to a derivative status. We need to understand and organize in cognizance of the specific community roots of both white supremacy and Black nationalism not assuming that these are merely ideological reflections of economic factors. And we need organizational forms and methods which embody principles which run counter to the logic of class and race oppression, rather than ones which at the deepest level tend to reinforce the logic of these oppressions.*

Some Other Ramifications of the
Orthodox Marxist Ignorance of Community

We have discussed, in very broad and general strokes, some issues regarding art, culture in general, and race. But there are related problems for the orthodox approach associated with other parts of the spectrum of cultural diversity in the United States. For example, by and large orthodox Marxists are insensitive to the importance and wisdom that may be gleaned from an on-going diversity of regional demarcations. For in addition to community differences along borders of race or ethnicity for that matter, there are also differences that arise due to geographic distances and the different experiences these may delineate. For example, urban and rural cultural norms are usually quite different. Moreover, in the U.S., people of Appalachia, the South, and Southwest don't like to be subsumed under East and/or West coast definitions of beauty, manners, linguistic norms, notions of celebration, morality, daily lifestyle, and pace. Even cities—New Orleans, Los Angeles, Boston, N.Y., Austin, Chicago—have their own characteristic cultural attributes as do different neighborhoods inside these cities, however further differentiated the same cities and neighborhoods may be

*The point here is comparable to points made earlier about the way economic, kinship, and political relations can invade the very contours of revolutionary movements. It isn't merely that such movements can have wrong positions or demands with regard to one or another aspect of social reproduction and struggle, but that the organizations of the movement can embody the oppressive characteristics of one or more realms. The division between conceptual and executionary labor may be present reproducing classist consciousness and behavior. A division between male and female modalities may be present reproducing patriarchal consciousness and behavior. A power hierarchy may be present reproducing political characteristics of the larger society. And similarly, an inter- and intra- community orientation may be present, usually in the form of sectarianism or the norms of dominant community groups, which reproduces the ways of thinking and acting constitutive of all types of inter-community oppression.

internally along race, ethnic, and class lines. Envision the fast talking, aggressive Yankee union organizer sent into Charleston, South Carolina. Any modern revolutionary practice is going to have to be sensitive to diversities, particularly to the many different positive cultural attributes that characterize the regional communities which make up the United States. Such a sensitivity does not easily emerge from an analysis which says culture is but a reflection of economic requirements. Where would the wisdom we should respect come from in that?

The orthodox Marxist understanding of the roots and implications of religious or national identification is also deficient. The dominant theme is that religion and nationalism are irrational and mere opiates. And this theme has profound implications for analysis. Religion and nationalism are seen as anachronisms that will progressively disappear under the weight of general scientific advance, though much more rapidly under socialism. How many Marxists of the earlier days of this century would have predicted the current proliferation of religious hostilities: Christians versus Moslems in Lebanon, Catholics versus Protestants in Ireland, Catholics versus Moslems in the Philippines, Greek Orthodox versus Moslems in Cyprus, Jews versus Moslems in the MidEast, Eastern Orthodox versus Jews in Russia, Hindu versus Moslem in India and Pakistan. How many Marxists at the beginning of this century would have believed that every successful advance of "socialism" would ride on the back of a powerful national liberation movement as in the cases of Yugoslavia, China, Korea, Cuba, Vietnam, Mozambique, and Angola? How many socialists would have believed that the preponderance of "shooting wars" between nations in the late 1970s would be between self-declared "socialist states" like Vietnam and Cambodia, China and Vietnam, Russia and China, Ethiopia and Somalia, Russia and Afghanistan and perhaps shortly, even as we write, Russia and Poland?

With no comprehension of the distinction between defensive and creative bases of cultural formations, and therefore no grasp of the positive social and cultural aspirations that religious and national identifications often address, orthodox analysts are hard pressed to explain the power and proliferation of these ties. Furthermore, with blanket condemnations, the real task of discerning what aspects are debilitating and deserve opposition, and which aspects are positive and to be elaborated, is avoided. The prospects for addressing communities with powerful national and/or religious affiliations will remain dim for Marxists as long as the Marxist theory of community relations continues to stagnate.

Of course the exception is the Leninist commitment to anti-imperialist struggles, but even this is compromised, for its motivation is primarily anti-capitalist and not pro-nationalist. There is some ability to discern what is superficially good and bad in nationalist movements: The Ayotallah Khomeini may reasonably be "supported" as an opponent to western imperialism and the Shah, but also opposed as a religious, anti-socialist, and patriarchal extremist. But then the analysis of the roots of his influence is never begun. Where personality politics is disavowed as ludicrously naive where class forces are to be discerned, it is the accepted norm for most Marxists where national or religious forces are at work. The Leninist analysis does not often pierce the full social relationships behind religious and/or nationalist movements. This is debilitating to analysis and program. Regrettably there is no time here for a comprehensive survey of orthodox discussions of religion or nationalism, but in context of the prior discussion of the orthodox failure to understand culture in general, and racism, we hope the brief paragraphs above will add further impetus to the effort to find a new way of understanding community phenomena. The idea of a socialist world with no nationalities, no religion, and proletarian "cultural oneness" which emerges from the orthodox view of culture-as-reflection, is an insufficient basis for developing a socialist program that will attract the allegiance of people with real and passionate community ties. As Harold Cruse suggests in an interview, "Black experience in the United States has shown that it is dangerous and non-productive for blacks to adopt Marxism, just as it has been historically detrimental for blacks to have adopted Christianity. The reason for this is that blacks have been unable to add anything original to either Marxism or Christianity. Thus both of these doctrines remain the intellectual patrimony, not of blacks, but of whites. If blacks continue to adopt these philosophies in the form that they received them from whites, then blacks will forever remain subservient to whites, intellectually, ethnically, morally, etc."[40] And indeed, given our analysis, if Marxism remains bound by economism to find the economy primary and all other spheres to one degree or another derivative, then this situation will prevail. For blacks will not be able to add anything substantial to this orthodox Marxism precisely because its fundamental concepts preclude such additions, at least insofar as they bear upon an understanding of racism as itself of fundamental importance. Whether the tenacity of orthodox beliefs is a function of confusion or of vested male, white, or academic interests—of "cultural capital" in Alvin Gouldner's interesting terminology—is unclear. That it has got to be overcome, either within the Marxist heritage or by stepping beyond that heritage, will be obvious. In the next section we present some ideas toward a new theory of community.

An Alternative Theory of Community and Culture

We are not born religious, members of a race, or of an ethnic group. Rather we *become* Hindu or Moslem, black or white, Greek or Turkish—at least insofar as these designations have real social content. For these community characteristics are products of community activity, just as kin differentiations, economic differentiations, and political differentiations are products respectively of kinship, economic, and political activity.

Individuals become members of a community. Of course, as in the other three spheres there are many other ingredients and products as well, and the process is affected by other dimensions of social life. When an individual becomes a black man or a Turkish woman, all four types of social activity are at work. But when we abstract to address community alone—an approach whose value we've argued already—we find a subset of institutions that are most crucial to these processes, as well as a network of community relations which extend throughout all of society.

"Only in community with others has each individual the means of cultivating his/her gifts in all directions; only in community is personal freedom possible."[41] Only via community do we evolve shared norms, body and verbal languages, moralities, religious and cultural identifications. As we pursue these ends, so we develop community institutions and social networks. Real needs are served. The developed cultures may be more or less able to serve as a basis for fulfilling human development, but in all instances they will be rooted in real human needs and potentials, even as these are historically formed and modified by changing social conditions.

Culture is certainly affected by economic, kin and political factors, just as class, sex, and political consciousness and social relations are affected by cultural processes. But still, it is useful in our opinion to see culture as rooted first in the sphere of community. For then we see that culture in all its forms is a *human product* aimed at the fulfillment of basic, albeit historicized, human needs. In this view cultural attributes are a product of all social interaction but primarily of community activity, and consequently have deeper roots than the rationalization of economic circumstances. Of course the family is the main initial *communicator* of cultural norms —whether religious, ethnic, or racial—but it is the family as a community institution rather than the family as a kinship institution that helps *create* these norms, while in the kinship mode it simply passes them along much as it passes along class and authority attributes as well. The Church, neighborhood, school, social club and workplace are other institutions which play both communicative and creative roles regarding community definition.

The development of a community means first and foremost the development of a common identity and language—not words but meanings—and a common understanding of the group's place in history. A heritage is shared. Solutions to various life problems—how we see ourselves, how we view birth and death, and how we approach various moral issues—are all community matters. But equally important is the fact that distinct communities must interface with one another. Each community must not only evolve internal modes and intra-community relations, but develop inter-community modes of interaction with other communities as well. Whether intra-community relations are restrictive or liberatory, and whether inter-community relations are respectful and fair, or unequal and domineering, will vary from case to case. And the particular relations between intra- and inter-community characteristics—how each affects the texture of the other—will also vary. But understanding these two sides of community relations and their interrelation is certainly one critical aspect of a full approach to understanding any particular social formation.

Looking at communities in isolation from one another, for a moment, we see a variety of *principal* (but not exhaustive) types— national, racial, religious, ethnic, and regional. To become a community of any of these "types," a group of people elaborates a variety of shared ways of seeing the world, relating to one another, viewing themselves in history, talking, celebrating, and otherwise engaging in cultural pursuits. Frequently groups develop community identifications encompassing two or more of the above types simultaneously. For example, Irish-Catholics, Southern-Baptists, and Italian-American-Catholics. The elaboration of such communities occurs to solve a host of problems of daily life. It is historical, yet once they are adopted solutions have a great deal of permanence. The evolved communities may be culturally enriching and supportive of human development or, on the contrary, very destructive of human potentials. More likely they will do some of both. Nationalism, for example, has included a disposition toward self-management of a group's own social life but whether this desire for sovereignty is liberatory, as was the case in post-revolutionary Cuba, or horribly restrictive, as in the case of nationalist pro-war sentiments in the United States during the Vietnam War, is always open to question. Similarly, religions have often included high moral precepts, opportunities for cultural advance, and dispositions toward human solidarity and mutual support. But religions have nonetheless more frequently been dominated by fetishism of gods, rationalizations of oppressive conditions, and manipulation of fear.

As opposed to some communities, racial communities, we should emphasize, cannot be understood even in a first approximation simply in terms of internal determinations. For a "race" is precisely the social product of inter-community relations. For this reason it would be especially pointless to study the American Black community or the American white community without studying the evolution of the interface between them—from slavery, to Jim Crow separatism, to predominantly legal forms of discrimination. Similarly, it is largely fruitless to study the Jewish community apart from anti-Semitism as well as Jewish racism toward Palestinians, nor to study the Palestinian nation without assessing the interface with Israel's Jews. For although all intra-community norms are very much affected by inter-community dynamics, racial communities are in the first instance the product of such dynamics. Robert Allen expressed it as follows:

> Ethnocentrism is a form of inward looking narrow
> mindedness whereas racism involves an outward facing

hierarchical ordering of human beings for the purposes of racial oppression. The former may or may not be a universal facet of human nature, but the latter is definitely socially conditioned. The two should not be confused."[42]

With some amendments and explication it is reasonable to say we subscribe to this view. Every community will have some inward looking view of itself, and in a hostile and oppressive context, this view will most often be narrow-minded and closed to ideas from without. Racism, on the other hand, is born in the hostile interface *between* communities. It is the view from a dominant community of a community which it dominates, and it is a rationalization of the oppression of the latter community by the former. But the resulting racism also has an inward focused effect.

As one example, consider the process of colonization. Members of one society subject the members of another to complete subordination. The process may initially be economically or politically motivated, but insofar as one community rules and terrorizes another, it also becomes a meeting of communities. Speaking of the Spanish conquest of Mexico, Magnus Morner says: "This colonial reality was characterized...by the dichotomy between conquerors and conquered, masters and servants or slaves.... People were classified in accordance with the color of their skin, with the white masters occupying the highest stratum. Theoretically, each group that could be racially defined would constitute a social stratum of its own."[43] Discussing the same instance, Tomas Almaguer argues "that five major *castes* came to characterize the social positions in colonial Mexico...1) peninsular Spanish, 2) criollos, 3) mestizos, 4) mulattos, zambos, and free Negroes, 5) Indios." The point, as Almaguer goes on to argue, is that social class divisions "came to correspond closely to the racial differentiation miscegination was to produce in the colony," so finally the "division of its labor system came to be defined largely in terms of race."[44]

The colonizer and colonized are therefore produced in the colonial dynamic. The former becomes racist to explain the treatment of the latter. The colonized are found less than human, or at best inferior humans requiring civilized administration from without. Of course it is all a sham that almost always accompanies a vast rip-off, yet the rationalization is quite real in the minds of the actors. The racism that develops has profound roots in the identities of the colonizer. This racism is, ironically, the only route to self-esteem in the face of the colonizer's barbarism toward "the natives." As Frantz Fanon makes clear, the aim of colonialism is not to deny the indigenous culture entirely, but to degrade and close it. "The aim sought is rather a continued agony than a total disappearance of the pre-existing culture." The culture of the colonized people, "once living and open to the future, becomes closed, fixed in the colonial status, fixed in the yoke of oppression." The paternal superiority of the colonizer is borne out by the stagnation of the colonized culture.[45]

The result among the *colonizers* is a racist overlay upon their own prior culture. And insofar as this racism flies in the face of humanism and the facts, the colonist too must become closed off to truth and sensitivity. "Racism bloats and disfigures the face of the culture that practices it. Literature, the plastic arts, songs for shop-girls, proverbs, habits, patterns, whether they set out to attack it or to vulgarize it, restore racism." The inter-community consciousness becomes a powerful force in the evolution of the oppressor community's own consciousness. And of course it is true for the effect of racism upon the colonized as well. For the *colonized* one route is "the negation of one's own ethnic origins or the art ingredients or cultural qualities of those origins."[46] The other route is revolt. And in between there is the debilitation of loving and hating oneself at once, of always giving in and rebelling simultaneously. For the colonized the inter-community pressures push one to see oneself as inferior and to emulate the colonizer—he is rich, he is learned, he is powerful; you are downtrodden, your culture closed, your integrity lost, save through identification. Colonization is the archetype oppressive relationship between two communities. Once it is established and has been operative for a considerable time both parties to the relation are powerfully affected. "The social constellation, the cultural whole, are deeply modified by the existence of racism."[47] Community activity in general produces "cultured people" who share solutions to diverse life problems. They develop a common identity. When inter-community relations are characterized by colonization, the ensuing racism disfigures all institutions of both communities, although one of course more powerfully and harmfully than the other.

According to Harold Cruse the Negro question is *essentially* a cultural question. This doesn't mean Blacks aren't exploited economically. It doesn't for a moment deny they have less political power. It doesn't denigrate the importance of familial norms to the reproduction of racism. It merely makes a useful abstraction from the whole to point out that the best angle to get at the "Negro question" is community. From there we are more likely to see things clearly, to discern the roots of the processes, and to be able to move on to a totalist analysis. [48]

"The one factor which differentiates the Negro's status from that of a pure colonial status is that his position is maintained in the 'home' country in close proximity to the dominant racist group."[49] This is obviously not a small difference, but it is not gargantuan either. It tells us to expect that Black people likely have mixed perceptions of themselves and of whites.

Dubois said of Black people in the U.S., "one ever feels his twoness—an American, a Negro; two souls, two thoughts, two unreconciled strivings; two warring ideals in one dark body whose dogged strength alone keeps it from being torn asunder."[50] The Black person in the U.S., like the more traditional colonized person, is fraught with a tension—to attempt assimilation, the adoption of the oppressor's ways—or to attempt the reassertion of one's own ways via rebellion. Roughly, Black nationalism, like all nationalist responses to community oppression, is an expression of the latter desire; passivity or a movement to assimilationist integration is an expression of the former. James Turner suggests that Black nationalism aims for Black control over the Black community, for Black unity, for Black resistance to subordination or assimilation, and for Black pride in Black history and norms.[51] Integration in the realm of the arts, for example, ignores the racist premises of white art and the fact that assimilation necessarily means self-denial for Blacks. Nationalism in the realm of the arts, on the contrary, notices that white art is generally white supremacist and that in any case Black people have their own art forms to further evolve and advance. There is no need to "integrate."

Black power is a nationalist expression as well. It is not explicitly anti-capitalist, though in our society the profound links between economic and community networks mean that the achievement of Black power would be impossible within capitalist economic constraints. Still, an analysis seeing nationalist and Black power movements as basically emanating from community forces will have no trouble discerning that such movements have *both* positive and negative potentials. They can be revolutionary with regard to community, and literally reactionary with regard to economics, kinship, or politics—much as class movements can be racist, and women's movements bourgeois. But while a nationalist approach which degenerates into a longing for African homelands is simply escapist, unsuited to effective implementation in the modern age, Black nationalism which stresses the need for a cultural revolution in the interface between the white and the Black community, and which seeks new intra-community definitions freed from both colonizing and colonized residues, can be a mighty force for socialist change in the U.S.[52]

Understanding racism as a product of the interface between white and Black communities in the U.S. also sheds light on the situation of whites.* White people's cultural identification, ways of viewing themselves, and assumptions about their history and life have all been affected by a three hundred year percolation of racism into all aspects of our culture. To counter racism means more than supporting demands for equality, however important that is. An analogy to the situation of men and women may provide a useful clarification.

When women began confronting men with their sexism in the late-1960s the issues were usually such highly perceptible things as

---

*Obviously there are also white/Asian, white/Native American, and white/Latino interfaces as well. Indeed though we have chosen to focus on Black/white dynamics, these others are important as well and the relative lack of attention they are receiving is more a function of the limits of our experience and learning than anything else. In many ways the life situation of Latinos in the U.S. is now approximating very closely to that of Blacks as is their population. The immense role of Chicanos in U.S. development is also comparable to that of Blacks—and certainly even if never slaves, Chicanos have been subject to colonial dynamics. For U.S. expansion, annexing half of Mexico, made Chicanos a minority on their own land and effectively a colony at once. Their subsequent contribution to U.S. development in agriculture, mining, and railroad construction and their racial mistreatment are well addressed in Tomas Almaguer, "Class, Race, and Chicano Oppression," in *Socialist Revolution*, No. 25, July-Sept. 1975.

language ("chicks," "broads" etc.), dress (bras, girdles, pants, etc.), and the most direct manifestations between men and women like "door-opening." Then the focus became men not taking women seriously—talking past them in mixed groups and acting as if women were helpless and dumb—and men brutalizing and raping women. Then came an emphasis on men exploiting women for nurturance while robbing women of access to knowledge, income, and power. (One can see the parallel to the manifestations of racism confronted by the Black movement a few years earlier.) But finally the women's movement began to suggest to men that male supremacy affected not only their behavior toward women, *but almost everything about themselves.* How men see the world, think, carry themselves; their personality, style, modes of expression, self awareness; how men compare themselves to others and how they feel, were all said to be infected by male supremacy. The dynamics of kinship had affected everything about men and women, not only things related to their direct interaction.

Black people have been saying the same thing to white people for some time now. But since Blacks aren't usually in as close proximity to whites as women to men, they have had a harder time communicating this penetration of white personality by racism. Yet one has only to watch Richard Pryor mimic whites to know that he understands something important about the very essence of "white culture," however much he may be parodying it for laughs.* The hostility that exists between whites and Blacks in the U.S. is not simply an economic phenomenon. Within prisons, for example, every inmate knows full well that racism is used by the warden and guards to divide and weaken them and thereby substantially reduce their well-being. They know all this, yet they stay separated despite the evident "material" loss. The whites are not about to admit that their community norms are infected with racism to such an extent that the Blacks have reason to not want to be around them, to not want to even eat at their tables, for example, even if the overt racism is kept under control. And so the separation, materially detrimental as it is, continues.

*Charlie Hill, an Oneida, presents a parody of white mores/attitudes/culture in much the same fashion as Pryor, though from a specifically Native American perspective.

It is often debated whether racism is beneficial to just a few whites or to all whites. Certainly it is beneficial to those whites who dominate society, the ruling class. For it does divide workers and thus serve to maintain capitalists' power. Or perhaps we should qualify this a bit. Given the existence of racism, it is put to good use by the capitalists within the economy. Whether a set of capitalist class relations is likely to finally last longer in a racially divided society than in a homogeneous one is unclear. It is plausible that racial divisions can propel revolutionary developments as well as delay them.

But whether or not whites as a whole benefit from racism is a question poorly put. A white racist has a view of the world, of himself or herself, and of Black people that is the product of his or her community involvement over a lifetime. Short of a revolution, this individual's self-image and psychic balance are well served by racist divisions and relations and highly threatened by anti-racism. Moreover, given the maintenance of capitalism for a period, it is not irrational during that period for whites to feel that there are only so many good jobs, nice houses, good schools, etc., and if these are open to everyone their own chances of getting them will diminish. It is irrelevant that white-black unity can increase the number of good jobs and redistribute wealth to the working class as a whole. The white person can seek this, and still continue to fight to retain the lion's share of the gains for "himself." Indeed, this has been the historical pattern.

No, to overcome racism it is essential to address it directly and fully. We can't make believe it is simply a confusion hoisted upon us which we can easily set aside. There can be no "end-run." We must uncover the processes by which the search for self-image and identity in a race-stratified society produce white supremacist racism, condescending white liberalism, Black passivity, and Black nationalism, as well as the process by which active practice can produce new community identifications for whites.

Manning Marable says of Blacks that "creating a positive, constructive image of blackness within the media must be viewed as a political effort."[53] Such a cultural revolution is necessary but not sufficient. In the first place kinship, economic, and political relations also help to reproduce racism and must be altered as well. In the second place the cultural revolution must occur on both sides of the community line, for Blacks but also for whites. As Blacks must assert their own culture and integrity rather than assimilating to white supremacy, so whites must reevaluate their culture. Whites must confront the effects of racism within themselves, and purge their racism rather than purging the most vulgar racists. This will only be possible if activists develop an analysis of culture as rooted in community relations and in efforts to meet human needs, even if in debased environments, and if we also stay sensitive to the other factors critical to the reproduction of racism and affected by its reproduction.*

For it is true that when extended the institutions of the community, of all communities within society, obviously encompass the institutions of the other spheres as well. As we saw earlier, along with commodities racism is also produced in the factory and along with laws racism is produced in the state. But the reverse penetration holds as well. The Black community itself is not homogeneous. The experience of being Black is different for Black men and Black women. Seeing Black people as paradigm proletarians is foolish since the Black community itself is class stratified—in particular there are many Blacks in intermediate positions "above the working class."[54] Some Black nationalist movements are aimed only at helping a few Blacks rise up the class hierarchy while the rest sweat below.[55] In this they are no different than some feminist movements which have a bourgeois (and racist) side. Yet feminism aimed only at redefining kinship relations and nationalism aimed only at redefining community relations are both as revolutionary and non-

---

*"The black and white worlds, although separate and distinct, are too closely intertwined—geographically, politically, and economically—for the social maladies of the one not to affect the other. Both must change if either is to progress to new and liberating social forms.... It goes without saying that black people should not postpone their freedom struggle until white America rouses itself out of its lethargy. On the contrary, blacks should never desist from struggle and agitation. But neither should black people deceive themselves into thinking that simple separation from white society will solve the problem.... In the quest for black liberation, white society cannot be ignored or cast aside with a sigh of relief. It must be changed. Otherwise, the racism and exploitative social relations which characterize that society will defeat even the best efforts of black freedom fighters.

revolutionary as a Marxism aimed only at transforming class relations.*

The extension of community into the factory means that Black and white work roles are impregnated with cultural expectations that reproduce the oppressed situation of Blacks and oppressor situation of whites as surely as they reproduce class divisions. This goes beyond the obvious issue of white foremen for Black work crews, to the fact that, for example, the salesforce of most companies is overwhelmingly white because selling involves socializing with the customers. The point is that economic features that come into accord with community dynamics may also become a very central factor in their reproduction. Consider Richard Nixon's expression of this relationship in the preface to a study conducted for leading corporations in 1959:

> In formulating a policy for broader employment of Negroes, a company cannot disregard the conventions and traditions within the community in which it operates. The community imposes itself on companies by providing a setting, both social and political, within which a plant operates. Employees of a company are residents of a community and they and the entire community are vitally concerned, as a matter of their own economic well-being, with the employment opportunities available in the company. Generally, company policy on the employment of Negroes will tend to reflect community attitudes, and reflection must be given to local practices, especially where a company wishes to go beyond them.[56]

Political decisions and programs, family behavior, and in fact all social activities have to at least conform to community generated

---

*But such an approach, autonomy in context of a larger united but multifaceted movement, is also contradictory to Leninist norms. Indeed, on two counts Leninism is strategically insufficient to struggles against community oppression. In the first place the vanguard approach precludes an autonomous and leading role for third world people especially to the extent that they proclaim nationalist principles; and in the second, Leninism's insufficient analyses of the roots and processes of community preclude successful struggles against various types of oppressive community behavior (including sectarianism) within Leninist organizations themselves, much less within society as a whole. A proper analysis of the

norms and they may also help reproduce and further develop those norms. The entwinement of male sexual privilege with racial dominance patterns is an obvious example. The fight against racism must therefore address all institutions in society; it must be part of a totalist movement with a diversity of aspects. But as Cruse argued in a passage quoted earlier, the struggle against racism will be led by Black and other third world organizations in coalition with other movements, but in no way secondary to them. Such a necessity arises as directly from our analysis as from the world we live in.

We should summarize some of the main theoretical innovations of the discussion to this point. Community is a concept which has many different manifestations and aspects. At the broadest level there is culture in general. With regard to the aesthetic mode, there is art per se. Regarding identification by origin or by socially emphasized characteristics, there is race and ethnicity. Regarding regional differentiation, there are neighborhoods and nations with gradations in between. And finally along what we might call a spiritual and moral axis, there is identification by religion.

In each case these phenomena have their "principal roots" in what we have termed community activity and in the community sphere of daily life. The basic common denominator is the process of people forging a shared identity: sometimes according to their own insular norms, other times according to requirements that emerge from an interface with another group of people, and often with elements of each of these pressures at work. Community activity is no more isolatable than economic, kinship, or political activity in either its effects, impacts, or reproduction. Yet, like them, it is sufficiently critical to warrant designation as a core moment of social life. The sphere of community activity and the network of community institutions is often as central to the character of social life and social possibilities within a country as are the spheres of kinship, economics, and politics. Moreover, it penetrates each of these other spheres often helping in their definition.

links in mode of perception and conceptualization between sectarianism and racism, for example, between vanguardism and segretgation, has yet to be done. But we would nonetheless contend that there is a reasonably clear parallel and interpenetration of causes, one that should not come as a surprise since Leninist organizational forms and aims are products of people living in oppressive societies, inculcated with the norms of those societies, and self-consciously disdainful of the need for self-criticism of their organizations along these lines.

Returning to the different possible community demarcations, these may be characterized a bit further. "Culture" actually refers to their totality, and to the community manifestations of class, kin, and authority dynamics as well. It seems useful, on the other hand, to reserve the term "art" for aspects of culture which are created for the conscious purpose of communicating with what we might call the human aesthetic sensibility. The fact that these creations also carry information meant for our historical and analytic sensibilities is secondary and not essential for their designation as art. "Ethnicity" seems to us to be most useful as a term referring to the creation of a community along lines which have to do with national origin and which then, however, transcend any geographic border. "Race," in this lexicon, should refer to those divisions which are a function of *relations between groups* embodying hierarchy and the use of physical features (socially chosen) for differentiation. "Nationalism," on the other hand, might best refer to community identification which *does* relate to a geographic boundary, whether one which exists or one which is desired—though of course, in fact the word nationalism has most often been used more generally to refer to a host of different kinds of community identification, especially when such identification becomes militant in its outward expression. Finally, "religion" seems to refer to a form of community which has both a cerebral and a spiritual side. In most instances of religious affiliation there need be neither a geographic origin, nor a physical characteristic, nor any other such trait held in common. Rather, what is required is simply a shared adherence to a particular body of thought and catalog of behaviors and customs. In this sense, religion is the most self-consciously social of the various community designations, recognizing as it does the possibility of "joining" and of "leaving" the community.

We make no pretense to having clarified the details of the character of community organizations or their operation, whether the church, the neighborhood gathering, the media, the ghetto, the school or any others. For the most part we haven't even mentioned these, much less analyzed them. Nor have we fully clarified the interrelations between community formations and types, nor their interface with other critical dimensions of social life. Part of the reason for this incompleteness of our discussion is certainly our relative lack of experience and knowledge of these matters. But there is another issue as well, one which distinguishes the study of community relations as compared, for example, to the study of kin, economic, or political relations.

With the latter three spheres there is generally an institution or a set of institutions which sets the parameters of the determinations of what interests and characteristics the evolved social group will have. Of course it isn't a mechanical simple determination, but in these cases it is generally possible to locate, label, and theoretically understand the functioning of institutions like the factory, state, and family as they relate in turn to economic, political, and kinship activity. These institutions can be x-rayed, in a sense, to show alternative economic, political, and kinship structures and associated role offerings which in turn tell us a great deal about the likely character of class, political, and sexual differentiations among citizens. But with community, the fourth sphere, things are different. There are only groups interfacing in endless ways which depend upon both the inward- and outward-looking relationships between the people involved. There is no single defining structure or set of structures that always recurs and can be labeled and easily dissected to show differences from one country, region, or race to another. There will always be specific institutions but in each new case they will have to be faced as if for the first time—always with fresh eyes rather than a "textbook preconception" of the sort which can indeed be useful in addressing the other spheres, particularly the economy. As a result it is difficult to avoid being either quite abstract or quite specific about matters of community. The middle ground discussion one can enter with regard to class relations, for example, applicable as a broad summary to all societies of a particular kind, is simply not attainable in discussions of culture. In any case short of a more complete theory and analysis, we have at least argued the importance of a sphere of social life that deserves critical attention both at the level of theory and social practice, and we have shown some of the failings that arise when this sphere is not given the serious attention it demands.

As a conclusion to this discussion of community theory, and to the theoretical discussions of the past three chapters as well, it is fitting to point out the greatest weakness of our work to date. Though we have put forward a framework emphasizing both an autonomous analysis of four spheres and *also of their interactive relations*, we have hardly begun to address the second part of this research program. At the broad level there are two areas of investigation we have in mind. First, community does not form in a vacuum isolated from prior effects governed by political, economic, and kin dynamics. What is the meaning for the logic of development of community groups that their members are also members of classes, kin groups, and political demarcations? And of course, the same question must be asked in turn for each other principal focus as well. What difference does it make for the operation of class demarcation, for example, that economic actors are also members of groups defined primarily by the historical evolution of other spheres of daily life? Second, however, how do community dynamics manifest themselves as additional moments to activity in other spheres? What is the community moment of class formation? It would seem, just to take this instance, that while classes evolve material interests and certain ideological perspectives from their particular economic position and activity, they also evolve a cultural dimension which transcends those economic positions and arises instead from their group dynamics and cultural innovations, that is, from the community moment of their class definition. Likewise, one must also investigate the community penetration of the definition of the very economic roles which precipitate class formations. Finally the reverse is also true, economic dynamics will affect community roles and an economic moment will help to fill out the defining character of all community activity. But to finally approach a holistic understanding, a totalist analysis is required. The difficulty of attaining such a goal shouldn't dissuade us from its pursuit, and the value of the partial syntheses we evolve in route, should help motivate the quest.

Community and the Orthodox Socialist Vision

Demands for socialism fail to impress many Blacks in the United States. Would there be on-going racism or assimilation? Certainly one or the other, for where is the socialist who speaks clearly of a serious alternative?

Historically, as we have discussed, community relations have come into being in diverse ways, but ethnic, racial, religious, and national community forms have most often taken shapes detrimental to human well-being. They have had a we-versus-they character. Providing a base for self-identification and sometimes even resistance to oppression, they have also often impeded experimentation and mutual learning between groups. Internal community cohesion has as often as not rested on a notion of self as superior or inferior to some other religion, nation, or race generating a catechism approach to self-definition. And external relations between different communities have been even worse, hostile to the point of grotesque forms of violence.

What should socialists do about community relations? Are present forms to be fostered, opposed, remolded, allowed to develop on their own, or repressed?

The orthodox socialist answer to these questions derives from the underlying orthodox theory of culture and economic primacy. As culture reflects economic relations, culture under socialism should reflect socialist economic relations. But religion is essentially bourgeois escapism. It is simply a means of rationalization of horrid circumstances, a way to give a thorn the appearance of a rose, or to justify the prick. Religion will disappear as this need passes. Similarly, racism and national identification are only means of dividing working people. They serve only false needs produced by bourgeois circumstances and bourgeois manipulation. Under socialism such identification should also pass. Of course, one must be patient. It takes time. The superstructure does not immediately follow the base—but it will eventually, and to aim in that direction is both reasonable and desirable.

So the most prevalent "socialist" answer for the existence of communities is to seek something we label "cultural homogenization." They have different names for it depending on the focus: working class culture, proletarian internationalism, and socialist realism are some. Local community forms are seen as backward, impeding the development of more general solidarity. There is perhaps a recognized right to "national self-determination," but it is a holdover right, a liberal right, one that is expected to become inoperative as time passes, and one whose implementation is seen not as a good in and of itself but as a tactical necessity for achieving working class solidarity in light of the legacy of previous imperialist caste oppression.[60] In any case, it becomes a weak second order principle at best, in the practice of most "socialist" governments.

The active aim becomes reduction of many cultures, ethnic and racial groups to one, of many religions to none. The goal is a society of socialists whose internal cohesion comes from an undivided identification with only the entire community. In the world of "art" the function of "socialist realism" has been to depict proletarian life as a realistic heaven of successful collective human struggle no matter the obstacles. The form is plain and the mode consciously reflective. The best art is the art that best teaches class consciousness—as defined by the most knowledgeable political authorities. There is no texture. Variety is threatening.

In theory, homogenization comes by "raising" the well being and the cultural standards of less "developed" internal communities, slowly integrating them into the dominant culture. Assimilation is not to be coercive. It is to be made desirable so it will be freely chosen over a reasonable period of time. In fact, however, the tenacity of ethnic, national, and religious cultures, and the elitist paternal mentality of vanguard leadership combine to make short work of the tolerant and voluntary aspects of this approach. In the end, the reduction of community to a single set of socialist norms is likely to be only partially accomplished even with doses of force accompanying the rhetoric of peaceful accommodation.

However, a proper verification of this chapter's worth, and of this final section's brief account of "homogenization," can only come through historical analyses of "existing socialism" and projections of an alternative "intercommunalist" community vision. These tasks are undertaken in the companion volume we will describe in the next and final chapter of this book.

SEVEN:
CONCLUSION AND ANALYTIC PROGRAM

> People's lives are in turmoil. There is a sense of crisis for men as well as for women, and for children too. Do we have a line or even a glimmering about how people can and should live, not as victims as in the past for women, nor as atoms just whirling around on their on their own trajectories, but as members of a human community and as moral agents in that community?
>
> Barbara Ehrenreich

In the first chapter of this volume we discussed a variety of philosophical issues concerning Marxism, science, and social theory. Paralleled by many subthemes, the paramount argument was that a rejuvenated social theory sufficient to contemporary socialist needs would have to transcend economism in all its guises and weave a number of complimentary analyses into a totalist framework. In the second chapter we set out such a theory premissed on a fourfold conceptualization of history and couched in a manner suited to use in contemporary industrialized societies. However, being very brief, this presentation had to be augmented in two ways in the following four chapters. First, it was necessary to critically evaluate *existing* theories of each of the focused spheres, and second, we had to further elaborate each side of the new totalist theory as well.

In chapter three we discussed politics, economics in chapter four, kinship in five, and community in chapter six. In each instance we criticized a variety of existing theories and models and elaborated our own alternative. Though the discussions were too brief to permit inclusion of extensive detail, hopefully this sacrifice was offset by the unusual scope of the presentation. In any case, a second sacrifice within this volume, the relative paucity of historical examples and analyses, will hopefully be alleviated by the existence of a companion volume, *Socialism Today and Tomorrow*. For there we test our theories more concretely. In three historical chapters we examine the post-revolutionary experiences of the Soviet Union, China, and Cuba including political, economic, kinship, and community spheres. Hopefully these case studies show the practical meaning of our approach, demonstrate its power, and also provide an encompassing analysis of the three most important examples of "existing socialism."

We find that none of the three societies present a viable model for emulation even though all have many positive and negative lessons to teach socialists. Moreover, we argue that none of the three countries has attained socialism. While the Soviet Union stabilized many years ago and China only very recently, both these societies are shown to be far from socialist and not moving toward socialism, not only in their economic relations—where they have established coordinator modes of production and consumption—but in all core aspects of social life. Cuba's status, on the other hand, is found to be more unsettled and undetermined. While the Cuban economy is more coordinator than socialist, its polity, kinship, and even community spheres nonetheless show signs of continued socialist initiatives.

In each historical discussion we try to understand the social forces and movements which have brought these countries to their current situations as well as the pressures for further change or stagnation in the future. But having criticized these societies and discussed forces for change within them, the time arises to discuss what new forms they might move toward. Likewise, having said that these societies are not workable models for emulation in the industrialized countries, we must suggest what a workable model would be like.

Therefore, the next chapters map a vision of what socialism might be like after a transformation of *all four spheres of social life* in an industrialized society. We discuss economics, including production, consumption, and allocation; politics, including basic decision-making structures, legal norms and law enforcement, and the role of parties; kinship including family structures, socialization, schooling, and issues of sexuality; and finally community, including the future of religion, culture, and relations between distinct communities.

None of the descriptions is complete, of course, but neither is the discussion merely a collection of glorious adjectives strung together without assigning any texture or shape to specific social institutions. Rather, the model includes an outline of institutional and ideological relations and a set of structural characteristics which can be elaborated, altered, and enhanced as movements choose. What we hope is that our description will provide a kind of scaffolding which can help socialists create a full vision as further efforts are undertaken. Obviously, however, the details and even many of the main contours of what a new society will look like are beyond anyone's immediate imagination and in any case, it is the place of millions of activists and then of tens of millions of citizens to elaborate these features and bring them into actual being, not on drawing boards or in books, but in the texture of real, sensual daily life.

Socialism Today and Tomorrow closes with a strategic chapter titled "Neither Leninism Nor Social Democracy" which presents some prospects for the eighties and argues in favor of a new type of social movement to supercede *both* Leninism and social democracy. For where these two approaches are generally economistic, subject to coordinator domination, and otherwise unsuited to bridging the immense gap between the way we live now and the way we might live under socialism, we argue that the new types of strategic orientation emerging from the theories in this book and the visions of the next are well suited to the tasks essential to this transition.

We have presented the material of these works in two volumes to make each more tractable and to allow readers the liberty of working with only one half or the other, should they so desire. For while each volume depends on the other for its full value, it is also true that they are nonetheless each able to stand alone. This first volume is addressed principally to active members of the left, to people who are quite familiar with many theories and theoretical arguments on the left, and concerned to resolve which of many available approaches has more to say about particular important concerns. It is meant to motivate a new totalist approach to problems of socialism and for people quite familiar with various existent theories and analyses and even adherents of one or more of them, such motivation obviously depends in part upon criticism of existing currently favored approaches. The second volume, however, is an application of theory to the experiences of certain countries and to a projected model for our own. It begins with a theoretical chapter which accessibly recounts the positive results of this volume. And then it continues as we have described above. Because it addresses history and vision and does not include excessive references to other theories, it is quite a bit more accessible than this volume. At the same time, it is the reason for being of this work, and this work is its foundation. Hopefully, as readers of this volume will turn to that for a continuation of our argument, many other readers who start with the more accessible historical/visionary volume will "come back" to this more theoretical work to better grasp the foundation for the entire project. That, at least, is our hope.

Marxism and Socialist Theory

There are three questions we would like to answer before concluding: Is Marxism a viable theory for socialists? Is our totalist approach an elaboration of Marxism or an alternative to it? And is the totalist approach superior? However, answers to these questions depend both on what one means by "Marxism"—we will give answers corresponding to two different definitions—and on how one gauges the relative merits of competing perspectives.

In the first chapter we described complexities inherent in comparing theories and also characteristic features of "theoretical progress." We explained how what one takes as "fact" depends on theory, thereby making empirical comparisons difficult. We countenanced the possibility that old theories can return even after being rejected making progress always somewhat tenuous. And we pointed out that since young theories will inevitably be incomplete, they may frequently appear inferior to predecessors even though when developed to maturity they will prove themselves superior. But without entering the maelstrom of controversy surrounding issues of falsification, fallibility, and the differences between anomalies and refutations, there are certain conditions under which *it is* relatively easy to choose the better of two theories or competing paradigms. Comparing theory 'a' and 'b' we can say 'a' is superior if it explains everything 'b' does, explains 'b's' relative success, and especially if it makes verified predictions 'b' does not. Between two paradigms 'A' and 'B', similarly 'A' is superior if it explains what 'B' explains, explain's 'B's' relative success, makes novel predictions compared to 'B', and if it instructs researchers to conduct successful analyses about which 'B' is silent.

In light of this methodology, if we equate "Marxism" with orthodox Marxism as discussed throughout this book, then our totalist approach would represent a progressive shift of the whole research programme: a paradigmatic revolution. For it explains everything orthodox Marxism explains and much that orthodox Marxism is blind to, corrects certain flawed analyses of orthodox Marxism, explains the level of success that orthodox Marxism enjoys, and makes numerous predictions (for example, about the expected importance of community dynamics and the existence of a non-capitalist and non-socialist coordinator mode of production) that are contrary to orthodox Marxism and either verified or capable of future verification. And if by "Marxism" one means orthodox Marxism, then the Marxist paradigm is insufficient to the needs of socialists and ironically better suited in many respects to the self-interest of coordinators, political bureaucrats, men, and members of dominant community groups than the oppressed sectors Marxism was supposed to serve.

On the other hand, if we identify "Marxism" with a broader paradigm or research program that consists of certain philosophical methods, the treatment of humans as beings of praxis, and an overall radical intent, then our totalist approach is a "progressive problemshift" *within* this heritage. In this growing and flexible form, Marxism remains a suitable intellectual framework for socialists and anathema to defenders of all oppressive social formations.

Though how socialists should label their philosophy and theory is technically a semantic issue, it has political and emotional overtones, and hopefully it will be resolved more by struggle and practice than exegesis. Our point, however, is that choosing labels is not nearly as important as a commitment to an "open theory" which supercedes orthodox Marxist economism in the many ways we have catalogued. If "Marxism" as a label becomes inextricably attached to the practice and thought of Leninist parties, political bureaucracies, coordinator movements, male chauvinists, and cultural homogenists, it will become necessary for participatory socialists to disavow any affiliation as Marxists. For in this event, "Marxism" will only mean orthodox Marxism despite any protestations we might make. On the other hand, if Leninist parties, political bureaucrats, central planners, male chauvinists, and cultural homogenists are successfully shown un- and anti-Marxist, then participatory socialists can embrace the label as our own giving it all the humanistic connotations we desire it to have. But it is important to realize that a resolution of this issue in favor of self-description as Marxists based upon the meaning "Marxism" might come to have in the West won't necessarily resolve a related problem. In coming years alliances with movements in the East are going to become increasingly important, and whether these liberatory movements will be able (or even want) to resurrect the label "Marxist" from the ignominy of its current identification with social stratification and regimentation, intellectual poverty, and Soviet tanks will influence how we describe ourselves. But in any eventuality, whatever label we adopt, our commitment to a totalist approach must be unswerving if our practice is to yield socialism.

Footnotes

Introduction

1. Michael Albert and Robin Hahnel, *Socialism Today and Tomorrow*, South End Press, Boston, 1981.
2. Ernest Bloch, "Notes and Commentary," Telos No 25, Fall 1975, p. 167.
3. Alvin Gouldner, *The Two Marxisms*, Seabury, N.Y., 1980, p. 12.
4. Rossana Rossanda, Introduction, *Power and Opposition in Post Revolutionary Societies*, Ink Links, 1979, p. 9.

One: Marxism, Science and Socialism

1. Gregory Bateson, *Mind and Nature*, Dutton, N.Y., 1979, p. 30. Also see Bertell Ollman, *Alienation*, Cambridge Univ. Press, London, p. 241, for a Marxist argument on the biological necessity of conceptualization via sharp boundaries.
2. Jacob Bronowski, *The Origins of Knowledge and the Imagination*, Yale, New Haven, 1978, p. 17-18.
3. Bateson, op. cit. p. 38. These ideas are referenced to Bateson as his is a recent, popular, and clear rendition. Paul Feyerabend's treatments in *Against Method* and *Science in a Free Society*, both New Left Books, London, 1978 and 1979 respectively, take the discussion in a variety of provocative and enlightening directions.
4. For a devestating critique of the whole Althusserian approach and intellectual framework, see E.P. Thompson, *The Poverty of Theory*, Monthly Review Press, N.Y. 1978.
5. For a full discussion see *Unorthodox Marxism*, Albert and Hahnel, South End Press, 1978, chapter two.
6. Feyerabend, op. cit. p. 29.
7. Ibid. p. 43.
8. Letter from Einstein to Maurice Solovine, May 7, 1952, quoted in Gerald Holton, *The Scientific Imagination*, Cambridge Univ. Press, London, 1978, p. 96-99.
9. Ibid.
10. Einstein, "Induction and Deduction in Physics," quoted in Holton, op. cit. p. 99.
11. This view is attributable to Noam Chomsky, for example in *Rules and Representations*, Columbia Univ. Press, N.Y., 1980 and see also Karl Popper, *Unended Quest*, Open Court, London, 1974, chapter ten.
12. Holton, op. cit. chapter one.
13. Ibid. p. 98.
14. Ibid.
15. For example, the most recent nobel prize for physics was awarded to Steven Weinberg, Abdus Salaam, and Sheldon Glashow for their efforts to synthesize our understanding of weak and electromagnetic interactions.

16. Lucio Colletti, *From Rousseau to Lenin,* Monthly Review, N.Y., 1974, p. 88.

17. Holton, op. cit. chapter four.

18. Niels Bohr, *Atomic Theory and the Description of Nature,* Cambridge Univ. Press, London, 1934. For a full discussion of the issues involved in modern interpretations of the quantum theory see Max Jammer *The Philosophy of Quantum Mechanics,* Wiley Interscience, N.Y., 1974.

19. Ibid.

20. *Unorthodox Marxism,* op. cit. includes a more complete discussion of these issues, and Ollman, op. cit. includes perhaps the most complete available discussion by a Marxist.

21. Ibid.

22. Bronowski, op. cit. p. 108.

23. The theorem in question is due to Kurt Godel, and a useful and comprehensive discussion can be found in Ernest Nagel and James R. Newman, *Godel's Proof,* N.Y.U. Press, N.Y., 1958 and further comment also appears in Popper, op. cit. p. 131.

24. Chomsky, op. cit. and also *Reflections on Language.*

25. E.P. Thompson, *The Poverty of Theory,* Merlin Press, London, 1978, p. 360-361.

26. Holton, op. cit.

27. Chomsky, *Reflections on Language,* op. cit.

28. Feyerabend, op. cit. p. 182.

29. Alvin Gouldner, op. cit. 317.

30. See C.F. Von Weizacker, *The Unity of Nature,* Farrar, Strous, and Giroux, N.Y. 1979.

31. See *Space, Time, and Spacetime,* Lawrence Sklar, Univ. of Cal. Press, L.A. 1978.

32. See Thomas Kuhn, *The Structure of Scientific Revolution,* Univ. of Chicago Press, Chicago, 1970 and *Criticism and the Growth of Knowledge,* edited by Lakatos and Musgrave, Cambridge Univ. Press, 1970.

33. Von Weizacker, op. cit.

34. Ibid. And see the excellent volume of writings by Imre Lakatos, *The Methodology of Scientific Research Programmes,* Cambridge Univ. Press, London, 1978.

35. Von Weizacker, op. cit. has lengthy discussions of all these ideas.

36. See *Unorthodox Marxism,* op. cit. for further discussions regarding Marxism in this light.

37. Although slightly less ambitious, the predominant view that a unified field theory is within reach, perhaps even as an adaptation of existing theory, is relevant. See Steven Hawking's monograph, *An End To Physics?,* Cambridge Univ. Press, 1980.

38. David Bohm, for example, believes there to be an infinite variety of qualities even while all are also interconnected so that however far one's knowledge may have progressed, there is always another level of insight to

be gained. The impossibility of reaching an end is not due to human limitation, in Bohm's view, but to the infinity of nature. Of course, one might also propose that we will reach an end to our theory development even though nature is infinite precisely because of limits on our own capacities. See David Bohm, *Causality and Chance in Modern Physics*, Univ. of Penn. Press, Phil., 1957.

39. Although the demarcation between these views are often not so sharp as we are implying, the bootstrap approach of Godfrey Chew can be offered as an example of this final type of approach.

40. See *Science and Liberation*, edited by Arditti, Brennan, and Cavrak, South End Press, Boston, 1980.

41. For a general discussion that is accessible without compromise, see Steven Rose, *Conscious Brain*, Vintage Books, New York, 1976.

42. Piaget took this position as did many of his supporters in *Language and Learning*, edited by Massimo Piatelli-Palmarini, Harvard Univ. Press, Cambridge, 1980.

43. Chomsky and his supporters took this view, Ibid.

44. Arditti, op. cit.

45. Steven Jay Gould, *Ever Since Darwin*, Norton, New York, 1977, p. 214.

46. Chomsky and Herman, *The Political Economy of Human Rights. South End Press, Boston. 1980.*

47. See Edward Wilson, *On Human Nature*, Bantam, New York, 1978; Marshall Sahlins, *The Use and Abuse of Biology*, The Univ. of Mich. Press, Ann Arbor, 1976; *The Sociobiology Debate*, edited by Arthur L. Kaplan, Harper and Row, New York, 1978; and *Sociobiology Examined*, edited by Ashley Montagu, Oxford Univ. Press, Oxford, 1980.

48. Chomsky, *Rules and Representations,* op. cit. p. 245.

Two: Society and History

1. *Western Marxism: A Critical Reader*, New Left Books, London, 1978.

2. For a presentation of what we mean by orthodox Marxism in more detail see *Unorthodox Marxism*, op. cit. chapter one and chapter two.

3. Naturally, many Marxists have undertaken similar efforts. See footnote 1 and, for example, *The Marxian Legacy*, Dick Howard, Urizen, Chicago, 1978.

4. Raymond Williams, *Marxism and Literature*, Oxford Univ. Press, Oxford, 1977.

5. Jurgen Habermas, *Legitimation Crisis, Theory and Practice,* and *Communication and the Evolution of Society*, Beacon Press, Boston. Louis Althusser, *Reading Capital, For Marx,* and *Lenin and Philosophy.*

6. Michael Albert, *What Is To Be Undone*, Porter Sargent Publishers, Boston, 1974, chapter one; Dick Cluster, *They Should Have Served That Cup of Coffee*, South End Press, Boston, 1979; and Sara Evans, *Personal Politics,* Vintage, New York, 1979.

7. Herbert Marcuse, *The Aesthetic Dimension*, Beacon Press, 1970.

8. Raymond Williams, op. cit. p. 92.

9. Ibid. p. 93.

10. Ibid. p. 97.

11. Ibid. p. 91.

12. Ibid.

13. Ibid. p. 97.

14 Ibid.

15. Ibid. p. 87.

16. Joan Robinson uses the motion picture analogy to discuss the vacuity of seeking to avoid all abstraction. Conflating all sides of life under a single concept amounts to such a program. See Joan Robinson, *Freedom and Necessity*, Vintage, N.Y. 1971.

17. Ollman, op. cit.

18. For a critique of orthodox Marxist economism see *Unorthodox Marxism*, op. cit. chapter two, and chapter five of this volume.

19. It is much like Ollman's view and what we proposed in chapter one.

20. See footnote five.

21. Thomas McCarthy's introduction to *Legitimation Crisis*, op. cit., is an especially helpful succinct presentation of many of Habermas' ideas.

22. "Historical Materialism," in *Communication and the Evolution of Society*, op. cit.

23. *Legitimation Crisis*, op. cit. p. 48-51.

24. See, for example, *For Marx*, op. cit. p. 166-167.

25. Ibid.

26. *Reading Capital*, op. cit. p. 27.

27. Ibid. p. 17.

28. *For Marx*, op. cit. p. 111.

29. Ibid.

30. Ibid.

31. For a more comprehensive critique of Althusser see E.P. Thompson, *The Poverty of Theory*, op. cit.

32. Albert, *What Is To Be Undone*, op. cit.

33. Ibid.

34. Melvin Rader, *Marx's Interpretation of History*, Oxford Univ. Press, Oxford, 1979, p. 101.

35. See footnote '47' chapter one.

36. Noam Chomsky, *Rules and Representations*, op. cit. p. 212.

37. Ibid, p. 45-46.

38. Numerous psychologists and philosophers have hypothesized about this possibility, though of course there is no scientific evidence to substantiate it.

39. Batya Weinbaum, *The Curious Courtship of Women's Liberation and Socialism*, South End Press, Boston, 1978, and *Unorthodox Marxism*, op. cit.

40. *Unorthodox Marxism*, op. cit. and a forthcoming volume on economics and welfare theory, Albert and Hahnel.

Three: Politics and History

1. Few Marxists pay much attention to anarchist writings on the state. Our own intellectual development owes much, however, to such works as Rudolf Rocker, *Anarcho Syndicalism*, Alexander Berkman's *What Is Communist Anarchism*, Dover, and the works of Bakunin and Kropotkin—for example, *The Political Philosophy of Bakunin* edited by G.P. Maximovv, Glenco, Ill., and *Kropotkin's Revolutionary Pamphlets*, two volumes, MIT Press, Boston.

2. Hal Draper, *Karl Marx's Theory of Revolution*, Monthly Review, N.Y., p. 239-243.

3. See also Joan Robinson, *Freedom and Necessity*, op. cit.

4. G.W.F. Hegel quoted in Melvin Rader, op. cit. p. 64.

5. Engels quoted in Draper, op. cit. p. 252.

6. See Engels, *The Origin of Private Property, the Family, and the State, op.* cit. or Marx and Engels, *The Communist Manifesto*, International Publishers, N.Y.

7. "The State and Socialism" by Mihaly Vajda p. 860, *Social Research*, Vol. 45. No. 4, Winter 1978.

8. Ibid.

9. The Trotskyiest approach to analyzing the Soviet Union's post revolutionary experience is of this sort.

10. There is additional discussion of these points in *What Is To Be Undone*, op. cit., *Unorthodox Marxism*, op. cit., and *Socialism Today and Tomorrow*, op. cit.

11. See the work of Alan Wolff, for example.

12. *Unorthodox Marxism*, op. cit.

13. Tom Hayden, *The American Future*, South End Press, Boston, 1980.

14. Bowles and Gintis' study on the state is in preparation for publication.

15. For our overall perspective on orthodox Marxism and its critics, see *Unorthodox Marxism*, chapters one and two.

16. Rader, op. cit.; Cohen, op. cit. and most other works on Marxist theory take positions that stem more or less from this simple idea.

17. See Jean Cohen and Dick Howards interesting essay in *Between Labor and Capital*, edited by Pat Walker, South End Press, Boston, 1979.

18. Vajda, op. cit. p. 852.

19. Paul Sweezy, *The Theory of Capitalist Development*, Monthly Review, p. 243.

20. Lenin, *State and Revolution*, International Publishers, N.Y.

21. Ibid.

22. This view is commonplace among many Eurocommunists. See Santiago Carrillo, *Eurocommunism and the State*, New Left Books, London, 1978, and *The Politics of Eurocommunism*, edited by David Plotke and Carl Boggs, South End Press, Boston, 1980.

23. For a discussion of various types of theory of the state, see *Kapitalistate*, special double issue, no. 4/5, Summer 1976 and also Erik Olin Wright, *Class, Crisis, and the State*, New Left Books, London, 1978.

24. Nicos Poulantzas, *State, Power, Socialism,* New Left Books, London, 1978.

25. Ibid.

26. *Kapitalistate,* op. cit.

27. Ibid.

28. See the concluding chapters of *Unorthodox Marxism* and *Socialism Today and Tomorrow,* op. cit.

29. It is as if one were to talk about understanding a modern capitalist economic arena without ever having even thought to assess the impact of market relations on social possibilities.

30. Richard Wright, *American Hunger,* Harper and Row, 1977, p. 92.

31. George Konrad and Ivan Szelenyi, *The Intellectuals on the Road to Class Power,* Harcourt Brace Jovanovich, N.Y. 1979, p. 183.

32. See *What Is To Be Undone,* op. cit.

33. Ibid. and Bahro, op. cit. chapters nine and twelve.

34. Bahro, op. cit. p. 212-213.

35. Sheila Rowbotham, *Beyond the Fragments,* Merlin, London, 1980.

36. Grace C. Lee, Pierre Chalieu (Cornelius Castoriadis), and J.R. Johnson, *Facing Reality,* Correspondence, Detriot, 1958, p. 130-131.

37. Albert, op. cit., *Unorthodox Marxism,* op. cit., *Socialism Today and Tomorrow,* op. cit.

38. *Left Wing Communism,* International Publishers, N.Y.

39. Ibid.

40. See *Socialism Today and Tomorrow,* op. cit. and Albert, op. cit.

41. Max Weber, *Economy and Society,* ed. by Guenther Roth, Bedminster Press, 1968, p. 1401.

42. Karl Marx, *Critique of Hegel's Doctrine of the State, Early Writings,* Pelican, London, 1974, p. 114-115.

43. Bahro, op. cit. p. 358.

44. Weber, op. cit. p. 991.

45. Agnes Heller, "Past, Present, and Future of Democracy," *Social Research,* op. cit. p. 870.

46. Ivan Szelenyi, "The East European Intelligentsia," p. 60, in *Critique 10-11,* Winter/Spring, 1978-1979.

Four: Economics and History

1. See the forthcoming volume on welfare economics, Albert and Hahnel, *Theories of Welfare and the Welfare of Economic Theory.*

2. Nicholas Georgescu-Roegen, *The Entropy Law and the Economic Process,* Harv. Univ. Press, Cambridge, 1971.

3. Ibid, and also Maurice Godelier, *Rationality and Irrationality in Economics,* Monthly Review Press, N.Y., 1972.

4. See *Unorthodox Marxism,* op. cit. chapter four.

5. Karl Marx, *Capital, Vol. 1*, International Publishers, N.Y., Part One.

6. *Unorthodox Marxism*, op. cit. appendix to chapter four, p. 364-368.

7. Karl Marx, op. cit. Part Three and throughout.

8. *Unorthodox Marxism*, op. cit. p. 159-166.

9. Karl Marx, op. cit. Part Two and throughout.

10. Albert and Hahnel, "A Tickit to Ride: More Locations on the Class Map," in *Between Labor and Capital*, edited by Pat Walker, South End Press, Boston, 1979.

11. There is a fairly extensive dual labor market literature and readers might want to consult the various RRPE bibliographies for futher references on these and other economics topics.

12. Thorstein Veblin, *Engineers and the Price System*, N.Y. 1932; John Kenneth Galbraith, *The New Industrial State*, Boston, 1967; Berle and Means, *The Modern Corporation and Private Property*, N.Y. 1932; Alvin Gouldner, *The Future of Intellectuals and the Rise of the New Class*, Seabury, N.Y., 1979; Erik Olin Wright, *Class, Crisis, and the State*, New Left Books, London, 1978; Simone Weyl, *Oppression and Liberty*, Univ. of Mass. Press, 1973.

13. Barbara and John Ehrenreich, "The Professional-Managerial Class," in Walker, op. cit.

14. Gouldner, op. cit. p. 19, 21-27.

15. Ehrenreichs, in Walker, op. cit. p. 18-30.

16. Sandy Carter, "Class Conflict: The Human Dimension," in Walker, op. cit.

17. Gouldner, op. cit. p. 17-18.

18. Ivan Szelenyi, "The East European Intelligentsia," *Critique 10/11*, Winter/Spring, 1978-1979.

19. Gouldner, op. cit. p. 75.

20. Rudolf Bahro, *The Alternative in Eastern Europe*, New Left Books, London, 1978, p. 134.

21. Albert and Hahnel in Walker, op. cit. p. 273-278.

22. Gouldner, op. cit. p. 82.

23. E.P. Thompson, *The Poverty of Theory*, Monthly Review, N.Y. 1980, p. 280.

24. Paul Sweezy, *The Theory of Capitalist Development*, Monthly Review, N.Y., *Unorthodox Marxism*, op. cit. chapter two and four, and Michael Albert, *What Is To Be Undone*, Porter Sargent Publisher, Boston, 1974, chapter three and seven.

25. *What Is To Be Undone*, op. cit.

26. E.P. Thompson, op. cit.

27. Ibid. p. 260-261.

28. Ibid.

29. See *Women and Revolution*, edited by Lydia Sargent, South End Press, Boston, 1981.

30. See Jean Cohen and Dick Howard, "Why Class," in Walker, op. cit.

31. See Williams, op. cit. and Manning Marable, *From the Grassroots*, South End Press, Boston, 1980.

32. Herbert Blumer, *Industrialization and Race Relations*, Guy Hunter, ed., Oxford, 1965.

33. Huberman and Sweezy, *Introduction to Socialism*, Monthly Review, N.Y. 1968.

34. See J.M. Montias, "Planning with Material Balances in Soviet-Type Economies," *American Economic Review*, No. 49, Dec. 1959, p. 963-985, or Benjamin Ward, *The Socialist Economy: A study of Organizational Alternatives*, N.Y., Random House, 1967, p. 45.

35. For alternative methods of this type see George Danzig and Philip Wolfe, "The Decomposition Algorithm for Linear Programs," *Econometrica*, Vol. 29, No. 4, Oct. 1961, p 767-777; Leonid Hurwicz, "The Design of Mechanisms for Resource Allocation," in *Frontiers of Quantitative Economics*, Eds. M.D. Intriligator and D.A. Kendrick, North Holland, 1974, Vol. 2, p. 10; William Baumol and Tibor Fabian "Decomposition, Pricing for Decentralization and External Economies," *Management Science*, Vol. 2, No. 1, Sept. 1964, p. 1-32; and E. Malinvaud, "Decentalized Procedures for Planning," in *Activity Analysis in the Theory of Growth and Planning*, Eds. Bacharach and Malinvaud, London, p. 170.

36. For alternative methods of this type see: J. Kornai and T. Liptak, "Two-Level Planning," *Econometrica*, 33, 1965, p. 141-169; S.A. Marglin, "Information in Price and Command Systems of Planning," *Public Economics*, Eds. J. margolis and H. Giffon, London, 1969, p. 54-77, and G.M. Neal, "Planning Without Prices," *Review of Economic Studies*, 36, 1969, p. 346-362.

37. See Hahnel, *Toward a Political Economy of Socialism*, chapter 5, Ph.D. Dissertation, The American University, Washington D.C., May 1979 for further elaboration.

38. Ibid.

39. Ibid p. 395-401 for a fuller discussion.

40. Ibid.

41. Bahro, op. cit. p. 213.

42. Ibid.

43. Quoted in Bahro, op. cit. p. 125.

44. Szelenyi, op. cit.

45. Marc Rakovski, *Toward an East European Marxism*, Allison and Busby, London, 1978.

46. Boris Weyl, "Marx and Lenin Read in the Camps," in *Power and Opposition*, Il Manifesto, Ink Links, London, 1979.

47. Ursula Schmiederer, "Politics and Economics in Capitalism and in 'Actually Existing Socialism,'" *Power and Opposition*, op. cit.

48. Branko Horvat, Jaroslav Vanek, and Herb Gintis are but three of the better known radical economists who embrace this view.

49. Marx describes this thoroughly in Chapter One of *Capital*, Vol!, op. cit.

50. Karl Marx in a letter to P.V. Annekov dated Dec. 28, 1846, *Collected Writings,* International Publishers, N.Y.

51. Gar Alperovitz, "Socialism as a Pluralist Commonwealth," in *The Capitalist System,* edited by Edwards, Reich and Weisskopf, Prentice Hall, N.Y., p. 527.

52. Frank Roosevelt, "Market Socialism: A Humane Economy?" *Journal of Economic Issues,* Vol. 3, No. 1, p. 18.

53. Kenneth Arrow, "Political and Economic Evaluation of Social Effects and Externalities" in *Frontiers of Quantitative Economics,* op. cit. p. 17.

54. Ibid. p. 18.

55. See any number of standard neoclassical text books on Public Finance, for example, R.A. Musgrave, *The Theory of Public Finance: A Study in Public Economy,* N.Y., McGraw Hill, 1959, which is one of the better ones.

56. Paul Sweezy, "The Nature of Soviet Society," *Monthly Review (MR),* Vol. 26, no. 6, Nov. 1974, p. 6.

57. Ibid. p. 14.

58. Bernard Chavance, "On the Relations of Production in the USSR," *MR* Vol. 29, n0. 1, May 1977, p. 5.

59. Paul Sweezy's reply, *MR,* ibid. p. 15-16.

60. Ibid. p. 17-18.

61. Ibid. p. 18.

62. Paul Sweezy, "Is There a Ruling Class in the USSR?" *MR* vol. 30, no. 5, Oct. 1978, p. 1.

63. Ibid. p. 16-17.

64. Ibid. p. 17.

65. Szelenyi, Ivan, *Critique,* 10-11, 1978-79, p. 60-61.

66. See Albert and Hahnel's piece in Walker, ed., *Between Labor and Capital,* South End Press, 1980.

Five: Kinship and History

1. Three volumes stand out as excellent collections on socialist feminism: *Toward an Anthropology of Women* and *Capitalist Patriarchy and the Case for Socialist Feminism,* both Monthly Review Press, New York, and *Women and Revolution,* South End Press, New York. Other volumes we have used are mentioned in the selected bibliography.

2. Gayle Rubin, "The Traffic in Women," in *Toward an Anthropology of Women,* edited by Rayna Reiter, Monthly Review, N.Y. 1975, p. 158.

3. Ibid.

4. Ibid. p. 183.

5. Rubin, op. cit. and Juliet Mitchell, *Psychoanalysis and Feminism,* Pantheon, N.Y. 1974.

6. Nancy Chodorow, *The Reproduction of Mothering,* Univ. of Cal. Press, Berkeley, 1980, p. 7.

7. Tschirhart, Evelyne, "On Chinese Asexuality," *Telos*, No. 32, Fall 1978.

8. See Chodorow, op. cit., and Dorothy Dinnerstein, *The Mermaid and th Minotour*, Harper Colophon, N.Y. 1977.

9. Edgar Snow, *Red Star Over China*, Grove Press, N.Y.

10. *Batya Weinbaum follows a similar line of argument in The Curious Courtship of Women's Liberation and Revoluton*, op. cit.

11. Engels, op. cit.

12. Weinbaum, op. cit. p. 18.

13. Heidi Hartmann, "The Unhappy Marriage of Marxism and Feminism," in Lydia Sargent, *Women and Revolution*, South End Press, Boston, 1981.

14. See articles by Slocum, p. 44, and Gough, p. 60 in Reiter, op. cit.

15. Ibid.

16. Ibid.

17. Ibid.

18. Rubin, op. cit. p. 165.

19. Sheila Rowbotham, *Women, Resistance, and Revolution*, Vintage, N.Y., 1972, p. 72.

20. Zillah Eisenstein, "Developing a Theory of Capitalist Patriarchy and Socialist Feminism," in *Capitalist Patriarchy and the Case for Socialist Feminism*, Monthly Review, N.Y., 1979, p. 27.

21. *Unorthodox Marxism*, op. cit.

22. Engels, op. cit.

23. Hartmann, op. cit.

24. Eli Zaretsky, *Capitalism, the Family, and Personal Life*, Harper and Row, 1976.

25. Sargent, op. cit.

26. The "wages for housework" view is best propounded by Mariarosa Dalla-Costa and Selma James, *The Power of Women and the Subversion of the Community*, Falling Walls Press, London, 1972. The mistake that this approach makes regarding determination of profit is twofold. First, there is the problem of attempting to develop a theory of the situation of women using sex-blind economic categories borrowed from orthodox Marxism. Second, there is the difficulty that these categories, obviously insufficient to analysis of a sexually differentiated workforce and the distribution of wealth where such a workforce exists, would also be insufficient to analysis even were such divisions absent. A full critique of the Labor Theory of Value relevant to these points is in *Unorthodox Marxism*, chapter two and the appendices. In a sense, Dalla-Costa is not falling prey to a trap here as she is consciously pursing the course we are criticizing. It is simply an ill-conceived plan. But consider Heidi Hartmann's assertion that "Marxist categories, like capital itself, are sex-blind." Despite noting the tendency for women to become trapped by the parameters of old theories and the pressures to

communicate with people holding those theories, she has here fallen into the same trap. For the implication of her statement seems to us to be that economic relations can be effectively explained by orthodox Marxist categories because, like the categories, the economic relations themselves also function obliviously to sex differences. But this is false and in practice it tends to give away the conclusion of debate before the first criticisms are even exchanged. For grant an orthodox Marxist the validity of economistic categories for evaluating the economy itself and the best he or she will ever yield is that there may be need for some sort of levels analysis with causality primarily running from economic to kinship factors. Veronica Beechy, in an article titled "On Patriarchy," in *Feminist Review*, 1979, Vol. 3, p. 78, makes a point quite similar to ours and the article as a whole provides an excellent overview of approaches to feminist conceptualization. "The second problem is that the separation of reproduction or patriarchy from other aspects of the mode of production has tended to leave the Marxist analysis of production untouched and uncriticized by feminist thinking. Yet, theoretically the Marxist analysis of the production process has been quite unsatisfactory—analyses of production are frequently economistic, the labor process has been divorced from the social relations of production as a whole, and female wage labor has frequently been left out of analyses of production."

27. *Beyond the Fragments*, op. cit.
28. Anne Bobroff,   p. 6.
29. Robin Morgan, "First Feminist Exiles From the USSR," *Ms.*, November, 1980.
30. Hartmann, op. cit.
31. Eisenstein, op. cit. p. 6.
32. Shulamyth Firestone, *The Dialectives of Sex*, William Morrow, N.Y., 1970.
33. A number of the essays in Sargent, op. cit. take up this type of analysis.
34. Mitchell, op. cit.
35. Rubin, op. cit.
36. Harstock, Nancy, "Feminist Theory and the Development of Revolutionary Strategy," in Eisenstein, op. cit. p. 63.
37. Rubin, op. cit. p. 209-210.
38. *Unorthodox Marxism*, chapter three.
39. Wilhelm Reich, *Sex Pol*, Vintage, N.Y., 1971.
40. See Ferguson and Folbre's contribution to Sargent, op. cit.
41. *Personal is Political*, Sara Evans, Vintage, 1979, and *They Should Have Served That Cup Coffee*, Dick Cluster, ed. South End Press.

Six: Community and History

1. It is simultaneously edifying and horrifying to skim contemporary leftist volumes on the state, economy, family, etc., taking note of the relative paucity of reference to issues of race, or, for that matter, religion.

2. A more substantial presentation of our view of orthodox Marxist theory is in chapter one of *Unorthodox Marxism*, op. cit.

3. See Harold Cruse, *Rebellion and Revolution*, chapter ten, Appolo editions, 1968.

4. Karl Marx, quoted in *Counterrevolution and Revolt*, Herbert Marcuse, Beacon Press, Boston, 1972, p. 79.

5. This argument appears in *The Aesthetic Dimension*, Herbert Marcuse, Beacon Press, p. 14-15.

6. This was Marx's explanation of the phenomenon in *The Introduction to the Critique of Political Economy;* see *The Aesthetic Dimension*, op. cit. p. 15.

7. Ibid. p. 15.

8. Ibid. p. 1.

9. Bertolt Brecht, quoted in Marcuse, op. cit. p. 32.

10. Unpublished these by Peter Bohmer, U. Mass. Amherst, 1981.

11. Robert Allen, *Reluctant Reformers*, Anchor, N.Y., 1974, p. 235.

12. Cruse, op. cit. p. 193.

13. Ibid.

14. Ibid. p. 92.

15. Ibid. p. 96.

16. Lenin, quoted in Horace Davis, *Toward a Marxist Theory of Nationalism*, Monthly Review, N.Y., 1978, p. 254.

17. Cruse, op. cit. p. 229.

18. Ibid. p. 87.

19. Frantz Fanon, op. cit.

20. Cruse, op. cit. p. 213.

21. Cruse, op. cit. p. 141.

22. Eugene Genovese, *In Red and Black: Marxian Explorations in Afro-American and Southern History.*

23. This position was presented in exactly this manner by Ernest Mandel in a speech given at Boston Univ. at which one of us happened to be present.

24. Cruse, op. cit. p. 88, 89.

25. Ibid. p. 244.

26. Robert Allen, *Reluctant Reformers*, Anchor, N.Y. 1975, p. 31.

27. Ibid. p. 18.

28. Ibid. p. 192.

29. Ibid. p. 208.

30. Ibid. p. 233.

31. Ibid. p. 232.

32. Ibid.

33. Ibid.

34. Ibid.
35. Ibid. p. 235.
36. Richard Wright, *American Hunger*, Harper and Row, N.Y. 1944, p. 37.
37. Ibid. p. 37-38, 39.
38. Allen, op. cit. p. 237.
39. Ibid.
40. Cruse, op. cit.
41. Ollman, op. cit. p. 116.
42. Allen, op. cit. p. 266.
43. Magnus Morner, *Socialist Review*, op. cit.
44. Almaguer, Tomas, "Class, Race, and Chicano Oppression," *Socialist Revolution* No. 25, July-Sept. 1975.
45. Frantz Fanon, *Toward the African Revolution*. Grove Press, N.Y., 1967 p. 34.
46. Ibid. p. 37.
47. Ibid. p. 36.
48. Cruse, op. cit.
49. Ibid.
50. W.E.B. Dubois quoted in Manning Marable, *From the Grassroots*, South End Press, Boston, 1980.
51. James Turner quoted in Alphonso Pickney, *Red, Black, and Green*, Cambridge Univ. Press, London, 1976, p. 4.
52. Ibid.
53. Marable, op. cit. p.
54. Cruse, op. cit. p. 89.
55. Marable, op. cit.

Bibliography

Albert, Michael, *What Is To Be Undone*. Boston: Porter Sargent Publisher, 1974.

Albert, Michael and Hahnel, Robin, *Unorthodox Marxism*. Boston: South End Press, 1978.

——————"Ticket To Ride: More Locations on the Class Map" in Walker, Pat, *Between Labor and Capital*. Boston: South End Press, 1980.

——————*Socialism Today and Tomorrow*. Boston: South End Press, 1981.

Ali, Tariq, *The New Revolutionaries*. New York: William Morrow, 1969.

Allen, Robert, *Black Awakening in Capitalist America*. Garden City: Doubleday, 1969.

——————*Reluctant Reformers*. Garden City: Doubleday, 1975.

Althusser, Louis, *For Marx*. New York: Vintage, 1970.

——————*Lenin and Philosophy*. New York: Monthly Review Press, 1971.

——————*Reading Capital*. New York: Pantheon, 1970.

Anderson, Perry, *Considerations on Western Marxism*. London: New Left Books, 1975.

——————*Arguments Within English Marxism*. London: New Left Books, 1980.

Aronowitz, Stanley, *False Promises*. New York: McGraw Hill, 1973.

Arrow, Kenneth J. and Hahn, F.H. *General Competitive Analysis*. San Francisco: Holden Day.

Arshinov, Peter, *History of the Makhnovist Movement*. Detroit: Black and Red, 1974.

Avinari, Sholomo, "Marx and the Intellectuals," *Journal of the History of Ideas*. xxxviii no. 2, April-June 1967.

——————*Karl Marx: Social and Political Thought*. London: Cambridge Univ. Press, 1968.

Avrich, Paul, *The Russian Anarchists*. Princeton: Princeton Univ. Press, 1967.

——————*Kronstadt 1921*. Princeton: Princeton Univ. Press, 1970.

Bahro, Rudolf, *The Alternative in Eastern Europe*. London: New Left Books, 1978.

Baran, Harold, *The Demand for Black Labor*. Somerville, New England Free Press, 1972.

Baran, Paul, *The Political Economy of Growth*. New York: Monthly Review Press, 1957.

Baran, Paul, and Sweezy, Paul, *Monopoly Capital*. New York: Monthly Review Press, 1966.

Bateson, Gregory, *Mind and Nature*. New York: Dutton, 1979.

Baxandal, Rosalyn; Gordon, Linda; and Reverby, Susan, *America's Working Women*. New York: Vintage, 1976.

289

de Beauvoir, Simone, *The Second Sex*. New York: Vintage, 1974.

Benjamin, Walter, *Illuminations*. Boston: Schocken, 1979.

Benston, Margaret, "The Political Economy of Women's Liberation," Somerville: New England Free Press, 1970.

Berkman, Alexander, *What is Communist Anarchism*. New York: Dover, 1972.

Bettleheim, Charles, *Economic Calculation and Forms of Property*, London: Routlage, Kegan and Paul, 1974.

——————*Class Struggle in the USSR*. Three Volumes. New York: Monthly Review Press, 1976.

——————*Cultural Revolution and Industrial Organization in China*. New York: Monthly Review, 1974.

Blackburn, Robin, Ed., *Ideology and Social Science*. New York: Vintage, 1973.

Boehm-Bawerk, Eugene, *Karl Marx and the Close of His System*. New York: Augustus Kelly, 1949.

Boggs, Carl, *Gramsci's Marxism*. London: Pluto Press, 1975.

Boggs, Carl, and Plotke, David, *The Politics of Eurocommunism*. Boston: South End Press, 1980.

Boggs, James, *Racism and Class Struggle*. New York: Monthly Review, 1973.

Boggs, James and Grace Lee, *Revolution and Evolution in the Twentieth Century*. New York: Monthly Review Press, 1974.

Bohr, Niels, *Atomic Theory and the Description of Nature*. London: Cambridge Univ. Press, 1934.

Bohm, David, *Causality and Chance in Modern Physics*. Philadelphia: Univ. of Penn, 1957.

Bookchin, Murray, *Post Scarcity Anarchism*. San Francisco: Ramparts.

——————*The Limits of the City*. New York: Harper Colophon, 1974.

Bottomore, Tom, *Karl Marx*. Englewood: Prentice Hall, 1973.

Bowles, Sam, "Economist as Servant of Power," *American Economic Review*, May, 1974.

Bowles, Sam and Gintis, Herb, *Schooling in Capitalist America*. New York: Basic Books, 1976.

Braverman, Harry, *Labor and Monopoly Capital*. New York: Monthly Review Press, 1975.

Bricianer, Serge, *Pannakoek and the Workers' Councils*. St. Louis: Telos, 1978.

Brecher, Jeremy, *Strike!* Boston: South End Press, 1977.

Brinton, Maurice, *The Bolsheviks and Workers' Control*. Montreal: Black Rose, 1970.

——————*The Irrational in Politics*. Montreal: Black Rose, 1974.

Bronowski, Jacob, *The Origins of Knowledge and the Imagination*. New Haven: Yale, 1978.

Brown, Phil, ed., *Radical Psychology*. New York: Harper Colophon, 1973.

Cabral, Amilcar, *Revolution in Guinea*. New York: Monthly Review Press, 1969.

——————*Return to the Source*. New York: Monthly Review Press, 1973.

Calvart, Greg and Neiman, Carole, *The Disrupted History*. New York: Random House, 1971.

Cammit, John, *Antonio Gramsci and the Origins of Italian Communism*. San Francisco: Stanford Univ. Press, 1967.

Cardan, Paul, *Workers' Councils and the Economics of a Self Managed Society.* Philadelphia: Solidarity.

——————*Crisis of Modern Society.* Philadelphia: Solidarity.

Carmichael, Stokely, *Stokely Speaks.* New York: Vintage, 1971.

Carmichael, Stokely, and Hamilton, Charles, *Black Power.* New York: Vintage, 1969.

Carrillo, Santiago, *Eurocommunism and the State.* London: New Left Books, 1978.

Carter, Sandy, *Mental Illness and Marxism.* Boston: South End Press, forthcoming.

Castro, Fidel, *Revolutionary Struggles.* Cambridge: MIT Press, 1972.

Cesaire, Aime, *A Dying Colonialism.* New York: Monthly Review Press, 1972.

Chailand, Gerard, *Revolution in the Third World.* New York: Viking, 1977.

Chodorow, Nancy, *The Reproduction of Mothering.* Berkeley: Univ of Calif, 1980.

Chomsky, Noam, *For Reasons of State.* New York: Pantheon, 1968.

——————*American Power and the New Mandarins.* New York: Pantheon, 1969.

——————*Problems of Knowledge and Freedom.* New York: Pantheon.

——————*Reflections on Language.* New York: Pantheon.

——————*Rules and Represenations.* New York: Columbia Univ., 1980.

Chomsky, Noam, and Herman, Edward, *The Political Economy of Human Rights.* Two Volumes. Boston: South End Press, 1980.

Claudin, Fernando, *Eurocommunism and Socialism.* London: New Left Books, 1978.

——————*The Communist Movement.* London: New Left Books, 1975.

Cleaver, Eldridge, *Soul on Ice.* New York: Delta, 1978.

Clegg, Ian, *Workers' Self Management in Algeria.* New York: Monthly Review Press, 1971.

Cliff Tony, *Lenin.* Four Volumes. London: Pluto Press, 1975.

Cockburn, Alexander, and Blackburn, Robin, *Student Power.* London: Penguin, 1970.

Cohen, G.A., *Karl Marx's Theory of History.* New York: Princeton: Princeton Univ. 1978.

Cohn-Bendit, Daniel, *Obsolete Communism: A Left Wing Alternative.* New York: McGraw Hill, 1968.

Colletti, Lucio, From *Rousseau to Lenin.* London: New Left Books, 1972.

——————*Marxism and Hegel.* London: New Left Books, 1973.

Commoner, Barry, *The Closing Circle.* New York: Bantam, 1971.

Cooper, David, *The Dialectics of Liberation.* London: Penguin, 1968.

——————*The Death of the Family.* New York: Vintage, 1971.

Cornforth, Maurice, *Historical Materialism.* New York: International Publishers, 1962.

Croll, Elisabeth, *Feminism and Socialism in China.* Boston: Schocken, 1978.

Cruse, Harold, *Rebellion and Revolution.* New York: Apollo Editions, 1968.

Dalla-Costa, Mariarosa and James, Selma, *The Power of Women and the Subversion of the Community.* London: Falling Walls Press, 1972.

Daly, Mary, *Gyn/Ecology*. Boston: Beacon Press, 1978.

Davin, Delia, *Women-Work*. London: Oxford, 1973.

Davis, Horace, *Marxism and Nationalism*. New York: Monthly Review Press, 1972.

Debray, Regis, *Revolution in the Revolution*. New York: Grove, 1977.

Debreu, Gerard, *Theory of Value*. New Haven: Yale Univ. Press.

Dellenger, David, *More Power Than We Know*. New York: Doubleday, 1975.

Desai, Meghnad, *Marxian Economic Theory*. London: Gray Mill, 1974.

Deutscher, Isaac, *The Unfinished Revolution*. London: Oxford, 1967.

Dinnerstein, Dorothy, *The Mermaid and the Minotaur*. New York: Harper Colophon, 1977.

Dobb, Maurice, *Welfare Economics and the Economics of Socialism*. London: Cambridge Univ. Press, 1968.

————————*Theories of Value and Distribution*. London: Cambridge Univ. Press, 1973.

————————*On Economic Theory and Socialism*. London: Routledge, Kegan, Paul, 1955.

Dolgoff, Sam, *The Anarchist Collectives*. New York: Free Life, 1974.

Draper, Hal, *Karl Marx's Theory of Revolution*. New York: Monthly Review Press, 1978.

Dumont, Rene, *Socialisms and Development*. London: Andre Deutsch, 1973.

Dunayeskaya, Raya, *Philosophy and Revolution*. New York: Delta, 1973.

Edwards, Richard C., "Alienation and Inequality: Capitalist Relations of Production in a Bureaucratic Enterprise," Unpublished Ph.D Thesis, Harvard, July, 1972.

Ehrenreich, Barbara and English, Deirdre, *For Her Own Good*. New York: Doubleday, 1978.

Emmanual, Arghiri, *Unequal Exchange*. New York: Monthly Review Press, 1972.

Engels, Frederick, *The Origin of the Family, Private Property, and the State*. New York: International Publishers, 1972.

Evans, Sara, *Personal Politics*. New York: Vintage, 1979.

Ewen, Stuart, *Captains of Consciousness*. New York: McGraw Hill, 1974.

Fanon, Frantz, *The Wretched of the Earth*. New York: Grove Press, 1968.

————————*Toward An African Revolution*. New York: Grove Press, 1967.

Feyerabend, Paul, *Against Method*. London: New Left Books, 1978.

————————*Science in a Free Society*. London: New Left Books, 1979.

Fiori, Guiseppi, *Antonio Gramsci: Like of a Revolutionary*. London: New Left Books, 1970.

Firestone, Shulamith, *The Dialectics of Sex*. New York: William Morrow, 1970.

Fleischer, Helmut, *Marxism and History*. New York: Harper Colophon, 1979.

Foreman, Ann, *Femininity as Alienation*. London: Pluto Press, 1980.

Freire, Paulo, *Pedogogy of the Oppressed*. New York: Herter and Herter, 1971.

————————*Education for a Critical Consciousness*. New York: Seabury, 1973.

————————*Cultural Action for Freedom*. London: Penguin.

Fromm, Erich, *Marx's Concept of Man*. New York: Frederick Unger, 1961.

————————ed. *Socialist Humanism*. Garden City: Doubleday, 1965.

Georgakas, Dan and Surkin, Marvin, *Detroit: I Do Mind Dying*. New York: St. Martin's 1975.

Georgescu-Roegan, Nicholas, *The Entropy Law and the Economic Process.* Cambridge: Harv. Univ. Press, 1971.

Gershenkron, Alexander, *Continuity in History and Other Essays.* Cambridge: Belknap Press, 1968.

Gerassi, John, ed. *Venceremous!* New York: St. Martin's, 1979.

Gintis, Herb, "Alienation and Power: Toward a Radical Welfare Economics." Unpublished Ph.D. Thesis, Harv. Univ. May, 1969.

————————"The Nature of the Labor Exchange: Toward a Radical Theory of the Firm," Harv. Univ. Paper No. 328, Oct, 1973.

————————"Welfare Criteria With Endogenous Preferences: The Economics of Education," Harv. Univ. Paper No. 329, Nov. 1973.

Godelier, Maurice, *Rationality and Irrationality in Economics.* New York: Monthly Review Press, 1972.

Goldman, Emma, *My Disillusionment in Russia.* New York: Appolo, 1970.

Gombin, Richard, *The Origins of Modern Leftism.* London: Penguin, 1975.

Gorz, Andre, *Strategy for Labor.* Boston: Beacon Press, 1964.

————————*Socialism and Revolution.* New York: Anchor, 1971.

————————*Ecology As Politics.* Boston: South End Press, 1980.

Gouldner Alvin, *The Two Marxisms.* New York: Seabury, 1978.

————————*The Future of the Intellectuals and the Rise of the New Class.* New York: Seabury, 1979.

Grahl, Bart and Piccone, Paul, eds. *Toward a New Marxism.* St. Louis, Telos, 1973.

Gramsci, Antonio, *Selections from the Prison Notebooks.* New York: International Publishers, 1971.

Guerin, Daniel, *Anarchism.* New York: Monthly Review Press, 1970.

Gurley, John G. *Challengers to Capitalism: Marx, Lenin, and Mao.* San Francisco: Stanford Univ. Press, 1975.

————————*China's Economy and the Maoist Strategy.* New York: Monthly Review Press, 1976.

Habermas, Jurgen, *Legitimation Crisis.* Boston: Beacon Press.

————————*Theory and Practice.* Boston: Beacon Press, 1975.

————————*Communication and the Evolution of Society* Boston: Beacon Press, 1976.

Harrington, Michael, *Twilight of Capitalism.* New York: Simon and Schuster, 1976.

————————*Socialism.* New York: Simon and Schuster.

Hartman, Heidi, "The Unhappy Marriage of Marxism and Feminism," in *Women and Revolution.* edited by Lydia Sargent, Boston: South End Press, 1981.

Hawking, Steven, *An End To Physics?* London: Cambridge Univ. Press, 1981.

Hayden, Tom, *The American Future.* Boston: South End Press, 1980.

Hegedus, Andras; Heller, Agnes, Markus; Maria; Vajda, Mihaly, *The Humanization of Socialism.* London: Allison and Busby, 1976.

Heilbrunner, Robert, *Marxism: For and Against.* New York: Norton, 1980.

Heitlinger, Alena, *Women and State Socialism.* London: MacMillan, 1979.

Heller, Agnes, *The Theory of Need in Marx.* London: Allison and Busby, 1976.

————————"Past, Present, and Future of Democracy," *Social Research.*

Hirsh, Arthur, The French New Left: An Intellectual History From Sartre to Gorz. Boston: South End Press, 1981.

Hinton, William, *Fanshen.* New York: Monthly Review Press, 1966.

Hobsbawm, E.J. "Karl Marx's Contribution to Historiography," in *Ideology and Social Science.* Robin Blackburn, ed. London: Penguin.

Hodgson, Geoff, *Trotsky and Fatalistic Marxism.* New York: Spokesman, 1975.

Holton, Gerald, *The Scientific Imagination.* London: Cambridge Univ. Press, 1978.

Horowtiz, David, *Marx and Modern Economics.* New York: Monthly Review Press, 1968.

Horn, Joshua, *Away With All Pests.* New York: Monthly Review Press, 1969.

Horvat, Branko, *Toward a Theory of the Planned Economy.* Belgrade: 1964.

Howard, Dick, *Selected Political Writings of Rosa Luxemburg.* New York: Monthly Review Press, 1971.

——————*The Marxian Legacy.* Chicago: Urizen, 1978.

Howard, Dick and Klare, Karl, *The Unknown Dimension.* New York: Basic Books, 1972.

Huberman, Leo, and Sweezy, Paul, *Introduction to Socialism.* New York: Monthly Review Press, 1968.

Hunnius, Garson, and Case, eds. *Workers' Control.* New York: Vintage, 1971.

Hunt, E.K., and Schwartz, Jesse, *A Critique of Economic Theory.* London: Penguin, 1973.

Hurwicz, Leonid, "Design Mechanisms for Resource Allocation," in *Frontiers of Modern Economics.* ed. M.D. Intriligator and D.A. Kendrick, North Publishing House.

Ignatin, Noel, "Black Worker, White Worker," in *White Supremacy.* Chicago: Sojourner Truth Organization, 1977.

Il Manifesto, *Power and Opposition in Post-Revolutionary Societies.* London: Ink Links, 1979.

Jackson, George, *Soledad Brother.* New York: Bantam, 1970.

Jacoby, Russell, *Social Amnesia.* Boston: Beacon Press, 1975.

——————"The Politics of Crisis Theory," Telos, Spring, 1975.

Jammer, Max, *The Philosophy of Quantum Mechanics.* New York: Wiley Interscience, 1974.

Jay, Martin, *The Dialectical Imagination.* Boston: Little Brown, 1973.

Johnson, Richard, *The French C.P. Versus the Students.* New Haven: Yale, 1972.

Kalecki, Michael, "Class Struggle and the Distribution of Income," Kylos, 1971.

——————*Selected Essays on the Dynamics of Capitalist Economy.* London: Cambridge Univ. Press, 1971.

Karol, K.S., *Guerillas in Power.* New York: Hill and Wang, 1971.

——————*The Second Chinese Revolution.* New York: Hill and Wang, 1973.

Kenner, Martin, and Petras, James, *Fidel Castro Speaks.* New York: Grove Press, 1969.

Keynes, J.M. *The General Theory.* New York: Harbinger Books.

Kolakowski, Leszak, *Towards a Marxist Humanism.* New York: Grove Press, 1968.

Kollantai, Alexandra, *The Workers' Opposition*. Chicago.
————————*Selected Writings*. New York: Lawrence Hill, 1977.
Konrad, George, and Szelenyi, Ivan, *The Intellectuals on the Road to Class Power*. New York: Harcourt Brace Jovanovich, 1979.
Koopmans, T.C., *Three Essays on the State of Economic Science*. New York: 1957.
Korsh, Karl, *Karl Marx*. New York: Russell and Russell, 1963.
————————*Marxism and Philosophy*. London: New Left Books, 1970.
Kovel, Joel, *White Racism: A Psychohistory*. New York: Vintage, 1972.
Kropotkin, Peter, *Kropotkin's Revolutionary Essays*. Cambridge: MIT, 1970.
————————*Fields, Factories, and Workships*. New York: Harper & Row, 1974.
Krupskaya, N.K. *Reminiscences of Lenin*. New York: International, 1970.
Kuhn, Thomas, *Structure of Scientific Revolution*. Chicago, 1962.
Laing, R.D. *Politics of the Family and Other Essays*. New York: Vintage, 1979.
————————*The Politics of Experience*. London: 1970.
Lakatos, Imre, *The Methodology of Scientific Research Programmes*. London: Cambridge Univ. Press, 1978.
Lakatos, Imre, and Musgrave, eds. *Criticism and the Growth of Knowledge*. London: Cambridge Univ. Press 1970.
Langer, Elinor, "The Women of the Telephone Company," *New York Review of Books*, XIV, no. 5 and 6, 1970.
Lange, Oscar, *Problems of the Political Economy of Socialism*. Calcutta, 1961.
————————*Political Economy*. New York: Pergamon Press, 1963.
————————*Theory of Reproduction and Accumulation*. New York: Pergamon Press, 1969.
————————"Marxian Economics and Modern Economic Theory," Review of Economic Studies, June, 1935.
Lefebre, Henri, *Dialectical Materialism*. London: Jonathan Cape, 1968.
————————*Everyday Life in the Modern World*. New York: Harper and Row, 1971.
Lenin, Vladamir Illych, *Collected Works*. Moscow: Foreign Language Publishing House.
Lichtheim, George, *From Marx to Hegel*. New York: Seabury, 1974.
————————*Marxism: A Historical and Critical Study*. New York: Praeger, 1961.
Leys, Simon, *Chinese Shadows*. London: Penguin, 1974.
Lowy, Michael, *The Marxism of Che Guevara*. New York: Monthly Review, 1973.
Lukacs, Georg, *Lenin*. Cambridge: MIT, 1971.
————————*History and Class Consciousness*. Cambridge: MIT, 1971.
————————*Tactics and Ethics*. New York: Harper Colophon, 1976.
————————*Marxism and Human Liberation*. New York: Dell, 1972.
Luxemburg, Rosa, *The Russian Revolution*. Ann Arbor: Univ. of Mich. Press.
————————*The Mass Strike and the Junius Pamphlets*. New York: Harper Torchbooks, 1971.
————————*Reform or Revolution*. New York: Pathfinder, 1970.

Lynd, Staughton, and Alperovitz, Gar, *Strategy and Program*. Boston: Beacon, 1971.

MacFarlane and Wheelright, *The Chinese Road to Socialism*. New York: Monthly Review, 1970.

Maletesta, Enrico, *Anarchism*. London.

Mandel, Ernest, *Marxist Economic Theory*. New York: Monthly Review Press, 1971.

——————*The Formation of the Economic Thought of Karl Marx*. New York: Monthly Review, 1969.

——————*Revolutionary Marxism Today*. London: New Left Books, 1979.

Il Manifesto, *Theses. Politics and Society*. Vol. 1, No. 4, Aug. 1974.

Mao Tse-tung, *Selected Readings From the Works of Mao Tse-tung*. Peking, 1971.

Marable, Manning, *From the Grassroots*. Boston: South End Press, 1980.

Marcovic, Mihailo, *From Affluence to Praxis*. Ann Arbor: Univ. of Mich. 1974.

Marcovic, Mihailo, and Cohen, Robert, *The Rise and Fall of Socialist Humanism*. London: Spokesman, 1975.

Marcuse, Herbert, *One Dimensional Man*. Boston: Beacon Press, 1964.

——————*An Essay on Liberation*. Boston: Beacon Press, 1969.

——————*Counter Revolution and Revolt*. Boston: Beacon Press, 1972.

——————*The Aesthetic Dimension*. Boston: Beacon Press, 1979.

Marglin, Steve, "What Do Bosses Do?" RRPE, Vol. 6, No 2. New York.

Marx, Karl, *Capital*. New York: New World Paperbacks.

Marx, Karl, and Engels, Frederick, *Collected Works*. New York: International.

Mattick, Paul, *Marx and Keynes*. Boston: Porter Sargent Publishers, 1969.

McAfee, Kathy, and Wood, Myrna, "Bread and Roses" Somerville: New England Free Press.

McClellan, David, *Karl Marx: His Life and Thought*. New York: Harper, 1973.

Meek, R.L. *Studies in the Labor Theory of Value*. London: Lawrence and Wishart 1973.

——————*Economics and Ideology and Other Essays*. London: Chapman and Hall, 1967.

Mehring, Franz, *Karl Marx*. London: 1936.

Meisner, Maurice, *Mao's China*. New York: Free Press, 1977.

Memmi, Albert, *The Colonizer and the Colonized*. Boston: Beacon Press, 1967.

Mermelstein, David, *The Economic Crisis Reader*. New York: Vintage, 1975.

Meszaros, Istvan, *Marx's Theory of Alienation*. New York: Harper Torchbooks, 1972.

Millett, Kate, *Sexual Politics*. Garden City: Doubleday, 1970.

Miliband, Ralph, *The State in Capitalist Society*. London: Oxford, 1969.

——————*Marxism and Politics*. London: Oxford, 1977.

Mills, C.W. *The Marxists*. New York: Dell, 1972.

Mitchell, Juliet, *Women's Estate*. New York: Pantheon, 1971.

——————*Psychoanalysis and Feminism*. New York: Pantheon, 1974.

Moore, Barrington, *Social Origins of Dictatorship and Democracy*. Boston: Beacon Press, 1966.

Morishima, Micnio, *Marx's Economics*. London: Cambridge Univ. Press, 1973.

Morgan, Robin, *Sisterhood is Powerful.* New York: Vintage, 1970.

—————*Going Too Far.* New York: Random House, 1977.

Myrdal, Jan, *China Notebook.* Chicago: Liberator Press, 1979.

Nove, Alex, *An Economic History of the USSR.* London: Penguin, 1969.

O'Conner, James, *The Fiscal Crisis of the State.* New York: St. Martin's Press, 1973.

Ogelsby, Carl, and Schaull, Richard, *Containment and Change.* New York: 1967.

Ogelsby, Carl, ed. *New Left Reader.* New York: Grove Press, 1972.

Ollman, Bertell, *Alienation.* London: Cambridge Univ. Press, 1971.

—————*Essays on Marx and Reich.* Boston: South End Press, 1980.

Orr, Robert, *Religion in China.* New York: Friendship Press, 1980.

Pannekoek, Anton, *Workers' Councils.* Detroit: Root and Branch.

—————*Lenin as Philosopher,* London: Merlin Press, 1975.

Pateman, Carole, *Participation and Democratic Theory.* London: Cambridge Univ. Press, 1970.

Petrovic, Gajo, *Marx in the Mid-Twentieth Century.* Garden City: Doubleday, 1967.

Piatelli-Palmarini, Massimo, ed. *Language and Learning.* Cambridge: Harvard Univ. Press, 1980.

Plotke, David, and Boggs. Carl, *The Politics of Eurocommunism.* Boston: South End Press, 1980.

Popper, Karl, *Unended Quest.* London: Open Court, 1974.

Poster, Mark, *Existential Marxism in Postwar France.* Princeton: Princeton Univ. Press, 1975.

Poulantzas, Nicos, *Classes in Contemporary Capitalism.* London: New Left Books, 1974.

—————*Political Power and Social Class.* London: New Left Books, 1973.

—————*State, Power, and Socialism.* London: Ne Left Books, 1978.

Rader, Melvin, *Marx's Interpretation of History.* London: Oxford Univ. Press, 1979.

Rakovski, Marc, *Towards an East European Marxism.* London: Alison and Busby, 1978.

Randall, Margaret, *Cuban Women Now.* Toronto: Women's Press, 1974.

Reich, Wilhelm, *Character Analysis.* New York: Farrar, Straus, & Giroux, 1961.

—————*The Mass Psychology of Fascism.* New York: Farrar, 1967.

—————*The Sexual Revolution.* New York: Farrar, 1961.

Reiche, Reimut, *Sexuality and the Class Struggle.* London: New Left Books, 1970.

Reiter, Rayna, *Toward An Anthropology of Women.* New York: Monthly Review Press, 1978.

Richards, Vernon, *Lessons of the Spanish Revolution.* London: Freedom Press, 1972.

Richmond, Al, *Long View From the Left.* New York: Delta, 1973.

Robinson, Joan, *An Essay on Marxian Economics.* London: MacMillan, 1949.

—————*Economic Philosophy.* Garden City: Doubleday, 1964.

—————*Economic Heresies.* New York: Basic Books, 1971.

—————*Freedom and Necessity.* New York: Vintage, 1971.

Robinson, Paul A. *The Freudian Left*. New York: Harper and Row, 1969.

Rocker, Rudolf, *Anarcho-Syndicalism*. London.

Rose, Steven, *Conscious Brain* New York: Vintage, 1976.

Rosenberg, Arthur, *A History of Bolshevism*. Garden City: Doubleday, 1967.

Rowbotham, Sheila, *Women, Resistance and Revolution*. New York: Vintage, 1972.

————————*Woman's Consciousness, Man's World*. London: Penguin, 1973.

————————*Beyond the Fragments*. London: Merlin, 1979.

Rubin, Gayle, "The Traffic in Women," in *Toward an Anthropology of Women*. New York: Monthly Review Press, 1975.

Rubin, I.I. *Essays on Marx's Theory of Value*. Detroit: Black and Red, 1971.

Sahlins, Marshall, *The Use and Abuse of Biology*. Ann Arbor: Univ of Mich, 1976.

————————*Culture and Practical Reason*. Chicago: Univ. of Chic. 1976.

Sargent, Lydia, ed. *Women and Revolution*. Boston: South End Press, 1981.

Sartre, Jean-Paul, *Search for a Method*. New York: Vintage, 1978.

————————*Between Existentialism and Marxism*. New York: Morrow, 1974.

Schaff, Adam, *Marxism and the Human Individual*. New York: McGraw Hill, 1970.

Schumpeter, Joseph, *Capitalism, Socialism, and Democracy*. London.

Sennet & Cobb, *The Hidden Injuries of Class*. New York: Vintage, 1972.

Serge, Victor, *Memoirs of a Revolutionary*. London: Oxford.

Sherman, Howard, *Radical Political Economy*. New York: Basic Books, 1977.

Silverman, Bertram, ed. *Man and Socialism in Cuba*. New York: Athenum, 1976.

Singer, Daniel, *Prelude to Revolution*. New York: Hill and Wang, 1976.

————————*The Road to Gdansk*. New York: Monthly Review Press, 1981.

Sklar, Lawrence, *Space, Time, and Spacetime*. Berkeley: Univ. of Ca. Press, 1978.

Smith, Adam, *The Wealth of Nations*. New York: Random House, 1937.

Snow, Edger, *Red Star Over China*. New York: Grove Press.

Spriano, Paolo, *The Occupation of the Factories*. London: Pluto Press, 1975.

Sraffa, Piero, *The Production of Commodities by Means of Commodities*. London: Cambridge Univ. Press, 1971.

Stojanovic, Svetozar, *Between Ideas and Reality*. London: Oxford, 1973.

Stone, Kathy, "The Origin of Job Structures in the Steel Industry," RRPE, Vol 6, No. 2.

Sweezy, Paul, *The Theory of Capitalist Development*. New York: Monthly Review Press, 1942.

————————*Modern Capitalism and Other Essays*. New York: Monthly Review, 1972.

Sweezy, Paul, and Bettleheim, Charles, *The Transition to Socialism*. New York: Monthly Review Press, 1971.

Szelenyi, Ivan, "The East European Intelligentsia," *Critique 10/11*, Winter/Spring, 1978-79.

Tanzer, Michael, *The Sick Society*. New York: 1978.

Tepperman, Jean, *Not Servants; Not Machines*. Boston: Beacon Press, 1976.

Terkel, Studs, *Working*. New York: Avon, 1972.

Thompson, E.P. *The Making of the English Working Class.* New York: Random House, 1966.

————————*The Poverty of Theory.* New York: Monthly Review 1978.

Timpanero, Sebastian, *On Materialism.* London: New Left Books, 1973.

Trotsky, Leon, *The History of the Russian Revolution.* London: Pluto Press.

Vajda, Mihaly, *The State and Socialism.* London: Alison and Busby, 1981.

Veblin, Thorstein, *Engineers and the Price System.* New York, 1932.

Venable, Vernon, *Human Nature: The Marxian View.* London: Meridan Books, 1946.

Voline, *The Unknown Dimension.* New York: Free Life, 1974.

Walker, Pat, ed. *Between Labor and Capital.* Boston: South End Press, 1978.

Ward, Benjamin, *What's Wrong With Economics.* New York: Basic Books, 1972.

Weber, Max, *Economy and Society.* New York, 1968.

Weil, Simone, *Oppression and Liberty.* Amherst: Univ. of Mass. 1958.

Weinbaum, Batya, *The Curious Courtship of Women's Liberation and Socialism.* Boston: South End Press, 1979.

Weinstein, James, *The Decline of Socialism in America.* New York: 1974.

Williams, Raymond, *Marxism and Literature.* London: Oxford, 1977.

Williams, William Appleman, *The Contours of American History.* Boston, 1973.

Williams, Gywn, *Proletarian Order.* London: Pluto Press, 1975.

Wilson, Edward, *On Human Nature.* New York: Bantam, 1978.

Woolf, Virginia, *Three Guineas.* New York: Harcourt Brace, 1938.

Wright, Erik Olin, *Class, Crisis, and the State.* London: New Left Books, 1978.

Wright, Richard, *American Hunger.* New York: Harper and Row, 1974.

Zahar, Renete, *Frantz Fanon: Colonialism and Alienation.* New York: Monthly Review, 1974.

Zaretsky, Eli, *Capitalism, the Family, and Personal Life.* New York: Harper,

Zeitlin, Maurice, *Revolutionary Politics and the Cuban Working Class.* New York: Harper and Row, 1970.

Zinn, Howard, *Disobediance and Democracy.* New York: Vintage, 1968.

Index